D1222063

IMPROBABLE WARRIORS

IMPROBABLE WARRIORS

WOMEN SCIENTISTS AND THE U.S. NAVY IN WORLD WAR II

Kathleen Broome Williams

NAVAL INSTITUTE PRESS
Annapolis, Maryland

Naval Institute Press
291 Wood Road
Annapolis, MD 21402

© 2001 by Kathleen Broome Williams
All rights reserved. No part of this book may be reproduced or utilized
in any form or by any means, electronic or mechanical, including
photocopying and recording, or by any information storage and retrieval
system, without permission in writing from the publisher.

Library of Congress Cataloging-in-Publication Data
Williams, Kathleen Broome, 1944–
    Impossible warriors : women scientists and the U.S. Navy in World
War II / Kathleen Broome Williams.
        p. cm.
    Includes bibliographical references and index.
    ISBN 1-55750-961-1 (alk. paper)
        1. Women scientists—United States—Biography. 2. United States.
Navy—Women—Biography. 3. World War, 1939–1945—Science. I. Title.

Q141 .W617   2001
500'.82'0973—dc21   2001030164

Printed in the United States of America on acid-free paper ∞
08 07 06 05 04 03 02 01   9 8 7 6 5 4 3 2
First printing

TO MY CHILDREN

CONTENTS

PREFACE

In 1996 the Naval Institute Press published my book *Secret Weapon*, a history of the U.S. development of high-frequency direction finding for use in the Battle of the Atlantic. In researching the book I examined the records of the U.S. Navy's technological bureaus and laboratories and those of academic and industrial labs with navy contracts. Gradually I became aware that not just men but women, too, were doing highly classified and important scientific work to aid the Allied cause. Yet who knew of this? So in 1996, when the City University of New York's Women's Research and Development Fund invited applications for grants to work on women's issues, I submitted a proposal for research on women and U.S. naval technology in World War II. Happily, I was awarded a grant enabling me to go first to the files of Lehman College in the Bronx, New York. During World War II, Lehman—then Hunter College—was the training center for enlisted WAVES. Later trips to the WAVES officer training center at Smith College in Northampton, Massachusetts, to various branches of the National Archives, and to many other document collections produced still more information. My first interviews were with a group of former Waves who had been sent to the Naval Ordnance Test Station, Inyokern (China Lake), California, in the 1940s.

Originally I had planned to look broadly at civilian and military women engaged with wartime naval science and technology. The rapid expansion of wartime science created many opportunities for women, especially in the science and technology–driven navy, whose increasing reliance on quickly emerging new technologies owed its success, in part, to their previously underutilized work. Much of that work was at the level of technician and mechanic, and the first chapter of this book gives an overview of the women who filled such positions. When I also found numbers of women with advanced educational and professional qualifications who made key contributions in technical fields I narrowed my approach, choosing four of those women as the main focus of this book. The four improbable warriors—all Ph.D.'s, each a scientist or mathematician—are

Mary Sears (1905–1997), Florence van Straten (1913–1993), Grace Hopper (1906–1992), and Mina Rees (1902–1997). All were college professors until service to the U.S. Navy intervened. Between 1942 and 1945 each held a position from which she influenced the navy's ability to wage a modern war dependent on science. Before discussing my improbable warriors in more detail, however, it is useful to look at what already exists in the field of women and naval technology in World War II.

The historiographical road documenting women's roles in World War II has been uneven. The military services have made some extraordinary and some paltry efforts in this regard. As part of its World War II series, the U.S. Army commissioned an official history of the Women's Army Corps that was published in 1954. In general, WACs have received more scholarly attention than women in other services, partly due to the establishment of the WAC museum. Following World War II the navy, the Marine Corps, and the Coast Guard also commissioned administrative histories, although none was published. Between 1991 and 1995 fact sheets on women in the war were published by the U.S. 50th Anniversary of World War II Commemoration Committee, and, with the exception of the navy, each service published small pamphlets on the wartime roles of their women's reserves. In 1994 the Naval Historical Center sponsored the preparation of a comprehensive history of women in the U.S. Navy (including nurses) by Susan H. Godson, which is forthcoming from the Naval Institute Press.

There are also some well-documented semiofficial works on American military women in each of the services, as well as accounts of Allied women in World War II. The small U.S. Marine Corps Women's Reserve has an extensive review of its formative years written by its first director. There are one or two good institutional histories of women in the U.S. Navy, and of military women in general, although these usually cover the whole span of American history, with only comparatively brief chapters on World War II. In recent years there has been an encouraging increase in general works on American women in World War II. More memoirs have been written. Collections of wartime letters and oral histories illuminate civilian and military women's varied personal experiences. Other accounts analyze the broad societal changes brought on by the war. Some studies focus on the home front and the ways women coped in wartime; others examine the traditional female role of nursing.

What is conspicuously absent, however, in even the best of the sources, is detailed information on women's scientific and technological activities. Most of the accounts of navy women in World War II give long lists of the jobs they filled—which included highly technical ones—but they seldom analyze Waves' occupations or give details of the specific skills and training their jobs required. Lively Wave memoirs continue to appear in growing numbers; the best recent one is *More Than a Uniform: A Navy Woman in a Navy Man's World*, by Capt. Winifred Quick Collins, former WAVES director and 1938 graduate of the Harvard-Radcliffe Program in Business Administration. These memoirs scarcely mention science and technology, however. Scholarly military and naval journals have published very little on navy women, nor has there been much consideration of women's war work in science and engineering journals. Female scientists barely appear in otherwise excellent accounts of American scientific developments in World War II, and none of the recent studies of naval technology identifies any specific contribution made by women. Two welcome exceptions are *Howard Aiken: Portrait of a Computer Pioneer*, by Bernard Cohen, and *Makin' Numbers: Howard Aiken and the Computer*, by Cohen and Gregory Welch, which recognize the wartime scientific contributions of Wave Grace Hopper.

Likewise, most sources on women and science offer little help with regard to their war work. An exception is Margaret Rossiter's two-volume *Women Scientists in America*, which is almost exhaustive in sweep and detail and convincing in analysis. However, Rossiter's one chapter on World War II gives only a taste of what women scientists accomplished, although it does point out the pervasive institutionalized downgrading of their positions and assignments. Rossiter also clarifies how little women were recognized for their contributions as soon as the first flush of victory faded. In addressing these deficiencies, my definition of activities affecting the naval scientific war is broad, although I exclude nursing, both because it was a well-established field long considered suitable for women and because it has been covered competently already. I do include the use of technical skills, work with technical equipment, scientific research, and the development and use of technological devices. I consider how the navy obtained the women it needed for war work, how it trained them to fill scientific and technical positions, and how women functioned in jobs for which many believed they were mentally and temperamentally unsuited. The results demonstrate the breadth and importance of the contribution of women to naval science and technology in World War II.

The four women who are the main subjects of this book—Sears, van Straten, Hopper, and Rees—came from similar middle-class backgrounds, and three of them grew up in New York City. Although they were expert in different scientific fields, their World War II experiences were similar.

Mary Sears, a Harvard and Woods Hole Oceanographic Institution planktonologist, joined the WAVES and spent the war years as head of the Hydrographic Office's Oceanographic Unit. She was responsible for developing and writing oceanographic intelligence reports used by the Joint Chiefs of Staff when considering landing conditions for proposed Pacific amphibious operations.

Grace Hopper, a Yale-trained mathematician teaching at Vassar, also joined the WAVES—or the U.S. Naval Reserve, as she insisted on saying—and was sent to the Bureau of Ships Computation Project at Harvard. There she worked on Howard Aiken's Mark I computer, churning out essential data for all sorts of ordnance and other projects, entering the new field of computer science at its very beginning.

Naval service also called Florence van Straten, a New York University physical chemist. She was one of the first group of two dozen WAVES officers trained as aerological engineers, and she spent the war in Washington analyzing the use of weather in combat operations in the Pacific. She, too, entered an essentially new field, because the science of meteorology did not really develop until the military needed it during World War II.

Mina Rees, a Hunter College mathematician, oversaw contracts for navy scientific projects as chief technical aide to the Applied Mathematics Panel of the National Defense Research Committee (NDRC). As the invaluable assistant to Warren Weaver, the panel's head, Rees was responsible for directing millions of dollars of government money to many scientific projects, including those in which the other three women were engaged. Indeed, the wartime interdependence of navy and civilian science, which permanently affected postwar ideas about the government's role in funding scientific research, is particularly well illustrated by the work of NDRC.

Although each of these women had a distinguished wartime and postwar career (and Grace Hopper is familiar for her later navy role), their contribution to wartime naval science is barely known. Fortunately, a number of institutions have preserved records of their war work in lengthy and probing interviews. Supplementing the women's own words with the recollections of their relatives and colleagues, archival sources, and published materials, I attempted to situate the women firmly in their occupational surroundings. I looked at their skills and training and how they acquired them, how they got into war work and what they did once there, and I tried to assess their contribution to the war effort. Finally, I considered how the war changed their lives, especially their professional lives, and how it affected their future careers. Their work is seen in the context of what their mostly male peers were doing at the same time and what other women in science—American, British, German, and Japanese—were able to contribute to the war. But the core of this book is the work of the improbable warriors themselves.

One of the most interesting of the questions I addressed concerns motivation. Why would three mature, well-established academic women join the navy, and the fourth—who considered such a move—also look for a way to serve the war effort? The women's choice of a career in science had already branded them as improbable, but I soon discovered that their motivation was not complex at all, or improbable, for them, in the mood of the time. Grace Hopper may have expressed the situation best, but they all felt it: "There was a war on, everybody joined something," she said.

Some may consider it presumptuous to call desk-bound scientists warriors; they did not put their lives on the line. It has only been since 1993, however, that women fly combat aircraft and serve aboard warships; and they are still restricted from service in ground combat units. So how was a patriotic woman to serve her country in the 1940s? The answer is no more complex than the motivation: she used her education and her skills to come as close to the action as she could. For every man who risked his life in battle there were other men, and women, too, fighting with all the strength they had to end the war victoriously and to bring everyone safely home. These women were intellectual warriors; moreover, all were volunteers.

In *Science and the Navy: The History of the Office of Naval Research*, Harvey Sapolsky uses the terms *basic* and *applied* to distinguish the two main categories of research. He defines *basic* as "research carried out by the investigator solely to increase knowledge," and *applied* as "research that is conducted with a potential application in view" (6). This is a useful distinction, and all the more so because war harnesses all scientists, whatever their personal inclination, into the service of applied research. In war, too, it is the gray area where science and technology merge that requires the most attention: scientists, theoreticians, engineers, and mathematicians all pitch in to solve the practical and immediate problems of national survival. This leads to a massive readjustment of priorities. Effective focus on the job at hand requires scientists, among others, to set aside their specialties and apply themselves wherever the need is felt.

The wartime needs of the U.S. Navy placed each of the three Waves in what van Straten called "an embryo science." All four women gave voluntarily and unstintingly of their time, energy, and abilities, and in return were rewarded with opportunities and experiences that shaped the rest of their lives. Because they were not tied down by family responsibilities they were able to serve where they were most needed and to profit afterward from what they had learned and from the contacts they made. The navy trained van Straten and Hopper in new areas they had not previously considered and changed the course of their professional lives. Mina Rees's administrative experience during the war and afterward moved her away from teaching and research and in the direction of academic administration. Only Mary Sears returned to her old work in oceanography at Woods Hole.

In a more general and profound way, however, the navy acted as an engine of change for all scientists. The intertwining of academic and military research during World War II placed government funding on university campuses to stay. The modest world of independent academic science Sears, van Staten, Hopper, and Rees left at the beginning of the war had changed forever by the end of it. For most women, however, the broader horizons of wartime contracted quickly with the advent of peace, and the promise of an equitable society for all women—not just the exceptional few—has still to be realized.

During World War II the U.S. Navy generally reflected society at large in its attitudes toward women and gender roles, and it would be churlish to criticize it merely for being of its time. In fact, in some ways the navy was more forward looking than other wartime organizations and agencies; certainly my improbable warriors found it so. They were grateful for the opportunities the navy gave them and the new vistas their war work opened up, and while they expected eventual changes in the status of women they did not expect the navy to be responsible for those changes. It is important to remember the sensibilities of the time and to respect the deep regard for the U.S. Navy felt by so many women who served.

ACKNOWLEDGMENTS

I owe an immense debt of gratitude to the many people who contributed to this book. Among them are Bob Campbell and the late Dick Bloch, who were in at its very beginnings and who helped with information, advice, encouragement, and several careful readings. Leila Sears (a World War II Wave) and Mary Murray Westcote shared with me many memories of their sisters, Mary Sears and Grace Murray Hopper. Mrs. Westcote very kindly gave me access to her sister's large collection of papers and photographs, and Miss Sears read several versions of the chapter on her sister, contributing telling anecdotes. Paul and Wendy Denton generously allowed me to use the several boxes of Mary Sears's papers in their possession. Gary Weir of the Naval Historical Center told me about Mary Sears and enthusiastically urged me to write about her. Joan Byers arranged for me to consult the Mina Rees Collection at the CUNY Graduate Center and read the chapter on Rees. Charles Bates, in addition to arranging for my use of his papers at the Texas A&M University archives, has also been a fund of information, a provider of leads to other sources, and a careful reader.

The following have also read parts or all of this book and I am grateful for their astute comments: Norman Polmar, Louis Brown, Nan Shaw, Norma Kenigsberg, Ruth Brendel Noller, Norman Friedman, and special thanks to World War II Wave Hazel Taylor.

Among others I am very much obliged to Bernard Cavalcante, Kathleen Lloyd, and Regina Akers at the Naval Historical Center; Tim Nenninger, Barry Zerbe, Vernon Smith, Sandy Smith, and Margery Ciarlante at the National Archives; Scott Price at the Historian's Office, U.S. Coast Guard; Nancy Cricco at NYU; Janet Butler Munch at the Lehman College Library, CUNY; Michael Nash at the Hagley Museum and Library; Jean Berry at the Wellesley College Archives; Elisabeth Kaplan and Lynne Leite at the Charles Babbage Institute; Stanley Tozeski and Helen Engle at the National Archives Northeast Region (Boston); Margot Garritt at the WHOI Archives; Susan Newman at the CUNY Graduate Center Archives; Evelyn Mazur at the American Meteorological Society; Brenda Stephens at the Bronx Community College Library, CUNY; and Pat Root at the Bronxville Public Library.

Many Waves allowed me to interview them, filled out questionnaires, or both. I take great pride in their accomplishments and wish to thank them all.

Kay Larson helped enormously with the early research for this book and has read it critically, and my mother, Jane Swift, was a willing research assistant. Such errors of omission and commission as may remain after all this help are entirely my own.

Successive PSC/CUNY grants made it possible for me to devote summers to the research and writing of this book, for which I am very grateful.

ABBREVIATIONS

AMG	Applied Mathematics Group
AMP	Applied Mathematics Panel
ASWORG	Anti-submarine Warfare Operational Research Group
BuAer	Bureau of Aeronautics
BuNav	Bureau of Navigation
BuOrd	Bureau of Ordnance
BuPers	Bureau of Naval Personnel
BuShips	Bureau of Ships
CNO	Chief of Naval Operations
DCNO	Deputy Chief of Naval Operations
JANIS	Joint Army-Navy Intelligence Study
JMC	Joint Meteorological Committee
Hydro	Hydrographic Office
NACA	National Advisory Committee for Aeronautics
NDRC	National Defense Research Committee
NOL	Naval Ordnance Laboratory
NRL	Naval Research Laboratory
ONR	Office of Naval Research
OSRD	Office of Scientific Research and Development
OU	Oceanographic Unit
SPAR	U.S. Coast Guard Women's Reserve (*Semper Paratus*)
SRG	Statistical Research Group
WAC	Women's Army Corps
WAVES	Women Accepted for Volunteer Emergency Service (U.S. Navy)
WHOI	Woods Hole Oceanographic Institution

IMPROBABLE WARRIORS

1

WOMEN AT WAR

an overview

On 30 July 1947, U.S. Navy women celebrated their fifth anniversary as WAVES: Women Accepted for Volunteer Emergency Service. In ceremonies across the country, flags snapped and young women saluted crisply. Congratulatory messages arrived from navy brass around the globe. The commander in chief (C-in-C) of the Atlantic Fleet, Adm. William H. P. Blandy, promised (perhaps too optimistically) that "the splendid services rendered by the WAVES . . . and their uncomplaining spirit of sacrifice and devotion to duty at all times" would never be forgotten by "a grateful navy."[1] Adm. Louis E. Denfeld, C-in-C Pacific, wrote more perceptively that "the vital role" played by the WAVES "in the defeat of the Axis nations is known to all and, though often unsung in peacetime, their importance has not decreased." Significantly, Admiral Denfeld added that he would welcome the addition of the WAVES "to the Regular Naval Establishment," an issue then hanging in the balance.[2] Indeed, for all the anniversary praise, the WAVES' contribution to wartime successes did not even guarantee them a permanent place in the navy once peace returned. Nor, until recently, has their "vital role" in the Allied victory received much scholarly attention. This is particularly true of their contribution to naval science and technology.

The navy has always been a technical service, but World War II was the first truly technological war. The demands of a two-ocean campaign placed enormous pressure on the U.S. Navy to develop new scientific and technical capabilities and to train skilled operators for increasingly sophisticated technical devices. While most people would agree with historian David Zimmerman that "the scientific war was won in large measure by the Allies because they were more successful than their enemies in mobilizing their scientific, technical, and engineering expertise," until now there has been little focus on the part women played in that mobilization.[3]

American women with scientific and technical skills had little incentive to join the navy—or any other service. Unlike women in Allied countries such as Britain and the Soviet Union, they were not subject to compulsory military service. The institution of the draft in September 1940, which took young male scientists and mathematicians away from their positions in industry and academia, enhanced the civilian careers and earning power of many women, stiffening the competition faced by the navy in acquiring their services.[4]

Further, the pool of technically skilled women for the navy to draw on was much more limited than that of comparably trained men. Before the war, few women graduated with technical degrees of any sort; fewer than a dozen a year graduated in engineering, for example. In 1941 the National Roster of Scientific and Specialized Personnel found only 144 women engineers in the whole country, or 0.3 percent of the total number of engineers. The navy was also handicapped in its effective use of women because of pervasive institutional (and societal) skepticism about women's technical aptitudes and abilities. Ultimately, however, women proved essential to the expansion of U.S. naval science and technology in World War II.[5]

In early 1942 the newly created War Manpower Commission declared itself unable to supply a sufficient number of men to satisfy the needs of the projected naval expansion, and a generally reluctant navy was forced to consider using unorthodox personnel instead—that is, women. As Dean Virginia C. Gildersleeve of Barnard College expressed it later, "if the Navy could possibly have used dogs or ducks or monkeys, certain of the older admirals would probably have greatly preferred them to women." However, the admirals were pressured by Congresswoman Edith Nourse Rogers of Massachusetts, who sponsored a bill to admit women to the army and then cast her eye upon the navy. Uncertain how to proceed, the navy directed Gildersleeve and a select group of academic women with no knowledge of naval affairs to draw up the initial plans for a women's naval force. This abdication of responsibility on the part of the navy led to unnecessary confusion and inefficiency during the WAVES' early days.[6]

Gildersleeve was appointed to chair the Advisory Council for the Women's Reserve United States Navy, and her national reputation attracted a remarkable group of very able women to head the proposed new force. Among them was Mildred McAfee, at forty-two the still youthful president of prestigious Wellesley College, who soon became the first director of the WAVES. Interviewed after the war, McAfee ruefully acknowledged that it might have saved the navy some confusion "had the supervision of the admission of women been put in the hands of an experienced naval officer."[7] On the other hand, initial weaknesses in operational procedures were offset by the caliber of the women Gildersleeve's academic connections drew into the navy and by the high standards these women established for the WAVES. While the Advisory Council received little guidance from the navy, it did have a precedent to follow. A small number of enlisted women—the so-called Yeomanettes—had served briefly in the navy in World War I. The loophole making that service possible had been plugged, however, and the Naval Reserve Act of 1938 confirmed the restriction of reserve service to "male citizens of the United States." Congressional action would be required to reverse this.

The Yeomanettes had generally filled navy yeomen's jobs ashore as clerical workers, telephone operators, translators, stenographers, and typists. But many legislators (and naval officers, too) believed that any clerical expansion required by war in the future could be met by hiring more civil service personnel. They failed to anticipate both the coming shortage of civilian employees generated by the military buildup and the rapidly increasing sophistication of warfare and weapons requiring not only clerical workers but also technically trained personnel. Although women with clerical skills would remain indispensable to the navy in World War II, the demand for technical and scientific skills burgeoned. In the absence of sufficient men, women would have to supply those skills.[8]

At the beginning of the war this need was far from apparent to most of the naval establishment. The WAVES' haphazard beginnings reflected the general dislocation of a service that grew from about a quarter of a million men in 1941 to more than three million men and 100,000 women by 1945. Yet in December 1941, when the Bureau of Navigation (BuNav, soon to become the Bureau of Naval Personnel, or BuPers) questioned naval commanders around the country on their need for navy women, the answers were almost unanimously negative. Even assistant navy secretary James Forrestal clearly indicated his belief that "the Navy had no place for a women's corps."[9]

Only the Bureau of Aeronautics (BuAer, the youngest and most technical branch of the navy) and the chief of naval operations (CNO) responded enthusiastically to BuNav's query. BuAer recognized "the educational and social changes which have taken place between the two periods of service," and quickly determined that it could employ women "in a wide variety of technical and skilled positions." Also looking ahead, the CNO foresaw an increasing need for communications personnel under military discipline and control to reduce security risks and to be available for work around the clock. To fill these needs, the CNO advised that an adequate women's reserve be begun without delay. On 2 January 1942, BuNav, ignoring the pervasive myopia of respondents to its survey, advised the secretary of the navy to request legislation permitting the employment of women in a naval reserve for duty ashore.[10]

After strong opposition from conservative senators led by Naval Affairs Committee chairman David Walsh, a bill was finally passed on 30 July 1942 accepting women into the naval reserve, but with limitations. They would be temporary emergency personnel only, signed on for the duration of the war plus six months and restricted to serving ashore within the forty-eight states. No numerical limits were set, but Rear Adm. Randall Jacobs, chief of navy personnel, had told the Senate that he thought numbers "will probably go up around 10,000 before we get through with it." By 30 September 1943, 776 WAVES officers and 3,262 enlisted personnel were working for the vice chief of naval operations in all communications areas, including cryptanalysis and hydrographics.

There was a low ceiling on rank and no chance of excess women officers. McAfee was to hold the top post as a lieutenant commander; only thirty-five WAVES lieutenants were authorized; and no more than 35 percent of the remaining officers could be lieutenants (junior grade). The Senate debates emphasized the legislators' parochial concerns. Instead of galvanizing the nation for all-out war, Senator Andrews of Florida wanted to be reassured that "there would not have to be another Annapolis, would there?"[11]

When a representative from the Bureau of Ordnance informed the Senate committee that his bureau already employed some civilian women engineers, quite a few women draftsmen, and some other women in technical and professional positions, several senators expressed disapproval. Far from being reassured, they insisted that women were suited only to clerical work or nursing. Admiral Jacobs explained to the legislators that navy women were needed not only for clerical work but also for communications jobs of all sorts—coding work, cryptanalysis, photographic interpretation, radio and electronics—and as laboratory technicians. Senators Harry Byrd (Virginia), Allen Ellender (Louisiana), Charles Andrews (Florida), and David Walsh (Massachusetts) still wanted to be assured that such jobs would involve only "desk work." A cornered Admiral Jacobs was finally driven to respond, "Yes; in some instances."[12]

The legislators were not the only ones who did not seem to grasp the nature and dimension of the wartime personnel problem. The navy, too, was hobbled by a service-wide patronizing attitude toward women. Nevertheless, in some ways the navy treated women better than the army did. For one thing, from the beginning women were granted reserve rather than auxiliary status, and even initially—particularly in the Bureau of Aeronautics—professional women were generally used in their field of expertise. The navy's deeper weakness was strategic, part of a general "slipshod planning system." Throughout the war the U.S. Navy remained unable to establish a reliable method of estimating manpower requirements. In early 1944, for example, there was still no comprehensive manpower plan for the summer of 1945.[13] Small wonder, then, that in 1942 BuPers estimated it would need only 10,000 Waves in total. When BuAer immediately requested 20,000, BuPers hastily revised its estimate upward. Ultimately, more than 100,000 women served in the wartime WAVES.[14]

The other military branches recruited women as well, all drawing from a common pool. The initial plan for the Women's Auxiliary Army Corps (WAAC) had been to recruit 12,000 women. Within three months the figure had risen above 65,000 and there was wild talk of an eventual 1.5 million. Finally, however, the army settled on a force of 150,000 women, the limit established by Congress. In June 1943 the WAAC was reconstituted as the Women's Army Corps (WAC) and was incorporated into the army reserve. The director of the WAC, its highest-ranking officer, held the rank of colonel. Of course, a man responsible for 150,000 soldiers would hold the rank of major general at least, more likely lieutenant general. The inequity of treatment (which was to last forty years) did not escape women's attention, and it both inhibited recruitment and lowered the WAC's reputation and morale. Nevertheless, by the end of the war some 150,000 American women had served in the WAC. The Marine Corps Women's Reserve, established in February 1943, similarly grew far beyond its initial planned size of 6,500 women; in the end 23,000 women marines had served. The Coast Guard Women's Reserve—the SPARs—set a more realistic goal of 11,000, which they reached. The total number of women in military service during World War II was small. In the end, women numbered less than 3 percent of the sixteen million wartime service personnel. They were not tokens, however, admitted to appease a constituency. They performed a wide variety of functions; without them the military could not have operated as successfully as it did. They filled in the gaps and were happy to do so. Most served at very basic levels, but a few— among them Sears, van Straten, Hopper, and Rees—operated at levels commensurate with their education and abilities.[15]

Many women were eager to serve the war effort in any way they could. When a ninety-seven-year-old woman volunteered for coast-watcher duty it was evident to those allocating manpower that women were prepared to tackle unconventional occupations during the national emergency. Three million women volunteered with the Red Cross, and others drove ambulances, worked at USO canteens, and sold war bonds. An additional six million women who had never before worked outside the home joined the labor force. As soon as rumors started that Congress was considering establishing a women's naval auxiliary, queries from interested individuals and groups flooded the Navy Department. Typical was the telegram from the chairman of the National Women's Council of the Navy League, which noted that the council had "at least twenty candidates all college graduates for the women's reserve of the navy. We are eagerly awaiting to hear where they may apply and when."[16] This, at a time when fewer than 10 percent of Americans attended college, is indicative of the high caliber of the women attracted to the U.S. Navy. Fewer than 5 percent of all men in the army at that time had sixteen or more years of education, and only twenty-eight of the ninety-six Marine Corps generals on active duty during the war had college degrees.[17]

A navy survey based on the 1930 and 1940 census figures estimated that the pool of women eligible for the WAVES, which excluded married women with husbands in the same service and women with dependent children, was around four million. In spite of the initial enthusiastic response, however, women did not flock to join. The navy was forced to go out and look for them. Vigorous recruiting began at once, particularly among women scientists from college faculties and student bodies. Eventually, strenuous publicity campaigns using newspaper and radio ads were also required to attract sufficient numbers. The limitations on rank and the restrictions of military discipline undoubtedly deterred many well-qualified women who held more responsible positions at higher salaries than they would ever attain in the navy.[18]

The other services, too, had trouble meeting their recruitment goals for women. An editorial published in the *Smithfield (N.C.) Herald* in February 1944 complained: "We have commented before on the failure of women to respond to the war needs of the nation. For some reason, the ladies show no great enthusiasm to wear the uniform of the country." Perhaps part of the answer might be found in the headline of another North Carolina newspaper of that same month: "Navy Is Seeking Women, While Men Still Direct the Show." The editor of the *Concord (N.C.) Tribune* thought he had a solution, though: "The foundation garment; nearly extinct in civilian life, it is General Issue to the auxiliaries. So now here's a new slogan: 'Join the services and get a girdle.'" "Stand aside and let 'em in," he concluded.[19]

Perhaps the publicity was directed to the wrong audience. In May 1942 Admiral Jacobs advised the secretary of the navy that "there seems to be a tendency on the part of male members of the family to discourage females from joining the armed services. This includes all branches." The negative attitude of the average serviceman toward women in the military kept many of their wives, sweethearts, and sisters from joining up. In fact, many of the women who joined did so, as one historian notes, "over the often vociferous objections of family and friends, in the face of scurrilous allegations directed their way by certain segments of society, and despite the crude reception they received from the men they were attempting to help." A patronizing paternalism in Congress also thwarted the navy's efforts to increase WAVES enrollment by lowering the enlistment age to eighteen. In Britain, too, the armed forces had trouble attracting sufficient numbers of women, even after March 1941, when all women between the ages of nineteen and forty had to register at employment exchanges so that the Ministry of Labour could direct them to essential war work.[20]

Nor was it only women who were failing to answer the recruitment call. By March 1944 the Selective Service was near a stalemate and still there were demands from all the services for more men. There were

"I'm sorry, but there's nothing for you now. And what's more, I'm not at all sure we'll be hiring men _after_ the war."

© The New Yorker Collection, 1943. Whitney Darrow Jr. From cartoonbank.com. All rights reserved.

suggestions to expand the pool by reducing the minimum draft age to seventeen or raising the age limit for active service from thirty-eight to forty-five. The urgent need for more men also brought up the issue of deferments. More than 900,000 nonfathers between the ages of eighteen and twenty-five were on the nation's draft-deferred list according to a congressional committee convened to review all deferment cases. More than 500,000 of these were farmers and 350,000 were in industry—occupations classified as essential for the war effort—but there was a strong sense that many of these jobs could be filled by men over thirty-eight or by women. "Is it an essential job in an essential industry," one editorial asked, "or is the gentleman just a non-father who doesn't like the idea of wearing a uniform?" Scientists were generally able to defend their deferred status, and the great majority much preferred the freedom of being civilians. Unfortunately, numbers of them also preferred not to become involved in government projects.[21]

Civilian scientists leading the war effort such as Vannevar Bush, an electrical engineer and the president of Carnegie Institution who headed the Office of Scientific Research and Development (OSRD), and James B. Conant, a chemist and the president of Harvard University, offered suggestions to alleviate the situation. In 1942 Conant suggested creating "by law, a Scientific Research Corps into which men would be forced by fear of the draft, as well as by patriotic motives," but neither the army nor the president supported the idea, and it came to nothing.[22]

Bush's Office of Scientific Research and Development itself drew large numbers of men away from military service. Through an effective contract system OSRD channeled huge amounts of government money into scientific research projects at universities and laboratories all over the country. But while it was one of the largest wartime employers of male scientists—tens of thousands were ultimately involved—only several dozen women scientists received wartime assignments in OSRD commensurate with their professional status and abilities. It appears that only three women actually supervised OSRD projects: Maria Telkes, an MIT metallurgist; Agnes Fay Morgan, a Berkeley nutritionist; and pathologist Virginia Frantz. Unlike the normal large research teams working on OSRD projects, however, each of these women worked alone: Telkes on a project to use solar energy to purify water on life rafts, Morgan testing dehydrated foods for their vitamin content, and Frantz developing her own new cellulose compound to stop bleeding. At least five women scientists worked on various OSRD radar projects, another four contributed to its penicillin project, and three women chemists worked on the antimalaria drug project. Other women scientists, like chemists Louise Kelley and Hoylande D. Young, who were employed as chemical librarians, had been shifted into traditional women's work.[23]

There are several reasons for the poor showing of women scientists at OSRD. Most of the projects were located at prestigious universities where the female presence was very small anyway. In addition, scientists recruited from other academic institutions to join in the wartime research were usually found through an old-boy network that either actively excluded women or simply did not know about them. Mathematician Mina Rees, who had made an effort to be widely known in her discipline, was one of the few exceptions. She profited from her experience with OSRD, even though her position was administrative rather than in research. But she was one of only a very few women scientists in OSRD projects.[24]

OSRD's Manhattan Project, on the other hand, employed at least eighty-five women scientists and engineers. Among them were Lilli Hornig, who helped to develop the high-explosive lenses used in the plutonium bomb, and physicists Rose Moony, Maria Goeppart Mayer (Nobelist in physics in 1963), and C. S. Wu. Ella Anderson prepared the first sample of uranium 235 for use at Los Alamos, and Elizabeth Riddle Graves helped monitor the Trinity test. Minerologist Helen Blair Barlett, geochemist Margaret Foster, and chemist Lotti Grieff were also engaged on the project.

A number of other civilian government agencies attracted women scientists during the war, although many of the women had to work in fields well outside their area of expertise. Among the best known was Rachel Carson, an associate aquatic biologist for the U.S. Fish and Wildlife Service who during the war wrote government food-conservation bulletins explaining how fish could be substituted for other, scarcer foods. Geologist Grace Stewart did geographical work for the Office of Strategic Services (precursor of the CIA), and other geologists did highly secret work preparing maps of battle zones in North Africa, Southeast Asia, and the Pacific Islands.[25]

Women who chose to enlist and serve in the military received even fewer guarantees than civilian women that they would be able to pursue their area of expertise and that they would be given an intellectually challenging assignment. Their commitment seems even more unusual when one considers that military service was not universally regarded as a patriotic step. A strong and rather aggressive women's antiwar movement flourished in the United States in the late 1930s and right through the war. Made up of a confederation of women's groups, the so-called Mothers' Movement was anti-Communist, anti-Semitic, and anti-Roosevelt. Part of the larger noninterventionist movement, the women joined forces with leaders of the extreme right like Father Charles Coughlin (the "Radio Priest"), Col. Robert McCormick (the Anglophobe owner of the *Chicago Tribune*), and such isolationist senators as Burton K. Wheeler, Gerald P. Nye, and Arthur H. Vandenberg. At its peak the Mothers' Movement had five or six million members, and far from disbanding after Pearl Harbor they continued to oppose the war until its end in 1945. Members of the movement blamed the war on British imperialism, supported Hitler as a barrier to communism, and claimed to be superpatriots defending their sons and husbands from the scourge of war. These women were predominantly upper middle class and college educated—the sort of women who should have been in the pool of potential women military officers. Nevertheless, in general American women supported the war and whether in uniform or as civilians contributed impressively to the Allies' eventual victory.[26]

Although no Japanese women served as soldiers, the entire Japanese population was mobilized for the war effort, with or without consent. Harrowing accounts exist of teenaged girls being sent to work in factories making balloon bombs, and an unknown number of women were forced into labor, in many cases to serve as "comfort women," or prostitutes for the military. Toward the end of the war, when an invasion of the Japanese home islands was expected, everyone—young and old, male and female—was prepared to take on a combat role. On Okinawa, students from the girls' high schools, middle schools, and normal schools were called up to serve in the students' corps, those from the elite schools joining the student nurses of the "Lily Corps." As in other countries, a substantial number of Japanese women participated in the nursing services, often working close to the front lines. In a nation where individual autonomy scarcely existed, however, and where opposition to the paternalistic and all-controlling government was almost unheard of and was in practice almost impossible, the degree of support for the war among Japanese women is very difficult to judge. Their occupations, often not voluntarily chosen, offer few clues.[27]

The situation was different for German women. It has been argued that the Nazis failed to persuade the women of Germany to respond to their appeal for cooperation in the war effort, and were therefore less successful in harnessing women's energies for victory than were the Allies. At first, certainly up until the failure to take Moscow in the winter of 1941, the German leadership remained confident of victory and saw no need to persuade women to work. The Nazi ideology favored keeping German women at home in the kitchen. Thus conflict between party and state in the Third Reich prevented taking full advantage of the energies and abilities of German women, even though they may have been better prepared at the higher professional levels—particularly in the sciences—than were their American counterparts. The effort to get women into the workforce was started late and was never pursued wholeheartedly.[28]

In the United States, on the other hand, after decades of isolationism and lack of preparation, the effort to attract qualified women for war work geared up fast once the war started. In August 1942, the week after the formation of the WAVES, *Newsweek* reported that engineering, astronomy, metallurgy, statistics, and physics were "especially desired" skills in WAVES recruits. The navy, however, faced stiff competition for such women from companies with navy contracts like Du Pont, Bell Labs, Grumman Aircraft, GE, Kodak, Raytheon, and Sperry, which had no mandated caps on salaries or promotions. By December 1942 the *New York Times* quoted a corporate director of engineering admitting, "We'll give an aeronautical engineer any job in the place she wants."[29]

As a group, the women who enlisted in the U.S. military were better educated than their male counterparts, nearly 20 percent of whom were found to be functionally illiterate. All military nurses were nursing school graduates, of course, and 7 percent of other female personnel were college graduates, 15 percent more had some college, and an additional 41 percent had completed high school; only 6 percent had never been to high school. Only 13.6 percent of the armed forces as a whole had some college, 24 percent were high school graduates, and 35 percent had only an elementary education. In fact, though women with formal academic scientific or technical qualifications were rare in those years, there were many more with technical skills than degree statistics suggested. The war brought many of these women to the navy. More significantly, this number was greatly enhanced by the rapid acceleration of technical training both outside the navy and within.[30]

Many women (and men, too) acquired skills specifically recommended by the army, navy, and defense industries in specially designed courses offered to the public at participating colleges across the country. As early as October 1940 Congress appropriated $9 million for condensed college-level engineering courses designed to meet the shortage of engineers trained in fields essential to the national defense. The Federal Security Agency of the U.S. Office of Education administered the Engineering, Science, and Management Defense Training program (ESMDT), and in 1941 more than twenty-three hundred ESMDT-sponsored courses were offered in 144 engineering schools in the United States and Puerto Rico. The following year Congress voted an additional $17.5 million to expand the program to include training for chemists, physicists, and production supervisors. Once the war began, the program accelerated and changed its name to ESMWT, for "war training." Although the courses had educational prerequisites, there were no restrictions on participants regarding their "age, sex, race, or color."[31]

Barnard College for Women at Columbia University established its own Faculty National Service Committee to examine the contents of all courses that might be of value as "war minors" to students majoring in the various departments. As far as possible such courses were to be related to "requirements of Civil Service, Army, Navy, or other war works demands" to help prepare students to join the war effort.[32] Barnard's Geology Department identified meteorology, geological survey work, photogrammetry, and courses in topographical drafting as suitable war minors. For each of these a good foundation in mathematics and physics was required. As well, Columbia University's School of Engineering contributed to the ESMDT and war minors programs with such courses as "Chemistry of Powder and Explosives," intermediate and advanced courses in electronics and radio frequencies, and a course in photomicrography. On 19 February 1942, Professor of Engineering Frank Lee suggested to Dean Gildersleeve, who headed the Faculty National Service Committee effort, that the college institute an ESMDT course in statistical drafting in response to "a request . . . by the Navy Department for chartists for immediate employment by the navy."[33]

Similar ESMDT/ESMWT and war minor courses were offered at many women's colleges, including Bryn Mawr, Manhattanville, New Jersey College for Women, Sweet Briar, Goucher, Pembroke, Skidmore, Radcliffe, and Wellesley. The Committee on College Women Students and the War, under the American Council of Education, was also active in promoting "significant plans or programs for the higher education of young women to prepare them to meet the specific needs already developed in the war period." One of the most successful of these programs was the joint NYU-Vought-Sikorsky venture, which was specifically instituted to train women as aeronautical engineers. Vought-Sikorsky Aircraft Division of the United Aircraft Corporation produced, among other navy items, shipboard fighter planes such as the F4U-1 Corsair.[34]

Mary Sears's younger sister Leila was at Radcliffe when the United States entered the war, and there was a mass movement of students motivated by patriotism to leave college and join the war effort. On hearing what was planned, Ada Comstock, the president of Radcliffe and member of the Navy's Commission on Women, addressed the students and persuaded them that the best service they could give to their country was to complete their education first. She then established a number of war courses at Radcliffe and organized the nearby sister colleges to do the same. Leila Sears took the course in cryptography and when she graduated was automatically placed in navy communications intelligence.[35]

Women also attended night schools set up in cities and towns to provide training in such essential fields as radio and electronics. Many graduates of these programs applied to the navy with their newly acquired credentials. Among these women was Sue King. Realizing early on that war was inevitable, King took a course in aeronautics at Louisiana State University and then a preflight course at Centenary College. Already holding a master's degree from the University of Texas, she completed a course in higher mathematics at Columbia, and when the navy opened its doors to women she signed on. In 1943 Ensign King went to the Naval Air Navigation School at Hollywood, Florida, for training. In March 1944 she was assigned to the Aviation Training Division of the Office of the CNO, where she worked on research and development of carrier navigation procedures and wrote a training manual entitled *Mark III Plotting Board— Instructions for Use and Problem Portfolio*. After fifteen months King went to Quonset Point, Rhode Island, for research on navigating by radio, radar, loran, altimetry, dead reckoning, and pilotage. In January 1947, after a short stint at the Naval Aeronautical Laboratory at Banana River, Florida, Lieutenant King was assigned to the Air Branch of the Office of Naval Research to develop an air navigation research program. Sue King represents the combination of education, prewar experience, and specialized training in the naval service that was at the heart of the WAVES' contribution to the scientific war.[36]

WAVES officers-in-training at the Naval Reserve Midshipmen's School (WR) at Smith College, Northampton, Mass.
National Archives, Northeast Region (Boston), First Naval District, RG 181

After their haphazard beginnings, WAVES recruitment, training, and job assignment soon settled into a well-organized and effective routine. The six-week boot camp for enlisted women became centralized at Hunter College in New York City, and WAVES officer candidates received two-month indoctrination training at the Naval Reserve Midshipmen's School (WR) on the Smith College campus in Northampton, Massachusetts. The efforts of McAfee, Gildersleeve, and the Advisory Council attracted many exceptional women to the navy in spite of the irksome restrictions. There were four college deans in the initial classes at Smith, and more degrees than there were WAVES. Of the professional and business women, some were specialists in technical fields such as engineering and radio. One 1942 Smith graduate recalled that nearly a quarter of her class was in the first batch of WAVES officer trainees. Pearl Harbor had shattered their senior year, and as soon as the navy moved on campus they were ready to serve.[37]

Enlisted women also sustained the WAVES' reputation for quality. Many were unsophisticated young women from rural America attracted by hopes of adventure, although in general most seem to have come from middle-class backgrounds. Strict chaperoning and social codes carefully maintained the impression of gentility. This was even more true of the British Wrens (Women's Royal Naval Service), whose motto was "Never at Sea." Their all-volunteer force was widely regarded as the most socially select of the women's services. U.S. WAC recruiting, on the other hand, was persistently hindered by "slanderous, mocking rumors" of general loose and immoral behavior in the corps.[38] Many enlisted Waves were college graduates qualified to become officers but initially unable to obtain commissions because of the tight numerical restrictions on them. Among this group was Emily B. Saltonstall, daughter of the governor of Massachusetts. Though pronounced eligible to join the next available officer class, Emily Saltonstall chose instead to accept immediate service in the navy. She was sworn in as apprentice seaman on 2 September 1942, even though she already held the rank of major in the Massachusetts Women's Defense Corps, where she was in charge of all communications. By fall 1944 the majority of WAVES officers were chosen from enlisted ranks.[39]

Soon Waves were serving in every bureau of the Navy Department and in every naval district in the continental United States. At first, the congressional mandate allowing Waves only to replace men needed for sea duty was adhered to strictly. This led to some peculiar assignments that often did not make the best use of the Waves' skills and training. At first, too, the practice of assigning three Waves to replace two men was widespread, as it was also for the Wrens, where heavy work was involved. But with the rapid expansion of the U.S. Navy, women were moved into many new positions, often gaining real scope for their particular skills. Eventually, Waves replaced fifty thousand men for sea duty and filled almost fifty thousand new jobs as well.[40]

After basic training, some enlisted women were assigned to duty as seamen second class, but most were selected by aptitude tests for specialist schools. It is no surprise that a majority of enlisted women ultimately served as yeomen and storekeepers. The next largest group, however, were medical specialists in the Hospital Corps, where they worked in the wards and offices, clinics, laboratories, and therapy departments. A report issued in 1951 showed that during World War II 390 WAVES officer medical specialists served as laboratory technicians, dental hygienists, and occupa-

U.S. Naval Training School (WR), Bronx, N.Y., Waves' Dress Review, August 1944
Courtesy Claire Horgan Twaddle, WAVES Memorabilia, Lehman College Library of the City University of New York

tional and physical therapists. Forty-one of the women were doctors, two were dentists, and two more were civil engineers. Many of these women, like Elisabeth Gaskill from Belmont, Massachusetts, were trained by the Bureau of Medicine and Surgery in much-needed specialties.[41]

On 2 September 1942, Gaskill was sworn in to the navy as an apprentice seaman second class. Because she had just graduated from Smith College with a premed major, Gaskill was soon assigned to the Hospital Corps for training; she made pharmacist's mate second class early in 1943. After studying at the Massachusetts General Hospital in Boston, Gaskill received a certificate from the Bureau of Medicine and Surgery as a qualified assistant in electroencephalography. By June 1943 Gaskill was the head technician at the Brain Wave Laboratory at the U.S. Naval Hospital in Chelsea, Massachusetts, where she performed tests on epileptic, seasick, and psychoneurotic patients, and those suffering from brain tumors or head injuries. She also gave EEGs to all applicants for the Aviation Cadet Corps in the First Naval District who had a history of head injuries. As a result of her good work in the Brain Wave Lab, Gaskill was recommended for officer training and was commissioned an ensign on 14 December 1943. By March 1944 Ensign Gaskill was on her way to the Naval Air Training Center in Pensacola, Florida, where she was instructed in the operation of low-pressure chambers. WAVES officers took the two-month course in low-pressure chamber technology in groups of ten, working closely with the navy's Altitude Training Unit to gain practical experience. Gaskill then put this training into practice at NAS Quonset Point, Rhode Island, where she, twenty-six other women, and two men made up the low-pressure chamber personnel.[42]

A number of Waves in the Bureau of Medicine and Surgery were also involved in devising tests and outlining procedures for the assignment of navy women to appropriate billets. This included establishing requirements for such medical specialties as clinical training in occupational and physical therapy. Waves also devised aptitude tests for women assigned as control tower and Jam Handy operators, cryptographers, and others thought to require specific personality and ability profiles.[43]

Almost alone in the navy, the Bureau of Aeronautics had correctly anticipated its wartime expansion. In the course of the war, one-third of all the women who joined the WAVES were assigned to the rapidly growing field of aeronautics. Many were yeomen and storekeepers, bakers, mailmen, and cooks, but many others had technical jobs in aerology departments, parachute lofts, control towers, and hangars. Enlisted women were sent to naval training stations in Norman, Oklahoma, and Memphis, Tennessee, where they learned to become aviation machinist's mates and aviation metal smiths. They took radio operator courses at the University of Wisconsin and trained to be Link Trainer instructors at the U.S. Naval Reserve Aviation Base in Atlanta, Georgia. They also went to NAS Lakehurst, New Jersey, for training as parachute riggers or as aerographer's mates to do technical work with weather instruments, charts, and weather observations. Once trained, Waves were used as instructors to pass on their new skills to male fliers and future aircrews. One thousand Waves taught instrument flying to four thousand men a day, and two WAVES officers and an enlisted woman were awarded the French Cross of Lorraine for training French pilots at Pensacola. WAVES aviation mechanics serviced and repaired planes and engines, for which they needed practical mathematics and knowledge of simple blueprint reading. Women were

Waves in low-pressure chamber training, 1944
U.S. Navy photo, courtesy Elisabeth Gaskill Coombs

trained as degaussers to demagnetize ships. For this, "knowledge of physics and/or electrical engineering [was] desirable." Waves with knowledge of telegraphy became Land Line supervisors handling single-traffic telegraph lines. A background in amateur or professional photography was necessary to strike for photographer's mate, and knowledge of developing, printing, sorting, and splicing was helpful, too. Aspiring licensed radio operators needed experience in coding and in operation of a radio set and, if possible, should have knowledge of electricity. Experienced ham radio operators were particularly valuable.[44]

Virginia Scott Potter of Kansas City was just the sort of person the navy needed. When she enlisted in the WAVES in 1942, Potter already had a short-wave radio operator's license. Through hard work and skill, Potter rose from apprentice seaman to chief petty officer, becoming the first Wave to serve as a chief radioman. In June 1945 CPO Potter was the supervisor of sending and receiving messages in the Communications Department at NAS Floyd Bennet Field, New York. She also wore the dark blue ribbon of an expert pistol shot. CPO Potter out-rated two of her brothers in the service and had leveled with the third, a navy chief storekeeper.[45]

A look at the Hydrographic Office, responsible for producing naval navigation charts, gives some idea of the magnitude of the navy's training task. Hydro's peacetime organization included about 200 officers and civilians who produced about two million charts annually. By October 1944 the Hydrographic staff—the majority of them enlisted Waves—had grown eightfold and their annual output had increased by forty million. Rear Adm. George S. Bryan, the navy's Hydrographer, admitted that "the training of hundreds of unskilled personnel in the highly technical art of chartmaking was a tremendous job, but we still got our work out without loss of valuable time." Among other assignments, Waves in the Hydrographic Office compiled and drafted air charts for combat areas in the South Pacific.[46]

During the war, under the guidance of Mary Sears, the Oceanographic Unit of the Hydrographic Office took on a variety of critical new responsibilities. When the war broke out, Dr. Sears was on the staff of the Woods Hole Oceanographic Institution. After Pearl Harbor she put her extensive scientific skills at the disposal of the navy, receiving a commission as lieutenant (j.g.) in the WAVES in 1943. Sent to Washington, Sears headed the navy's oceanographic effort and was chiefly responsible for writing oceanographic intelligence reports. After the war Sears remained active in the naval reserves until 1963, finally retiring as a commander.[47]

For the most part, the navy succeeded in obtaining Waves with the required skills by a judicious and practical combination of selection and training. This policy is indicated at the top of a list of billets dated 1 December 1942:

> Which billets will be filled by WAVES is presumed upon the qualification of a good, all-around education, not necessarily specifically or technically directed toward the duty to be assumed. Where training and experience prior to Navy enlistment is considered either *necessary* or especially *desirable,* such notation is made. In other classifications, experience is as a rule *helpful,* and of course where candidates with specific training are available, such training whenever practicable will be a basis for further instruction and assignment. But willingness and interest in the type of work, plus adaptability as shown in aptitude tests, will most frequently be relied upon to determine special technical training and assignment of the individual.[48]

Even without specialized training, Waves often contributed to technically significant projects by fulfilling routine and boring assignments with scrupulous care. When vivacious, outgoing twenty-year-old Seaman 2d Class Terry Wiruth arrived at China Lake Naval Ordnance Testing Station, Inyokern, California, in December 1944, she was sent straight to Harvey Field, probably, she thought, because of her service with the civil air patrol back home in Dubuque. "They had the airplanes at Harvey Field," she recalled, fifty-two years later,

> and they would have the ordnance on the planes, and then they had sailors giving the numbers off the hardware, and the sailors thought this work was beneath them so they would put down any old numbers.
>
> So when there was a . . . bad batch of rockets or something, the scientists had no idea which batch it was, and this messed up all their calculations. So they decided, well let's try a Wave. And my job was to get the right information off of the rockets and the information off of the airplane, and everything that was necessary.[49]

There was no more confusion over batch numbers after Seaman Wiruth took over. After the war, Rear Adm. W. A. Buck, the chief of the Bureau of Supplies and Accounts, explained women's usefulness at such tedious tasks: "In performance of work which consists of a repetitive and, therefore, monotonous task, . . . [women] are more capable since they tire less easily and retain enthusiasm for that type of work longer than do male personnel."[50] Terry Wiruth agreed with the admiral's observation about job performance, if not with the patronizing tone, but the reason for her enthusiasm might have surprised him. When she arrived at Harvey Field "there were sixty-five guys and me," Wiruth noted. "I had a ball." In general, the slightly older age of the Waves also affected the care with which they undertook even monotonous tasks. Waves had to be at least twenty years old to sign on, whereas men could enlist at seventeen with parental permission. Many Waves, moreover, had fathers, brothers, husbands, or sweethearts overseas; they were very much aware that how they performed their work might affect their loved ones' chances of survival.

WAVES officers—who had to have a college degree or two years of college combined with suitable job experience—were drawn from a wide variety of backgrounds. Among the 185 WAVES officers assigned to the Third Naval District (New York) in March 1943, one had been a postal censor, thirty-nine had held secretarial positions, eight had sales experience,

Waves at Harvey Field, Inyokern, Calif., with World War II ordnance they
helped test, spring 1945. Terry Wiruth is seated, far left; Ida Rambo is standing
right behind her
Courtesy Terry Wiruth

seven were librarians, and twenty-seven had been teachers. Five women had
research backgrounds, and there were nine statisticians, one physiologist,
one chemist, one lawyer, one botanist, and one clinical psychologist.[51]
After indoctrination training, some of these women went directly to their
assignments, while others, like the enlisted Waves, went on to specialized
training.

Advanced training for many WAVES officers took place in coeducational classes. Some women who had an M.A. or a Ph.D., like Florence
van Straten, were selected to take the nine-month meteorology course at
the Massachusetts Institute of Technology or the University of California
in Los Angeles. More than one hundred Waves with similar high educational qualifications went to the University of Chicago for a nine-month
course in aerological engineering (meteorology) and then ran aerological

operations at various naval facilities. MIT and UCLA also offered radio courses, and other colleges offered training in chemical warfare or general ordnance. Some WAVES officers trained at the Naval Aviation Training School in Hollywood, Florida; the Navy Pre-Radar School at Harvard; and the Naval Technical Training Command School in Corpus Christi, Texas.[52]

Additional training programs were established to keep up with the navy's rapid expansion. As the CNO had predicted, the need for communications officers grew exponentially, so a special training course was set up at Mount Holyoke College, a few miles from Smith College. Graduates of this course and enlisted WAVES radiomen were essential to the smooth flow of information and orders. Until the last two or three months of the war, for example, Radio Central in Jacksonville, Florida, was run entirely by Waves with the exception of one male chief. Waves also made up three-quarters of the personnel at "Radio Washington," the nerve center of the entire navy communications system.[53]

From its founding in 1867, the navy's Civil Engineer Corps (CEC) had been open to men only; but in September 1943 Ens. Kathleen F. Lux became the first woman admitted to the Corps. Ensign Lux, who had an engineering degree from Purdue University, had been commissioned the previous March and had been on duty in the Bureau of Yards and Docks for several months before being granted her CEC status.[54]

The navy sent a number of Waves, such as Ens. Charlotte Potter, for diplomas in electricity, magnetism, alternating currents, electronics, cathode-ray tubes, and radar to Harvard University's graduate school of engineering. Lt. (j.g.) Rose Nudo, who had a math degree from Penn State, was assigned to NAS Norfolk, Virginia, in May 1944, where she taught celestial navigation in the Celestial Link Trainer. Nudo flew in PB4Ys for additional training and experience in sun line approaches and radar-jamming techniques. She was one of a select group who qualified as air navigation instructor, received flight pay, and wore technical observer wings—a precursor to the present naval flight officers.[55]

Officers of the women's reserve also held many demanding and responsible positions in laboratories doing research and testing, and compiling scientific information. At the Indian Head, Maryland, rocket power plant early in 1945, Waves operated the laboratory, completely staffed one of the firing bays, and did approximately half the ballistics calculations. By August 1945 sixty WAVES officers and two hundred enlisted Waves were among the 2,555 uniformed personnel engaged in scientific and technical work at the Naval Research Laboratory (NRL) in Anacostia, Washington, D.C. In September 1944, five WAVES officers arrived at the NRL together. They had just spent six months at Harvard and three months at MIT studying radio and radar engineering in a class with more than one hundred men from various branches of the military. Four of the women were assigned to radio and radar work, but Marie Klein, who had worked for Southern Bell before the war doing statistical work, was assigned to a civilian scientist and "spent all day punching a calculator, working on air-to-air-missile trajectories."[56]

Perhaps the most notable American woman scientist of World War II was the Wave who ran calculations for the navy on the Mark I computer. With a Ph.D. in mathematics, Grace Murray Hopper joined the navy and spent the war at the BuShips Computation Project at Harvard University. There she was one of a team (including one other woman, Ens. Ruth Brendel) who operated the navy's only computer, the Mark I.[57] Yet the story of the WAVES is significant not only for its star performers but also for the high level of competence achieved generally by its members in World War II in professions completely new to them. In spite of deep initial reservations, assessments of Waves' performance by those in a position to know were ultimately favorable.

In July 1943, for example, a survey was conducted among fourteen representative activities to obtain a cross-section of opinion on how Waves handled their communications duties. In general, the comments were favorable, although it was suggested that WAVES officers, in particular, needed more practical training before being assigned. The district communication officer for the Fifth Naval District wrote on 10 August that "it might be of interest to you to know that two of the original WAVE officers who reported here in January are standing 'top watch' as CWOs [communication watch officer] and also are handling the job of Staff Duty Officer for ComFive."[58] The chief of BuShips, replying to the survey in September, noted that there were eighty-three WAVES officers on duty at the bureau in administration, in maintenance, and in the radio and shipbuilding divisions. In addition, there were ninety-six officers on duty throughout the country at the offices of the supervisors of shipbuilding and the inspectors of machinery. "The most cogent proof of their efficiency," wrote the chief, "is the continuous demand for more WAVES, not only from divisions which have already had some assigned to them, but also from divisions which previously did not consider them as potential replacements for male officers."[59] Even Senator Walsh had softened by 1943. "I see some of the charming young ladies who represent the WAVES here," he gushed during a Senate hearing. "We are pleased to note that we have got very excellent reports from naval officers as to the very excellent work you are doing."[60]

Unfortunately, some other legislators proved incapable of moving beyond their prejudices. Soon after the end of the war, the House Naval Affairs Committee debated an initial proposal to establish the women's reserve on a permanent basis. Congressman Carl Vinson, committee chair and longtime opponent of women in the military, was particularly mulish after having "seen some comments in the newspapers saying that the women were going to run the navy." His resistance did much to prevent an early favorable resolution of the issue. In fact, by 1947 the final dissolution of the WAVES was imminent, and the navy had to launch a vigorous campaign to save them. A Navy Department press release of 27 June 1947 urged retention of women, going so far as to admit that "in certain specialized fields the performance of WAVES was superior to that of men." During this time of rumor and uncertainty, however, many women who might otherwise have stayed in service left the WAVES, believing they had no future there. A number of the WAVES meteorologists, for example, asked for discharges in 1946 although they would have preferred to remain. They took civilian jobs in the field in which the navy had trained them, but they received little official encouragement in the job market. Serious concern was given to channeling male military forecasters into government and private-sector meteorology, but the women were generally ignored.[61]

Acrimonious congressional debate on the permanent admission of women to the regular navy and to the naval reserve dragged on into 1948. In February of that year, Adm. Louis Denfeld, by then the CNO, told the House Armed Services Subcommittee on Organization and Manpower that it was essential to provide careers for women in the regular navy in order to secure the strength and resources of "womanpower." The last war had shown that "this is particularly applicable to problems of medical and technological development . . . which must continue during peacetime."[62] In a House committee debate back in June 1944, Congressman Frederick Bradley, though objecting to most Waves going overseas, had not minded the idea of Waves in the Medical Department doing so because "that is a natural function of a woman—to take care of the sick."[63] This was not at all the kind of work Admiral Denfeld praised in 1948, and his view was supported by the testimony of Rear Adm. H. L. Pugh, the deputy surgeon general, who described the "wide scope of the usefulness of the Women's Reserve to the Medical Department in the technical and clinical fields." They had been, and would continue to be "needed in technical specialties allied to medicine, in the laboratory, in research, in rehabilitation."[64] Finally, Rear Adm. Earl E. Stone, the chief of naval communications, made his pitch to the House committee to admit women to the regular navy. He stressed that during the war Waves had shown themselves particularly well fitted for work in coding rooms, for message traffic handling, for linguistic assignments, for cryptanalytic work, and for all phases of naval communications.[65]

On 2 June 1948, after more than a year of debate, Congress finally passed the Women's Armed Services Integration Act. This act saved the WAVES, making them for the first time an integral part of the regular navy. In spite of testimony about their varied capabilities, they were finally retained mostly to perform clerical functions and as a nucleus for expansion in case of a future emergency. As before, the terms of admission were grudging; numbers were limited to 2 percent of the regular navy strength, and there was a lid on promotions.[66]

The cumulative accomplishments of the WAVES—sometimes with the support of their male coworkers and sometimes in the face of daunting opposition—were important in winning the navy's scientific war. Yet recognition of their contribution to naval science and technology still lags far behind awareness of their achievements in more traditional female roles such as nursing. Perhaps, in part, this is because the prewar resistance to scientific and technical careers for women was reasserted once the men returned and wanted to reclaim their jobs. Evidence suggests that unlike Sears, van Straten, Hopper, and Rees, most women who had performed technical and scientific work in the navy during wartime never used, nor indeed even spoke of, those skills once peace was restored. In general, they returned to civilian life, participating in the new national prosperity as housewives. Their technical and scientific prowess was quickly forgotten—by others if not by themselves.[67]

The same was generally true for most of the women who served, whether in the military or in wartime jobs as civilians. So what did those women who married and moved on get out of their war work? One recent account gives some insight. Hazel Parker Taylor signed up for officers' training school in 1943 and became paymaster at the naval air station in Sanford, Florida. "Being a Navy officer was a boost for me," she wrote fifty-three years later.

> Even with a college degree, job opportunities weren't great in 1941, when I graduated [from college]. Women had little expectation for advancement, except perhaps to become an executive secretary. In the Navy I was given equality of opportunity, total respect as an officer, and management responsibilities. As paymaster each month I disbursed about a quarter of a million dollars in cash, kept all financial records of the pay office, and supervised eighteen military and civilian workers. It was so gratifying to have a chance to be an executive and not be handicapped for being female. I'm almost ashamed to say how much I enjoyed the whole experience.

Hazel Taylor left the navy as a lieutenant (j.g.), married in 1947, and had five children. Later she got a graduate degree and taught for more than twenty years. When Taylor signed up for the navy her mother wanted to join her but was a year too old, so she joined the army instead. Her daughter remembers how good those years were for her mother, too, serving as a private first class working the telephone switchboard at Fort Sumter, South Carolina, proud of her service and of the uniform she wore.[68]

Most of the literature on military women in World War II emphasizes —like Hazel Taylor's story—the personal benefits women believed they derived from their wartime service, even when it did not visibly affect their later lives or their careers. The four women whose contributions we will now examine in detail—Sears, van Straten, Hopper, and Rees—were exceptions in many ways. They were exceptional in their prewar careers, exceptional in their wartime service, and exceptional in what they got out of it and where they went from there. In each case their experiences during the war deeply affected their postwar professional lives in positive ways. They each gave in full measure and they received much in return because they were ready and able to perceive new challenges.

2

MARY SEARS

oceanographer

An interest in the possible military uses of oceanography had begun to develop in America even before the commencement of hostilities at Pearl Harbor, particularly in anticipation of anti-U-boat warfare in the Atlantic. By the end of 1942, however, amphibious assaults like Operation Torch in North Africa and seaborne attacks on Japanese-held islands in the Pacific had made oceanography a crucial element of the war effort. The problem was how to land large numbers of troops from the water onto strongly fortified beaches. Costly mistakes continued to occur in the amphibious assaults of 1943, particularly at Tarawa in the Gilbert Islands, where unusually low tides grounded landing craft on the surrounding reef, forcing troops to wade slowly ashore into devastating enemy fire. Typical was the experience of Col. David M. Shoup, commander of the 2d Marine Regiment, who landed on Betio Island, Tarawa Atoll, on 20 November 1943. Shoup

> leaped out of his disabled tracked landing vehicle . . . into the turbid green waters of Betio's lagoon—and into unimaginable hell on earth. It was 1000. In less than an hour the carefully designed amphibious

assault plan of the 2d Marine Division had degenerated into chaos. Shoup himself had already been wounded in the leg, and as he waded painfully toward the long pier, he saw knots of demoralized troops clinging to the pilings.[1]

Tarawa drove home the necessity for improved strategic planning based on intelligence assessments that must include the best and most up-to-date hydrographic information.

It had been to collect, organize, and present such oceanographic intelligence that planktonologist Mary Sears had been ordered to Washington in April 1943. Disasters like Tarawa in November ensured that planners at the highest levels would pay close attention to her oceanographic intelligence reports for future amphibious operations. Indeed, during the remainder of the war, Sears's oceanographic reports were considered so vital that on 20 May 1946, the chief of naval operations himself, Adm. Chester W. Nimitz, commended her for her "outstanding contribution to the war effort as Chief of the Oceanographic Unit of the Division of Maritime Security of the Hydrographic Office." Even allowing for the standard boilerplate language of letters of commendation, something of the immediate, practical impact of Sears's work crept in when Nimitz added that she was "frequently called upon by the Joint Chiefs of Staff to furnish critically valuable information for use in combat operations."[2]

How did this short, arthritic, shy, forty-year-old specialist in minute plankton—and a self-styled inbred New Englander to boot—arrive at a position to influence the combat effectiveness of the U.S. Navy in World War II? The journey was a long and arduous one.[3]

Mary Sears took on her challenging role when women became a numerically small but important part of the navy's solution to its scientific manpower needs. In mobilizing for total war, the United States successfully harnessed a broad spectrum of previously overlooked resources: women. Particularly hard-pressed for scientists to direct its rapid technological expansion, the navy turned, albeit reluctantly, to Mary Sears and others like her, and both sides profited from the exchange. Though very able, without the national emergency these women scientists would almost certainly not have attained such significant positions, nor would they have enjoyed the boost their military achievements gave to their later civilian professional lives. Sears herself was convinced of this benefit. Looking back later she wrote: "The years in the U.S. Navy in charge of oceano-graphic intelligence reports gave me an opportunity as a woman to further my career that nothing else could have."[4]

Yet because the sciences continued to be dominated by men—even after World War II—until very recently there was not even a way to acknowledge success in science except in masculine terms. Just as Grace Hopper was to win a "Man-of-the-Year" award, Mary Sears's accomplishments won her a place in the tenth edition of *American Men of Science* (1960–61). Clearly, then, Sears's chosen educational and professional path was unusual for a woman, though little in her early life suggests the direction she would later take. She herself always said she was a "victim of happenstance: nothing in my life was ever planned."[5]

Mary Sears was born on 18 July 1905 and raised in rural Wayland, Massachusetts, about ten miles west of Boston, where her great-grandfather had been a Unitarian minister and the author of the words to the well-known Christmas carol "It Came upon a Midnight Clear." She grew up in comfortable surroundings, though the loss of her mother in 1911 and her father's subsequent remarriage gave her responsibility at an early age for her two younger siblings and a half-brother and two half-sisters. She always had the security, however, of a very close relationship with her stepmother, who had been her homeroom teacher. Sears, twelve years old when her father remarried, was in on the secret of the marriage ahead of time, which gave her a double tie with her new mother.[6]

A competent girl with tenacity and drive, Sears graduated from the private Winsor School in Boston in 1923, distinguished in her yearbook for her reserved nature and her keen ability. Her classmates believed she was destined for a political career representing the farm bloc in Congress because she knew everything there was to know about farming, particularly about raising Guernsey cows. This knowledge might have surprised some of her colleagues later in life, though perhaps her love of gardening, which they all knew well, reflected her early agrarian bent. Besides farming, Mary Sears's other chief interests were listed as children, housekeeping, and knitting; nothing in the yearbook suggested a long career devoted to the sea.[7]

From Winsor, Sears went to Radcliffe College, where she planned to study Greek but was encouraged by her stepmother, a Radcliffe graduate, to try other subjects. A course in biology led to one or two summers spent in Bermuda studying corals, where she began her lifelong pursuit of collecting specimens. Her fascination with marine invertebrates led her to major in zoology, in spite of the generally inhospitable atmosphere suggested by the absence of bathrooms for women in Harvard's Museum of Comparative Zoology, where she had to do most of her studying.[8] In 1927 Sears received a bachelor's degree, magna cum laude, from Radcliffe and was elected to Phi Beta Kappa. Her younger half-sister Leila maintained the family tradition by following Sears to Radcliffe some years later. Like Sears, she, too, ended up in the WAVES in World War II, also serving in Washington, where the two "Radder-Gradders" got together for dinner from time to time. Another sister, Katharine (Kit), graduated summa cum laude from Smith College in 1931 but had no military leanings, and the two Sears brothers were unable to serve in the military because of defective eyesight.

After completing her undergraduate work, Mary Sears continued at Radcliffe, earning a master's degree in 1929. At that time her focus was on amphibians, which were abundant in the Wayland-Sudbury area where she lived. Leila remembered Sears taking her and another sister on frog- and salamander-hunting excursions in boggy pools and brooks, impervious to the dangers of mud and quicksand. One time the younger girls were amazed to see their sister, up to her waist in mud, struggle out without help. "She was always very strong," Leila recalled.[9]

These adventures were in aid of Sears's doctoral dissertation, to be entitled "Migration of Pigment in Frogs' Eyes." She had hoped to find a method for changing the color of human eyes, but in the end shifted topics to "The Deep-Seated Melanophones of the Lower Vertebrates," for which she was awarded a Ph.D. in zoology in 1933. On that foundation Sears began her career as a biological oceanographer.[10]

Oceanographic studies in the United States had languished after World War I, following a promising beginning in the nineteenth century with the work of Harvard professors Louis Agassiz and his son Alexander. In the 1920s, much of what would today be considered oceanography was taking place at the Museum of Comparative Zoology at Harvard as the work of Henry Bryant Bigelow—a former student of Alexander Agassiz—who had become, according to Sears, "a one man task force." Dr. Bigelow was engaged in writing two large monographs, one on the plankton of the Gulf of Maine, the other on the physical oceanography of the Gulf of Maine. His work developed both aspects of a field that was usually divided between marine biology and physical oceanography.[11]

As a graduate student, Sears worked at the Museum of Comparative Zoology with Dr. Bigelow, whom she later described as "perhaps the *only* person who was ever competent to write about *all* aspects of oceanography . . . not only from the United States but also from Europe." In her first year of graduate school (1927), Sears climbed the stairs to the fourth-floor laboratory in the museum, where Bigelow set her to work identifying (under his supervision) the plankton he had collected in Monterey Bay, California, the previous summer. This was, Sears remembered, "an education not otherwise to be had at Radcliffe—or even at Harvard." Far from seeing her work as the routine drudgery to which most graduate students are liable, Sears viewed the frequent conferences with Bigelow as, in effect, private tutoring in oceanography from one of the few people competent to teach it.[12]

Sears's devotion to planktonology was set, and so, too, at the same time, was her lifelong association with the Woods Hole Oceanographic Institution (WHOI). In a small way, Sears was even instrumental in the very creation of WHOI. Her assistance with his cataloging gave Bigelow the time to write up a report for the Committee on Oceanography of the National Academy of Sciences recommending the establishment of a major oceanographic center on the East Coast of the United States to equal in stature the Scripps Institution of Oceanography in La Jolla, California. Frank R. Lillie, the chairman of the National Academy of Sciences Committee on Oceanography and the president and former director of the Marine Biological Laboratory at Woods Hole, had long advocated such a center and urged Bigelow to write the report. In 1930 WHOI was established next to the Marine Biological Laboratory in the village of Woods Hole, Cape Cod, Massachusetts, with an initial grant of two million dollars from the Rockefeller Foundation.[13] From the very beginning, WHOI's mandate was to encourage all aspects of a general oceanographic program.[14]

Henry Bigelow, having helped to found WHOI, became its first director. In addition to supporting both Woods Hole research facilities, the Rockefeller Foundation also gave money to the Bermuda Biological Station, the Scripps Institution, and the University of Washington's program in marine science, thus ensuring that the United States was in a good position to respond aggressively to the challenges of maritime and amphibious warfare in World War II.[15]

When WHOI was founded in 1930, however, according to Sears there were only three people in the whole country who could really be considered oceanographers. Few scientists on the East Coast had undertaken sustained research at sea, the most notable exception being Bigelow himself, who had sailed on various fisheries vessels, including the schooner *Grampus* and the aging R/V *Albatross*. Otherwise, like Henry Stetson at the Museum of Comparative Zoology at Harvard, sea scientists were mostly just scientists with yachts. Even Scripps was without a research ship for some years after World War I due to lack of funding, and the institution survived only by allying itself with the University of California. In the early days, and with some justification, the WHOI staff were sometimes referred to as "the Harvard Yacht Club."[16]

Almost nobody earned degrees in oceanography at that time, including Sears. Instead, they concentrated on the marine aspects of the more traditional disciplines of physics, chemistry, and biology. Spurred by the dynamic oceanography coming out of Norway, however, especially the work of Vilhelm Bjerknes, interest in the marine sciences began to pick up in the 1930s. At that time there were a dozen or so students at Scripps working in marine biology—several of them women. Nevertheless, biological oceanography as a distinct discipline did not develop until the 1950s, when it emerged as part of the expansion of all sciences made possible by the increased interest and funding generated during World War II.[17]

The U.S. Navy was no newcomer to the field. Even before the Civil War the navy had been collecting meteorological and oceanographic observations. Lt. Matthew Fontaine Maury, superintendent of the Depot of Charts and Instruments, prepared ocean charts showing winds, currents, ice floes, and other physical characteristics of the ocean. By the 1880s all the navy's marine oceanographic activities came under the supervision of the Hydrographic Office. The U.S. Coast and Geodetic Survey was also active in the nineteenth century sponsoring hydrographic and other scientific surveys. During World War I, the U.S. Navy (and the British Royal Navy) had major hydroacoustic research organizations, although most of the research involving cooperation with civilians was dropped as soon as peace returned. Some sonar/asdic research continued, however. In the United States this work was made possible by the establishment of the Naval Research Laboratory in 1923. The following year, when the navy had hoped to launch an oceanographic expedition, Congress refused to vote the funds, and this pattern generally continued in the Depression years. In the first half of the 1930s, therefore, there had been little support for marine research for military purposes in the United States. The Germans, on the other hand, were already making some progress in this regard, and the Japanese were assiduously charting the waters around their new Pacific mandate islands. The ripples of approaching conflict finally brought change in the United States, too, and Mary Sears was in at the beginning of the new developments.[18]

During the early 1930s under the tutelage of Dr. Bigelow, Sears spent winters at the Museum of Comparative Zoology in Cambridge and summers in Woods Hole at the Marine Biological Laboratory, where she gave nearly every waking moment to her work. One time her stepmother and sister Leila came to visit and take her out to lunch. Providing her relatives with seats, Sears refused to even talk to them until the stroke of noon. When she was finally allowed to converse, Mrs. Sears asked her daughter what was in the several mason jars on the shelf behind her. "The contents of fishes' stomachs," Sears replied. When asked why there were so many, Sears responded a bit testily that each was very different and came from a different part of the ocean. When they went to a restaurant in town, Sears would spend only forty-five minutes with them because she had already squandered fifteen minutes of the lunch hour walking and chatting. These were the Depression years, and Sears spent the summers living in various boardinghouses, always in very frugal accommodations. One year her pillowcases were discarded feed bags, one of which still showed the slogan, "Lay or Bust."[19]

Although Sears had no way of knowing it then, the contacts she made while a graduate student working for Henry Bigelow and her early association with WHOI would prove of great importance to the effective fulfillment of her assignment in the navy. On the floor above Bigelow's office at the Museum of Comparative Zoology, for example, in an enclosure off the hall next to the elevator, sat Columbus O'Donnell Iselin, another graduate student in Bigelow's coterie. Iselin, also a yachtsman, was to become the energetic wartime director of WHOI with close ties to Sears's office in Washington.[20]

Working with Bigelow exposed Sears to everyone of importance in marine science. A broad array of visitors came to see him, including many from overseas. There were frequent conferences with personnel from the U.S. Coast Guard and from the U.S. Bureau of Fisheries. Coast Guard ice observation officers wrote up their annual reports for the western North Atlantic's International Ice Patrol while stationed ashore at the Harvard museum, becoming, according to Sears, "competent oceanographers" at the same time. Bigelow also offered hospitality to representatives of the International Council for the Exploration of the Sea (ICES) who came to Harvard from Norway, Denmark, England, Scotland, and France, among other places. Sears got to know "essentially every distinguished oceanographer including [as she put it] fisheries, biologists, physical oceanographers, etc."[21]

These contacts were extended, and friendships developed, in the congenial atmosphere of Cape Cod. For most of the 1930s, WHOI, like the Marine Biological Lab, was only a summer research center attracting faculty members from several universities. Sears began working there in 1932 as one of the first ten research assistants. Five of the original staff, all men, had their roots at Harvard, which long remained the dominant influence at the institution. Life at WHOI was very informal then. It was a small place where everyone knew everyone else and people were addressed by first names only; no one, not even distinguished foreign visitors, was "Doctor" or "Professor." For the first decade of its existence there was only one secretary for the whole institution, and the sole telephone in the place was in her office. When calls came in, the secretary would go into the hall and yell up for whomever was wanted, and they would have to run down to her office to take the call. After the war, when WHOI had grown in size and reputation with generous government funding, Sears recalled the earlier times with nostalgia.[22]

Sears worked at WHOI every summer from 1932 until 1943, becoming an integral part of the small fraternity of oceanographers. She began as a junior biologist, and from 1940 onward she was a planktonologist with a year-round appointment, one of only two women on the professional staff of nineteen. After her war service in Washington, Sears returned to WHOI full time in 1947. In 1963 she was named a senior scientist in the Biology Department, a position she held until her retirement in 1970. In 1978 Sears was named scientist emeritus. She was also a longtime member of the WHOI Corporation, serving as clerk of the corporation from 1947 to 1973, and as deputy clerk from 1973 to 1975. The following year Sears was named an honorary trustee and an honorary member of the corporation.[23]

During the early years, Sears spent only summers at WHOI and worked the rest of the year as a research assistant at Harvard, continuing her work with Henry Bigelow on studies of the waters of the continental shelf (1933–49); as a tutor in zoology at Radcliffe (1934–40); and as an instructor in zoology at Wellesley College (1938–43). Apparently, she was not a gifted teacher, candidly describing herself as "lousy," and she was not reappointed to teach at Wellesley. Nevertheless, Wellesley did give Sears what she called "a graceful exit": a faculty fellowship enabling her to do research in Pisco Bay off the coast of Peru for six months beginning in August 1941. This opportunity to study the effects on the guano industry of the phytoplankton of the Humboldt Current afforded Sears the only chance she had in her life for sustained work afloat.[24]

Research at sea is essential for a marine biologist, but for many years WHOI policy prohibited women from sailing on Woods Hole research vessels. The usual reason given was that there were no "facilities" for women onboard, especially on the original ketch *Atlantis,* which had only two "heads," of notorious reputation. Similarly primitive conditions did not prevent women from going to sea in other countries, however. Nor were women prevented from sailing at the Bermuda Biological Station, which welcomed them, or on the University of Washington's research ship *Catalyst,* sailing out of Puget Sound. As Sears noted, there may not have been facilities, "but there were pails!" and that is exactly what she used when aboard the guano company boat in Peru. At least one young woman who was initially accepted for a research position at WHOI was quickly rejected when it was learned that she expected to go to sea. It was hard even for men to get a berth on a research vessel, and this seems to have been a closely guarded privilege among them. It was more than thirty years after Sears's graduation, in fact, before women were generally accepted on oceanographic ships, and it was not until 1963, with the acquisition of *Atlantis II,* that WHOI finally got its first research vessel equipped with "facilities" for six women among a scientific party of nineteen.[25]

Noted oceanographer Roger Revelle once remarked that an oceanographic institution without a research ship is like an astronomical observatory without a telescope. If that is true, then for a marine biologist, to be shorebound is to be blind. Revelle, a former director of the Scripps Institution of Oceanography and founder of the University of California at San Diego, certainly knew what he was talking about. Columbus Iselin, Sears's fellow graduate student at Harvard, became an eminent physical oceanographer, but Sears's entire professional career was defined by her restriction to shore. Yet far from succumbing to this handicap, she found other ways to establish a place for herself in a relatively new, male-dominated, seagoing field.[26]

Early in 1942, at the end of her only real research cruise, Sears returned to the States from Peru by plane; passenger steamers were no longer sailing because of the war. Everyone at WHOI was already engaged in war work, and Sears "found the Institution alive with many new faces." Director Iselin's committed patriotism and enthusiasm coupled with the needs of the U.S. Navy had turned WHOI essentially into a laboratory for naval oceanographic research. Members of the regular staff were joined by scientists from many universities and from industry, as well as by assigned naval officers. Those lacking experience in marine studies soon received it. Before she even had time to sort out her notes, Sears was enlisted to prepare a bibliography on marine fouling of ships' bottoms (and anti-fouling methods) for a National Defense Research Committee–sponsored Navy/Harvard/WHOI project.[27]

The project was directed by Harvard associate professor of zoology George L. Clarke, who was also a marine biologist on the staff at WHOI. Alfred C. Redfield, of Harvard and WHOI, adviser to the Navy Department on the investigation of fouling, was a consultant. In collaboration with other researchers surveying correspondence and reports on fouling at the Bureau of Ships in Washington, Sears completed a search through the published zoological literature from 1928 through 1939, as well as looking up all significant references from other biological sources. She summarized much of the material on barnacles and other groups of organisms that play a part in fouling—including hydroids, bryozoa, and Pacific tubeworms—and created the sort of comprehensive index on file cards for which she justly became famous. Among the characteristics that enabled her to keep such meticulous records was the "ultra tidiness" particularly noted by her sister Leila.[28] At any rate, in March, when she joined the project, Dr. Clarke had described Sears as "particularly well qualified to undertake this part of the work as she has had long experience with the research work and literature of marine biology."[29] The shortage of trained oceanographers to handle the great rush of navy-sponsored oceanographic projects made very important the help of this specialist in the minute plankton called siphonophores.

Although many Americans remained isolationists until Pearl Harbor, the opening of hostilities in Europe in September 1939 infused urgency into much scientific work. In June 1940 President Franklin Roosevelt established the National Defense Research Committee (NDRC) to mobilize, direct, support, and arrange financing for the nation's scientific activities for war. This act was the first major involvement of the U.S. government in the funding of science, and it permanently affected the dynamic as well as the speed of scientific change. In part by means of NDRC sponsorship, the navy soon became a major patron of oceanography, a role it maintains today. Though late getting started in the application of science to war, America caught up quickly, even while the initial mobilization of resources was frequently rocky.

Late that summer of 1940, NDRC began to pour funds into WHOI for a broad study of the role of oceanography in naval warfare. Ten years had passed since WHOI was founded, but there were still few well-trained physical oceanographers. About half the staff of WHOI were biologists, which was typical for marine labs before the war, and they were mostly engaged in pure research, not projects directly related to specific applications. A WHOI report written after the war acknowledged the cost of failing to start a training program for oceanographers in 1939, noting that it was too late to do so in 1942. By then the practical uses of the marine sciences in modern warfare were very clear, but "almost overnight the number of qualified physical oceanographers in the country became entirely inadequate."[30]

By contrast, Germany and Scandinavia had institutionalized the ocean sciences and were making strong strides in the field. Germany, especially, quickly established close ties between oceanographic research and the needs of the navy. Between 1925 and 1927, the German navy had loaned a converted gunboat, the R/V *Meteor,* to the University of Berlin for a research expedition to the South Atlantic Ocean that collected data in an area that was to prove crucial in the next war. In fact, since 1935, according to Iselin, the German navy had had "a relatively large group of oceanographers . . . working on a number of naval problems." Admiral Bryan, looking back in 1945, had a different view. "It was widely known before the war," he wrote,

> that many of the German oceanographers and fisheries men were outspoken in their dislike of the Nazi regime. During the war German oceanographers did not produce any work of military value. In fact, the oceanographers deliberately "slowed down" their work and one of

the most outstanding was actually reported to have been completely uncooperative.

Germany's failure to mobilize its oceanographers was in sharp contrast to America's ability to do so and represented an important weakness.[31]

In 1937 WHOI scientists had been asked to undertake underwater sound transmission observations in collaboration with the U.S. Navy destroyer *Semmes*. This joint project emphasized the relationship of physical oceanography to subsurface warfare, a connection that was confirmed in 1939 when WHOI was engaged by the navy to investigate the slime film that formed on antifouling paints. In 1940 WHOI signed a contract with the newly created Bureau of Ships to examine organisms, such as barnacles, that substantially reduced the speed of ships by fouling their bottoms, and to assess the efficacy of antifouling paints as a deterrent. By the time Sears returned from Peru to assist with this project, it was already clear that even a few extra knots of speed could be crucial in the close-run contest between German U-boats and Allied merchant and warships then raging in the Atlantic. From this point onward, government funding poured into research establishments throughout the United States. While some scientists grumbled about the navy's emphasis on application, not fundamental research, in the long run they all stood to gain, oceanographers along with the rest.[32]

The sudden influx of funds for oceanographic studies ran up against a lack of personnel qualified to undertake them. The navy addressed this deficiency by calling on scientists—women included—in fields related to oceanography such as geology, physics, chemistry, and biology. This creative approach continued as the applications of oceanography to warfare multiplied. WHOI was only one of a number of institutions in the country engaged by NDRC and the navy to develop military oceanography; others included the Scripps Institution and the Museum of Comparative Zoology at Harvard. Usually, each organization worked on only part of a given project, though a close collaboration was maintained, and the navy itself undertook the final assembly.[33]

A similar rapid militarization and expansion was occurring in many other scientific fields at the same time, forcing the navy to compete for scientists with other branches of the armed forces as well as with NDRC. The WHOI annual report for 1940 noted that several of the institution's researchers might soon be recruited by the military; and indeed, during

WHOI Boat Basin with research vessels and lobster boats, 1945
© *Woods Hole Oceanographic Institution*

the course of 1941, one man went into the army, one to the navy, and two to the Coast Guard. In 1942 WHOI lost 7 staff members to the military, including Mary Sears, and by the end of the war the number had reached 63. On the other hand, increasing war work at the institution (mostly for NDRC, BuShips, and the navy's Hydrographic Office) led to an increase in local staff from 60 in 1940 to a high of 335 by 1945. The augmentation came principally from universities, from industry, and from naval officers assigned to assist with classified research.[34]

In Sears's words, the war created a "revolution" at WHOI: "money became available for instrumentation and the reversing thermometer, and the Nansen bottle almost, but not quite, became obsolete!" A group of researchers including Paul Fye and James Coles, known to their colleagues as the "bang boys," were engaged to study underwater explosives. Another group worked on studies of ocean water temperatures, developing a bathy-thermograph, which could make a continuous temperature plot on a grid while being towed behind a ship under way. Other studies undertaken for the navy tested underwater acoustic echo-ranging gear for tracking submarines; advances were made in sea, surf, and wave forecasting; and an air thermograph was used to measure the drift of smoke at sea for smoke-screen experiments.[35]

Clearly, Mary Sears's expertise could have helped the WHOI war effort had she chosen to remain, although alone she could not have done much to rectify the gender imbalance. Of the 105 scientists hired by WHOI to work on government contracts between 1942 and 1945, only 2 were women. The demand for technically trained women was there at last, but the available pool was small and pulled in many directions. Toward the end of 1942, for example, and by her own account "feeling very full of patriotism," Sears had tried to join the WAVES. She evidently also felt some pressure to join her male WHOI colleagues who were already in the naval reserve or in the process of applying for admission. Initially Sears failed the medical exam, however, rejected as unfit because of an earlier bout of arthritis.[36] The navy counted on the old-boy network to supply critical scientific personnel. Because Mary Sears was a member of that network—by profession if not by gender—when her skills were needed, bureaucratic hurdles such as failed medicals were brushed aside and she was catapulted to a position of influence and authority within the military-scientific brotherhood.

Throughout the war, the navy, the army air forces, and NDRC continued to contract for increasing numbers of research projects with WHOI and other institutions to develop field and laboratory techniques for the burgeoning field of military oceanography. They created instruments and equipment for obtaining information on tides, currents, sea state, and other hydrographic factors, and began to integrate meteorological considerations into their studies. The war effort also required access to existing oceanographic intelligence and its analysis and presentation for immediate strategic planning at the highest levels. It is this aspect of the new military oceanography with which Mary Sears became involved.

In order to speed the delivery of oceanographic information for the rapidly expanding military operations, as well as to coordinate research activities, the various military establishments began to reorganize their own technical branches. In mid-1941 1st Lt. H. Richard Seiwell, famed at WHOI for being able to make drinkable alcohol out of almost anything, left for military duty. By March the following year the now Captain Seiwell was chief of the Oceanographic Unit, Weather Research Center,

Headquarters Army Air Forces. Seiwell acquired marine biologists wherever he could find them, and within a year the section had turned out forty operational reports for use in mission planning. Moreover, despite the navy's unwillingness to allow Prof. Harald Sverdrup and his assistant, Walter Munk, to work on classified projects because they had close relatives in Nazi-held territory, Seiwell arranged army clearances for them. As a result, both were soon under contract with the Scripps Institution not only to develop sea, swell, and surf forecasting techniques but also to teach these techniques to graduates of the USAAF's meteorological training program.[37]

The navy's reorganization of oceanography began in September 1942 when Rear Adm. Julius A. Furer, coordinator of research and development, convened a meeting attended by Rear Adm. George S. Bryan, the hydrographer of the navy, and Cdr. Rawson W. Bennett, director of electronics design, BuShips, among others. At the meeting it was decided to transfer Lt. Roger Revelle, USNR—an oceanographer from Scripps—from his initial posting at the Navy Radio and Sound Laboratory at Point Loma, California, to duty at the Hydrographic Office, with collateral duty at BuShips to coordinate the navy's oceanographic work. According to various accounts left by Sears, as well as stories she told to others, Revelle, a misfit at Hydro, was soon spending most of his time at BuShips. He still needed someone to cover oceanographic intelligence at Hydro, so in mid-December 1942, he stopped off at WHOI to see who was available.[38]

In later years Sears maintained that since all the men at WHOI were already busy at sea because of the war, Columbus Iselin, a reserve naval officer himself, palmed her off on Revelle. The first she knew of the assignment was when she looked up to see a tall figure in navy uniform leaning against the doorjamb of her office. In retrospect, Sears came to the conclusion that given WHOI's wartime concentration on underwater sound research, Iselin believed the lab could spare a marine biologist more easily than, say, a physicist or a chemist. Anyway, networking paid off for Revelle. Because the navy wanted a serving officer to head its oceanographic effort, Revelle apparently even managed to get Sears a waiver for her medical disability. On 13 February 1943, she began an abbreviated officer training course at the Naval Reserve Midshipmen's School (WR) at Northampton, Massachusetts. On 27 March 1943, Sears was commissioned a lieutenant (j.g.) and was posted directly to the Hydrographic Office in Washington. A year later another improbable warrior, Grace Hopper, would undergo

Lt. Mary Sears, USNR(W),
Chief, Oceanographic Unit
Courtesy Denton Family

similarly speedy training and a direct assignment to the Bureau of Ships Computation Laboratory, where her mathematical skills were also in immediate demand.[39]

Established by an act of Congress in 1866, the Hydrographic Office had long been a division in the Bureau of Navigation working with the Coast Guard and the U.S. Maritime Commission to provide maritime navigation charts and to coordinate the collection of oceanographic data. In April 1942, reflecting its increasing operational significance, Hydro was transferred to the Office of the Chief of Naval Operations. There it underwent a number of internal reorganizations, but most of the work continued to be done by the Division of Maritime Security, the Division of Air Navigation, and the Division of Chart Construction.[40]

Among her personal papers Sears kept several copies of the letter ordering her to active duty with Hydro. One was the copy that had gone to the Division of Maritime Security (where she was due to report) on which someone had penciled: "She is an oceanographer recommended by Revelle." At Hydro, Sears reported to Lt. Cdr. B. E. Dodson, head of the Pilot Charts Section, but she was responsible, more or less, to Roger Revelle, with whom she worked closely throughout the war. As project officer, Revelle guided the navy's contract work with WHOI, Scripps, and others from his post at BuShips. There, as the officer in charge of Water Studies, Sonar Design Section, Revelle provided the fleet with information and instructions about new devices and techniques, especially with regard to hydroacoustics and oceanography. He also continued to make the arrangements with Scripps and with the University of California Division of War Research, and established the scheduling for the production of Submarine Supplements. While leaving Sears to handle the elusive realm of long-range strategic forecasting, Revelle busied himself with the more tangible aspects of oceanography, the products of the labs and field tests.[41]

The Division of Maritime Security was primarily responsible for collecting and disseminating information on minefields, swept channels, ice, and all other factors affecting the navigational safety of shipping on the high seas. In addition to broadcasting and publishing warnings of immediate dangers and changes in aids to navigation, the division produced written descriptions of the coasts of the world, radio navigational aids, light lists, tables of distances between ports, and pilot charts. When Sears first arrived at Hydro in April 1943, she was assigned a desk in the Pilot Chart Section, where she was the only person doing oceanographic work. Awareness of the significance of military oceanography was growing rapidly, however, as was the need for marine intelligence for future waterborne landings. It was just at this time that the Allied invasion of Sicily (Operation Husky, July 1943) was being planned.[42]

The requisite military oceanographic data for that assault would already have been supplied by Dick Seiwell's group within the army air forces. However, shortly after Sears arrived at Hydro the Joint Meteorological Committee made a decision that was significant for the war effort, and for Sears personally. In a highly successful and far-sighted joint planning initiative for interservice cooperation, the oceanographic activities of the army and the navy were ordered centralized in the navy's Hydrographic Office. The majority of the personnel of the Oceanographic Section in the AAF Weather Service were accordingly transferred to the U.S. Navy Hydrographic Office in June 1943, thereby providing the nucleus of the new navy Oceanographic Unit (OU) headed by Lt. Mary Sears. Simultaneously Dick Seiwell was transferred to beach intelligence work in Europe, where he was involved in planning the Normandy landings, and then later in the Pacific. Thereafter, all requests for oceanographic intelligence, even from the army, had to go via the Navy Department, to Hydro's Oceanographic Unit.[43]

The main work of Hydro remained, as it had long been, the making and printing of navigation charts, but the commencement of hostilities injected a frenzied pace into this normally leisurely and mostly civilian occupation. Rear Admiral Bryan, who returned from retirement to head Hydro, called the nautical chart "an essential instrument of war," a truism which yet conveys the pressure imposed on Hydro. Under these circumstances change was inevitable. The personnel shortage was severe, but the navy resisted filling the vacant slots with women. Back in April 1942, in response to a Bureau of Navigation survey on shore jobs that might be filled by women should they be admitted to the navy, Hydro had replied in the same negative vein as most other departments that "there are no billets . . . now filled by commissioned officers which might be filled by one of the proposed auxiliary reserves." As Roger Revelle somewhat puckishly reminded people many years later, "at that time the Hydrographic Office was a *macho* organization."[44]

Before admitting women, the navy scraped the bottom of the barrel. A letter of August 1942 from the Office of the Assistant Secretary of the Navy, for example, authorized Hydro (as well as other affected offices) to reappoint employees whose removal had been requested previously by the Civil Service Commission on the grounds of fraud. Those who had made false claims as to experience or who had colluded to secure false vouchers could be reemployed "as long as their services are needed but not to extend beyond the duration of the present war." By that December, "older persons and the physically handicapped could also be employed," and finally, navy women were taken on, too, though on the same temporary terms.[45]

Less than a year later, the demand for oceanographic intelligence had intensified so much that the Hydrographer himself urged the Bureau of Naval Personnel to send him two WAVES ensigns to assist in the compilation and publication of data for the Air Navigation Division. "The demand for this data is increasing at a very rapid rate," wrote Admiral Bryan, and "any delay in making the information available to the fleet will seriously delay the war effort. These [WAVES] officers are urgently needed to help speed the program outlined above." As in most navy shore establishments after the outbreak of war, the Civil Service Commission—in spite of early fears of loss of positions to military women—could not

fill the required complement. Apparently there were not enough employees, or even lawbreaking ex-employees, to handle the increased workload.
In a letter written the next day asking for still more Waves, Admiral Bryan
stressed that the data produced by Hydro were for fleet- and shore-based
aircraft "in direct combat operations" and that any delay in disseminating the information would "seriously delay the war effort."[46]

The skills required of suitable candidates were experience with coded
records and files, knowledge of world geography and the use of maps and
atlases, general knowledge of aviation, and research experience with documentary material. In addition, the Chart Construction Division sought
cartographic engineers from among WAVES officers. Women with these
and many other skills were found and put to work. By April 1944 the
Hydrographic Office had become totally reliant on Waves. Admiral Bryan
bluntly summed up his dependency: "The degree with which the Hydrographic Office can meet the ever-increasing demand on production of priority and strategical navigation facilities is in direct proportion to the
WAVES that can be supplied [for] this activity."[47]

This dependence continued through the end of the war. In June 1945
the navy was still actively recruiting Waves, and the Waves of Hydro were
asked to participate in a widely publicized drive with a live exhibit demonstrating how they pieced together photographic surveys and made them
into charts. Hydro declined the request, noting that their workload was
still at a peak and they could spare no one for demonstrations for the
foreseeable future.[48]

When women already trained to perform the highly specialized tasks
of Hydro were not available, they were trained on the job. This was especially true in the Photogrammetric Unit, where a great many enlisted Waves
were involved in the preparation of target maps and surface and air navigation charts from aerial photographs taken by the navy in various theaters of operation. Most of the young women performing these tasks had
had no previous special training in photogrammetry, according to the
Hydrographer, but they were "a high type of American girl anxious to
learn and be of help to our Navy."[49] Hydro established a close liaison with
the Bureau of Naval Personnel in order to get women of the highest caliber possible for this work. They must "have superior intelligence and be
highly efficient in their respective operations [and], in addition, they must
be absolutely reliable from a security standpoint." The work was consid-

ered so essential that once trained, these enlisted Waves were given the same specialist (P) rating approved for enlisted men doing similar work.[50]

By the time Roger Revelle put forward Mary Sears's name for the Hydro post at the beginning of 1943, 10 enlisted Waves had already reported there and more had been requested. Seven WAVES officers had been assigned: some to the Division of Research's secret loran (radio navigation) project, some to the Division of Air Navigation, and the rest to the Division of Maritime Security. On 1 June the Hydrographer requested an initial assignment of 10 enlisted Waves supervised by one officer to work in the Geographical Research and Information Section. They were to compile a list estimated to consist of somewhere in the region of two million geographical names, with latitude, longitude, and reference map citations. By 23 June 1943, there were already 43 enlisted Waves at Hydro, with 85 due by 5 July, and a projected goal of 250 by 1 September. In June 1944 the number of WAVES officers at Hydro had grown to 30, and the number of enlisted Waves to 332. The personnel crunch was exacerbated by the requirement to operate in three shifts, seven days a week. Eventually, Waves filled the majority of the new positions at Hydro and replaced most of the navy and civilian men. The general rapid wartime expansion coupled with the new functions undertaken by Hydro required an infusion of personnel that overcame the initial reluctance to employ women.[51]

To give him proper due, by all accounts Admiral Bryan was much more open to the employment of women than were some of his peers. After a visit to Hydro in December 1943, WAVES director Capt. Mildred H. McAfee wrote to thank Bryan for all he had done "to maintain the pride and efficiency of women in the service," noting, in particular, his "cordial reception of them." A report of an inspection of Wave activities at Hydro in April 1945 commented on the great ability of the women there, both commissioned and enlisted, and noted the high regard in which they were held. Admiral Bryan, with possibly a touch of humor, was quoted saying of his Waves, "We would have been sunk without them."[52]

The Oceanographic Unit relied as much on women, both military and civilian, as did the rest of Hydro. Perhaps because Admiral Bryan was also on the board of directors of WHOI and knew the caliber of the scientists there, when Mary Sears arrived she got a job commensurate with her abilities. Thus, with new commission in hand, a prim WAVES lieutenant (j.g.) became "the first Oceanographer of the Navy in modern times," directing twelve other women and three men in the application of oceanography to war.[53]

Sears's little band included Dora Henry, a civil servant originally from the University of Washington oceanography program in Seattle and an expert on barnacles; another civilian, Mary Grier, also from the University of Washington, "the only oceanographic research librarian in the country"; and army air forces captain Fenner Chace.[54] Dr. Chace, a carcinologist well known to Sears, was the former curator of crustaceans at Harvard University's Museum of Comparative Zoology. In addition, there were an algologist and a limnologist and, of course, Sears the planktonologist. With the Hydrographer's sympathetic support, this predominantly female group of marine biologists was given practically free rein to do the work that came its way from the navy and from whichever other of the armed services needed oceanographic information. Growing awareness of the intelligence it could provide caused a corresponding rise in importance of the Oceanographic Unit within Hydro. This rather quickly changed the balance of power in the organization, and by the end of the war, Mary Sears (in due course promoted to lieutenant and then to lieutenant commander), along with Dodson and Revelle, had transformed the tiny Oceanographic Unit into a major division. Years later she witnessed the evolution of the Hydrographic Office itself into the Naval Oceanographic Office headed by an admiral bearing the title Oceanographer of the Navy.[55]

When Sears took over the Oceanographic Unit, information provided by physical oceanography was already recognized as essential in submarine warfare for improving search, attack, and evasion procedures, and in air-sea rescue for locating survivors drifting in rubber rafts. Physical oceanography was also required in the development of underwater ordnance, for determining the effect of sea and swell on certain types of mines, and for understanding the effect of turbulence on moored mine endurance and on the dispersal of floating mines. Much of the sea and swell work was being done by Scripps director Harald Ulrik Sverdrup, the world's leading physical oceanographer, and Walter Munk, a former army ski trooper who had worked for Seiwell on predictions for the North Africa landings. Revelle had been pivotal in getting Sverdrup and Scripps the navy contract for sea, swell, and surf forecasting, and their reports were an important source of information for the Oceanographic Unit. Biological oceanography had achieved a recognized military role as well; for example, in assessing the effect of certain organisms on mine mechanisms, in predicting how noise-making animals interfered with underwater listening devices, in identifying luminescent organisms that could give away the presence of a vessel by lighting up its wake, and in locating large kelps that might interfere with amphibious operations.[56]

As head of the Oceanographic Unit, Sears's role was to supervise the selection and transformation of research data from oceanographic centers on the East and West Coasts into oceanographic reports, charts, and pamphlets accessible to decision makers at the highest levels. She had to translate the technical manuals produced by scientists into practical language for the use of military commanders. Her responsibilities were generally confined to the Pacific and Indian Oceans after an arrangement was formalized with the British that gave their Admiralty's Hydrographic Department control over oceanographic intelligence for the Atlantic and its tributaries (e.g., the Mediterranean and the North Sea). The most crucial of her tasks, and the most taxing, was to provide—from whatever sources were available—intelligence reports demonstrating the main overall hydrographic factors affecting the location and timing of long-range operations. These reports were required for immediate strategic and tactical planning, especially for amphibious operations in the Pacific. Since forecasts were often demanded on extremely short notice, the Oceanographic Unit could not always wait for the results of research, but had to rely on already existing scientific literature, which was usually scanty. Even when information was available, it was often woefully out of date. The best available data on sea and swell in the Indian Ocean, for example, came from a Dutch publication from 1896, and this was far from exceptional.[57]

Time was a decisive factor in the war emergency, and it could not be wasted in "the pursuit of impossible perfection" and minute accuracy. According to Sears, the pressure to produce was especially severe "whenever Roosevelt and Churchill got together." At such times "there were always quickies. We'd have to work all night." One time, Sears remembered, the secretary to the Committee on Meteorology of the Joint Chiefs of Staff, or somebody similar, arrived very late with some tide tables he wanted computed for Pacific localities so secret that he insisted she do all the calculations herself. Although already exhausted, Sears worked on the tide tables all night, "doing just plain arithmetic," and wondered by morning if she was even getting the addition right.[58]

Sears and her Oceanographic Unit were often forced to rely on informed guesswork to prepare their intelligence reports on ocean currents, wave and tide predictions, amphibious landing sites, and the presence of propeller-fouling kelp or bioluminescent marine life. By pulling together information from diverse sources the OU provided operational intelligence for imminent Pacific island campaigns—including a number that never came off.

Some of the intelligence used by Sears in her reports came from overseas. Every ship in the navy reported on sea conditions during the war, and once a month all the logs were forwarded to the Office of the CNO and could be used by Hydro. In addition, other information went directly to Hydro, at least in theory. Five U.S. Navy survey vessels conducted surveys in the Pacific Ocean under the direction of Commander, Pacific Ocean Areas, but with technical supervision from Hydro. They employed teams of divers, conducted special studies of harbor defense installations, and established ranges for testing equipment. They also had lithographic printing and photographic plants onboard which enabled them to reproduce special charts and maps for the speedy dissemination of vital information. All the information obtained by these survey vessels was supposed to be relayed back to the Oceanographic Unit directly, although this aspect of the relationship was obviously not as efficient as it might have been. In August 1944 Admiral Bryan complained to C-in-C, U.S. Pacific Fleet, that on several occasions Hydro had compiled new charts based on outdated information because the survey vessels had been dilatory in sending their latest field charts. Not unreasonably, Bryan requested that he be advised of any future contemplated surveying operations in advance so that he could avoid duplication of effort and provide better service.[59]

The collection of all kinds of empirical data was vital for accurate forecasts, and efforts in this direction improved markedly between 1943 and 1945, during which time Sverdrup and Munk perfected their Sverdrup-Munk technique, a quantitative method for predicting sea, swell, and surf conditions for amphibious assaults. Accurate forecasting of the effect of waves on amphibious operations required accurate knowledge of three main variables: (1) the length and height of the waves in the open sea, (2) the swell that would affect conditions in the anchorage area, and (3) the height of the breakers on the beach. The waves themselves were also affected by three major variables: the strength and direction of the wind at the surface of the sea; the fetch, or distance of water over which the wind blew; and the length of time that the wind blew. Studies of these phenomena were carried on at an accelerated pace during the course of the war, at WHOI and at other marine laboratories. The navy also sent groups of aerological officers to special classes run by Sverdrup at Scripps for training in oceanographic forecasting. The officers were then sent to the fleet to implement the collection of data on sea and swell conditions in the open ocean and on the probable characteristics of surf on given beaches. In spite of these efforts, the information reaching Sears at Hydro was still far from complete.[60]

Sears's Oceanographic Unit also obtained information from a variety of beachhead intelligence-gathering groups. Members of underwater demolition teams, Marine Corps reconnaissance companies, terrain intelligence teams, harbor companies, and above all aerologists working with the fleet and task forces supplied valuable data. In addition, specific information was sometimes requested directly from forces overseas. In May 1944 Sears endorsed a confidential message to the naval officer in charge at New Guinea to pass on to two Royal Australian Navy hydrographic survey vessels, *Moresby* and *Benalla*. The Australians were informed that it was "essential to obtain tidal observations of important forward bases as early as possible. Readings every 20 minutes required with wind observations for period 15 days or 6 weeks if possible. Progressive results to be forwarded direct by air to Hydrographic Office Washington."[61]

Sometimes the information-gathering methods on which Sears had to rely were rudimentary. After the conquest of Tarawa, the U.S. commander on the island was asked to instruct the 74th Naval Construction Battalion to collect tide records to be forwarded to Hydro on the first and fifteenth of each month. A letter describing how this was to be done noted that the benchmark elevation of 13.26 feet above zero of the tide staff on the main dock on Betio Island (Tarawa Atoll) was taken from "the top of an arrow-head shaped piece of iron on the north corner of the triangular concrete base of the range beacon." A local benchmark established at the end of the dock near the tide staff consisted of "a row of five nails driven into the butt end of a log." As Columbus Iselin dryly noted in his postwar history of WHOI's war work, "during the study of waves it was found that proper devices to measure and record tides, swell and waves were lacking."[62]

A similar crude source of information received by the Oceanographic Unit was a sketch made by Captain R. Ohlund of the SS *Albert E. Watts* showing Cape Moreton and the sea approach to Brisbane, Australia. The *Watts,* owned by the Sinclair Refining Company, had been allocated to the navy and had made many successful trips to the Southwest Pacific carrying valuable cargo. Captain Ohlund's map was forwarded to Hydro by the Naval Transportation Service, which regarded it as a significant addition to existing navigation information.[63]

And such it may well have been, although perhaps the Naval Transportation Service was just reacting to the pitiful state of U.S. Pacific cartography. In fact, both the Japanese and America's European allies were well ahead of the United States in Pacific navigation. Japanese charts of Pacific areas were found to be far better than anything available in America, and superior British, Dutch, and Australian charts of the Pacific were also hastily reproduced for the use of the U.S. Navy. The prewar shortage of personnel and appropriations had hobbled Hydro for many years, and the newly established Oceanographic Unit particularly felt the consequences of being unprepared. Charts in general were "sadly lacking," and even those available to Sears were "rather inferior" and mostly covered areas of peacetime interest to the United States such as the coasts of the Caribbean Sea and the Atlantic and Pacific approaches to the Panama Canal. This narrow focus was of little help when the picture was changing so rapidly that the Hydrographer himself complained, "We do not know when or where our forces may be called to go into action."[64]

Fortunately, information from Japanese charts was often available to Sears. Before the war, the Japanese had surveyed Pacific waters with more than ninety vessels of all different sorts, actively collecting oceanographic data that had been published in scientific journals subscribed to by many American libraries. Additional documents were captured during the course of the war, such as the classified air charts and publications of the Japanese Hydrographic Office found on Kwajalein Atoll, Marshall Islands. In February 1944 Sears penciled on a cover letter accompanying Japanese tide tables captured by the 4th Marine Division on Namur (Kwajalein) that she was forwarding them to the Coast and Geodetic Survey for comparison with charts from earlier years.[65]

Among the domestic resources Sears could turn to for information were other organizations also involved, either partially or fully, in maritime studies. Output from these organizations increased dramatically during the course of the war. As mentioned before, NDRC was responsible for extensive research in subsurface warfare, as well as for studies necessary for mine warfare including investigation of corrosion, currents, wave action, and water transparency. Important research, compilation, and publication in the marine sciences were also undertaken by the Beach Erosion Board, the Aerology Section of the Office of the CNO (where Florence van Straten worked), and the Division of Tides and Currents in the Coast and Geodetic Survey.[66]

The Oceanographic Unit also made extensive use of the observations of merchant captains sent to Hydro from the Office of Naval Intelligence, and even the Office of Strategic Services provided useful facts. Sears obtained up-to-date information from reconnaissance photographs requested from the navy's Photographic Interpretation Center at Anacostia, D.C., and made good use of the increasingly sophisticated weather observations of the army and navy weather sections and the civilian Weather Bureau. Sears used her connections with WHOI and Harvard to good effect as well; navy travel documents indicate that she made numerous trips to each institution for conferences concerning OU work. Some of the research groups at WHOI also worked closely with the Anti-submarine Warfare Instruction School in Boston, expanding still further the network of sources on which Sears was able to draw for information. Indeed, it may have been her reputation at Harvard and WHOI that was responsible for getting Sears assigned to the Joint Meteorological Committee of the Joint Chiefs of Staff and as secretary to the Joint Subcommittee on Oceanography. She served in both capacities from her arrival in Washington in April 1943 through her departure in 1946.[67]

Pursuit of information also put Sears in touch with other oceanographers throughout the country, and she made numerous contacts that would prove helpful in her postwar career. In one of her draft memoirs she noted the constant stream of visitors to the Oceanographic Unit from other institutions and also from overseas. Information culled from visitors, especially from those working out of Pearl Harbor for Pacific intelligence, enabled the Oceanographic Unit to create much better and more accurate reports to send out to the fleet. One particular local visitor attracted considerable notice whenever he appeared. This was the Scripps oceanographer who, inexplicably, had been put into uniform as an enlisted man and assigned to the Pentagon. When he visited the Oceanographic Unit he could not carry the classified reports on forecasting he had just written because as an enlisted man he did not have the required security clearance. Therefore, he was always accompanied by an officer whose sole task it was to carry the reports. This was, for Sears, the height of absurdity. It also suggests two other important points: first, that the question of properly assigning scientists had not yet been completely solved, and, second, that even men did not always get appropriately challenging assignments.[68]

In the process of exchanging information with her many visitors, Sears learned much that was new to her. She found it "amazing" that bioluminescence could be a real menace to pilots and ships. In some places, for example, it was so bright that pilots flying at night became light-adapted or it could reveal the presence of submerged submarines. The Oceanographic Unit was asked to make charts predicting where this phenomenon might cause trouble for U.S. subs.[69]

By pulling together information from sources both domestic and foreign, Sears and her unit produced reports whose accuracy she could defend at the highest committee levels, in spite of the relatively primitive state of much of the practical science involved. Coordination of data was an essential part of the job, and this involved dealing with constituencies whose responsibilities often overlapped her own. Information presented to the Joint Meteorological Committee, for example, for forwarding to the Joint Chiefs was always a composite effort. It is also true that in the tricky business of predictions and forecasts, the fusion of sources brought a comparable diffusion of responsibility.

In retrospect, though, while the cooperation was duly recognized, there was some disagreement about the weight of the different contributions. After the war, Dick Seiwell wrote of the importance of his early contribution to the use of oceanography in warfare. He maintained that it was the problems experienced in the first amphibious operations that alerted the military to consider expertly analyzed oceanographic information a vital part of preinvasion planning. He extolled the importance of the work done by the army units he organized and commanded—the 6812th Engineer Technical Team, Oceanography and Beach, and the 6211th Beach Intelligence Unit—successors of the defunct Air Corps Weather Directorate's Oceanographic Unit, which, to his regret, disappeared into Sears's Oceanographic Unit. In general, however, while he was concerned to some extent with sea and surf, Seiwell's appreciation of the importance of the principles of oceanography was specifically aimed at increasing the efficiency of such engineering activities as port construction and operation, supply over beaches, and large-scale surveying of ocean and coastal areas.[70]

On the other hand, Capt. Charles C. Bates, USAAF, one of the first eight graduates from the Scripps program in military oceanography (August 1943), emphasized the importance of joint preparation and presentation of information relating to oceanographic and hydrographic factors vital to amphibious operations. He believed that separate army and navy oceanographic services were unnecessary, and yet in an article published in 1947 he was careful to preserve an unassailable role for oceanographic meteorology, claiming that the already existing network of weather service observers in combat areas could handle all local information gathering. "It should always be remembered," he insisted, "that forecasts of sea, swell, and surf conditions, if they are to be reliable, must be made at a weather station, as a wave forecast is no better than the wind forecast or diagnosis upon which it is based."[71] Setting aside such postwar jockeying for recognition, nothing could make clearer Sears's skill in fusing information from diverse sources into a meaningful whole than the introduction to Hydrographic Office Report No. 234 of November 1944, "Breakers and Surf: Principles of Forecasting," which carried a Confidential classification:

> This manual is based on data obtained by the Bureau of Ships and the Hydrographic Office, by the Scripps Institution of Oceanography and the Woods Hole Oceanographic Institution, and the collaboration of the Beach Erosion Board, Office of the Chief of Engineers, War Department, and the College of Engineering, University of California. The aerial photographs were taken by the Photographic Training Unit, Fleet Air Wing Fourteen.[72]

Sears's work, drawing from each of these sources as well as many others, was a part of an intricate mosaic of information on which the planners in Washington depended to form their battle plans.

To assist in rapid retrieval of information for their reports, the Oceanographic Unit compiled an extensive bibliography under the guidance of oceanographic librarian Mary Grier. Because pertinent libraries were scattered throughout Washington, Grier was always off at one of them looking for information, but she would periodically check back with the OU by telephone. When an urgent assignment came in to the office— "a request for a quickie," as Sears called them—and Grier was out, they would have to tell her what information was needed over an unsecured phone line as soon as she called. To avoid giving away place-names, they would refer to the number of a report they had just worked on and then add, "but northwest," or whatever. Grier always caught on and would quickly return with the urgently required data.[73]

Information was not always as easy to come by in Washington as might be expected. Sears believed the library at the Marine Biological Laboratory at Woods Hole was "far superior to any in Washington," thanks to Mrs. Priscilla Montgomery, a librarian with a passionate disregard for the restrictions of budget. In addition to budget-conscious librarians, Washington was awash in civil servants who had the infuriating habit of cutting out sentences from library volumes when they needed the information. Sometimes the vandalism left behind an insubstantial lace, a serious impediment to research.[74]

Even when the Oceanographic Unit was not asked for an immediate report, it usually faced tight deadlines. During the first months of 1944, for example, the unit was working on oceanographic reports for Sakhalin, the Kuriles, and northern Hokkaido due in manuscript form by 15 March; a report on Palau due in manuscript form on the same day; and a report on the Mariana Islands previously due 21 March but postponed. Also in early 1944 the Oceanographic Unit was developing streamline and steadiness of ocean currents charts for "certain Pacific areas," as well as bottom-sediment charts for Java, western portion; Makassar Strait, southern portion; Camranh Bay to Cape Varella; Singapore Strait to Banka Strait; and Naikai or Setouchi, Inland Sea.[75]

The success of the Oceanographic Unit's reports is illustrated by the Allied landings on Luzon in the Philippines in January 1945. The surf was low on the western part of Lingayen Gulf in western Luzon, making it the most attractive location for an invasion. For that reason it was also the area most heavily fortified by the Japanese. With good weather data and wave refraction charts developed by task-force aerologists, Sears and her team were able to produce a report indicating that the surf on the less heavily defended eastern part of the gulf would be less than six feet high, making it safe to go ashore there.[76]

Thanks in part to this report, the invasion of the island was set. A convoy of eight hundred Allied ships approached the west coast of Luzon, moved northward around the Japanese fortifications, and entered Lingayen Gulf to their rear. Thus began the invasion of the main island of the Philippines, which the Japanese had taken thirty-seven months earlier. Six months after the Normandy landings, the amphibious operation in Lingayen Gulf—facilitated by a small group of marine biologists—was described by observers as "the greatest of them all." "This work got easier and easier as we approached the Japanese home islands," reported Sears modestly, "because we were able to use the very complete and excellent data [about Japanese coastal waters] published by Japanese scientists before Pearl Harbor."[77]

Sears also put together a report indicating which Okinawa beaches would have the least surf during the planned invasion of the island on 1 April 1945. According to one newspaper account of the landings, "A moderate eastnortheast breeze rippled the calm sea; there was no surf on the Higashi [landing] beaches. More favorable conditions could hardly be imagined." In November 1945 the WAVES Newsletter ran an article on the Hydrographic Office, particularly noting the WAVES lieutenant who, along with a team of scientists, edited and prepared manuals that were used in planning and executing invasions in the Pacific. But while many know the story of the meteorologist on whose weather forecast Eisenhower depended for his decision to go ahead with the D-day landings in Normandy on 6 June 1944, few are aware that a woman working at her desk in Washington was responsible for compiling a report indicating where the Okinawa invasion forces could land with least danger from currents and surf.[78]

Writing to a fellow scientist in Peru in 1949, Sears described, in broad outline, the techniques she had used, which followed the Sverdrup-Munk method:

> During the war, if good meteorological forecasts were available, it was possible to forecast wave conditions quite accurately and, if a sufficiently detailed chart were also available, the height of the surf breaking on a given beach. Such forecasts had very obvious advantages for "amphibious landing operations." Conversely, if one records wave data, it becomes possible to estimate not only the strength of the wind in the generating area but also its distance from the recording station.[79]

The interdependence of meteorological and oceanographic reports is obvious and will become even clearer with an examination in a later chapter of the work of Florence van Straten, an aerological engineer assigned to the Aerology Section in downtown Washington.

In addition to providing intelligence information requested for specific operations, the Oceanographic Unit also prepared reports, charts, and manuals for general operational use. The WAVES Newsletter of November 1945 noted that "the oceanographic unit, . . . in conjunction with air-sea rescue manuals," created a chart for locating aviators at sea on rubber rafts. By following a scheme for showing currents devised in 1910 by Scandinavian scientists but never before put to practical use, they contracted with Scripps to produce streamline current and prevailing winds charts printed on cloth handkerchiefs. These were issued to fliers in both the army and the navy as navigation aids should they have to bail out or ditch their planes. The newsletter claimed that these handkerchief charts "brought about the safe return of many fliers lost at sea." In addition, the Oceanographic Unit produced a manual for forecasting swell in offshore anchorages, and another for forecasting surf on beaches, based once again on Sverdrup's wartime research at Scripps.[80]

A letter from Sears to the secretary of the Joint Meteorological Committee demonstrates the sort of work for which she was directly responsible. Writing with regard to proposed changes to the Steere Surf Code (created by navy aerologist Cdr. Richard C. Steere), Sears explained that "the justification for proposing changes at this time is that . . . certain modifications have been suggested as a result of experience gained by field work." One of the proposed changes concerned Primary Data Group D:

> The old definition was for the direction from which breakers were approaching. The result of recent work indicates that the actual direction is not as important as the angle at which the breakers approach the beach. Since the angle is always small the 45-degree compass sectors are not sufficiently accurate. This angle is determined in large part by the underwater topography and is important in determining the velocity of the alongshore current caused by breakers approaching at an angle. Furthermore, if the direction of the oncoming breakers is not at right angles to the beach, the landing craft will be more exposed to enemy fire as they land.[81]

One of the requests Sears received from the Naval Research Laboratory was for "a report on the mean, maximum, and minimum salinity in various strategic areas where amphibious operations might be carried out by the United States Naval Forces." The velocity of sound in seawater is affected by temperature, by hydrostatic pressure (depth), and somewhat by salinity, and accurate measurement of the velocity of sound was required for radio acoustic ranging (RAR) used in hydrographic surveys of coastal areas. Soon the responsibilities of the Oceanographic Unit included producing regular Confidential Submarine Supplements for Sailing Directions with charts showing characteristics of underwater sound, such as sonar charts; bottom sediment and current charts; and charts showing the distribution of water temperature, salinity, and density. These supplements were compiled and written by scientists working at Scripps and the University of California Division of War Research.[82]

Many of these supplements and other Oceanographic Unit reports were put together with data from bathythermographs (BTs), comparatively new instruments developed at WHOI to measure water temperature and pressure and record them automatically and graphically. Submarine bathythermographs (SBTs), also developed by WHOI scientists, eventually became standard equipment on all submarines, where they were useful to both diving officers and sonar officers. Their purpose was to help determine effective sonar range, to find acoustic shadow zones, and also to take advantage of the density stratification of the sea to evade detection and depth charging by the Japanese.[83]

As they roamed the Pacific in places for which there was not much oceanographic information, the subs paid for the use of the SBTs by submerging daily to collect a temperature trace which they forwarded to the Oceanographic Unit with their war patrol reports. Often the card with the recorded traces arrived at the OU with "Thank God for Allyn Vine" scribbled on the back. Allyn Collins Vine was the WHOI physicist who taught many submariners how to read the BT trace. Vine's admirers may have had even more reason to be grateful to him than they knew because he was one of the WHOI scientists who had opposed Washington's notion that the BT readouts should be metric. As Vine recorded many years later, "We felt that the poor kids from Kansas that were dragged into the Navy shouldn't have to learn the metric system while they were seasick. So we made the first 200 [BTs] in the English system, and by that time the die was cast, and it all went English."[84]

Bathythermograph data collected by weather vessels in the Atlantic were used by the Oceanographic Unit to predict the effect of wind force on the mixing of water temperature layers as well as to measure the effects of diurnal warming and internal currents. Atmospheric stability information was also compiled and charted for use in connection with radio, radar, and the behavior of smoke for smoke screens.[85] Eventually, about seven hundred surface ships and submarines were equipped with BTs and nearly 100,000 BT temperature-depth records were obtained and forwarded to Hydro. In the postwar words of Rear Adm. Earle W. Mills, the acting chief of BuShips, Hydro's BT reports "formed one of the greatest stores of oceanographic information ever assembled." It was a store consulted frequently by Sears and her unit.[86]

In July 1943, because of the "probability of amphibious operations in many theaters," the Office of Naval Intelligence had instructed Sears's unit to "compile and disseminate . . . as soon as possible" information for use in forecasting wind, waves, swell, breakers, and surf for the oceanographic chapter of monthly reports put out by JANIS (Joint Army-Navy Intelligence Studies). Barnacle expert Dora Henry became the chief editor of the OU reports, and Sears praised her fine work. By June 1944 the Oceanographic Unit had supervised the production of 10 sound-ranging charts, 15 bottom sediment charts, 112 anchorage charts, 24 current charts, 7 sea and swell charts, and 6 JANIS charts, among others. During the war most of this work was classified because of its direct military significance.[87]

The continuing junior rank of the women in the Hydrographic Office was hardly commensurate with the importance of their work. Of the twenty WAVES officers at Hydro in September 1943, nineteen were ensigns and only one (Mary Sears) was a lieutenant (j.g.). Yet their workload increased. In October 1944 Hydro was still losing about a man a day to the draft, although by then the staff had grown to sixteen hundred officers, enlisted Waves, and civilians, and the output had reached an annual high of nearly forty-two million charts.[88]

Modest as always, Sears credited her high position in the navy to good luck. Among WAVES officers she believed she had the "best deal" of any she came across "because they were all in charge of enlisted barracks, or something like that, and very very few were working at what they might be competent to do." There is ample evidence to support this view, including the report of an April 1945 inspection of WAVES activities in the Potomac River Naval Command encompassing the Waves of Hydro. The report noted that while "some [WAVES] officers have entirely technical assignments . . . most have also administrative and supervisory duties." Sears also maintained that she never met another WAVES officer, even at Hydro, who really had a position of responsibility. Perhaps that is why, of all the individual awards and citations presented to personnel of Hydro in 1945, Sears was the only woman honored. She received a letter of commendation and the commendation ribbon.[89]

While luck, and the small size of the fraternity of oceanographers to which she belonged, certainly played a part in getting Sears her job at Hydro, it was in no way responsible for her performance there. What qualities of character did Sears possess that equipped her to succeed in her wartime work? Roger Revelle called her a "powerful natural force," and another close observer suggested that would-be contributors to *Deep-Sea Research* subjected to her rigorous critique of their writing would not have been surprised to learn of her military background. Perhaps that statement was a reflection of the determined, competent, and highly professional nature that assured Sears a respected position in an otherwise largely male world.[90]

Though basically shy, Sears was a woman of great enthusiasm and strong opinions. Characteristic was her lifelong habit of punctuating her writing with frequent exclamation marks and underlinings. She was also persistent and determined, and no pushover. She avoided ceremony, fanfare, and fuss, but she did not avoid taking charge. Until late in her life Sears insisted on doing the driving whenever in a group, disdaining the skills of her male colleagues and devoted to her beloved BMW. While the war years forced a suspension of many of her activities, as it did for so many people, after the war Sears returned to a life devoted to vigorous physical and mental activity. She was an avid gardener, an early- and late-season swimmer in Vineyard Sound, a keen sailor, a cross-country skier, and a committed student of languages. Above all, Sears was a bibliophile whose overburdened office shelves and bulging card index files seemed an infallible source of difficult or obscure references. All of these attributes combined to make of Mary Sears a well-organized and indefatigable researcher who could marshal a mass of disparate and disembodied facts into a coherent and plausible forecast.[91]

Sears was also a tireless worker, and one on whom her boss could and did rely. Because her commanding officer lived in Virginia while she herself lived across the street from Hydro (in the World War II apartment complex called Suitland Manor), Sears had to attend to teletype messages that came in for him at night. Never one to fuss about red tape, Sears admitted that sometimes the enlisted men on duty at Hydro saved her a trip to the office by bringing the messages across to her and carrying back

Dr. Mary Sears in her WHOI office
© *Woods Hole Oceanographic Institution*

her answers for transmission—even when the messages were classified, for which only officers had clearance. In this fine disregard for bureaucratic niceties, even in the navy, Sears was very much like another forceful pragmatist, computer pioneer Grace Hopper. However, Sears does not seem to have held the same relaxed view of rules and regulations when it came to communicating with others. Her sister Leila was a WAVES officer assigned to the Communications Intelligence Division at Ward Circle, in northwest Washington, from November 1943 until March 1946. She had a very comprehensive security clearance and yet she noted that even with her,

"Mary was so secretive about her work that our dad used to tell everyone she was training barnacles to fasten onto Japanese vessels."[92]

Mary Sears apparently got on well with most of the young enlisted Waves reporting to her, and in this regard, too, she was far from a martinet. To meet the tremendous demand for all types of charts and nautical information needed for the war at sea, Hydro had moved from the downtown main navy building to a new three-story building of its own on the pastoral Suitland Federal Reservation ten miles southeast of the Capitol. By then the office was working two shifts a day and even three when that was practicable. Facilitating this effort was the erection of a large WAVES barracks, including a mess hall, just to the southeast of Hydro, which added to the Waves' social isolation. Perhaps this was the reason for Sears's indulgent attitude toward her charges. She has left humorous stories of scrapes narrowly avoided by the more adventurous of these women, and of her own good-natured myopia with regard to their absences without leave or late returns. In later years, these women often called on Sears to write letters of reference for them, which she always did with grace. While she was very much aware of the rarity of her position of responsibility in the navy, did this make Sears a feminist? She certainly was not one in today's meaning of the word. When she retired from the naval reserve she was asked about issues of equality and responded that wartime conditions did away with much sex discrimination. "We were working so hard for a common cause, I was hardly aware of any barriers," she recalled in words almost identical with those used by Grace Hopper. Once, for instance, a marine officer used to bullying his secretaries found himself bellowed back at by a female scientist. But "he believed the navy needed my knowledge," Sears explained, "so he accepted me as an equal." In fact, Sears found that the stiffest resistance to employing women in responsible positions came from the civil service, which "didn't want to give women professionals anything but the lowest grades." Asked about issues of pay, Sears noted that while "female technicians and those who begin with only a bachelor's degree may be paid less than men, a doctoral degree guarantees equal pay." Such a view does more credit to Sears's optimism than to the record, as the facts do not bear her out. Similarly, she pointed out that even before the war, opportunities abounded for women who set their sights high enough, but most of the women who began careers in science with her in the 1930s soon married and left the field. She cited famous women oceanographers like

Rachel Carson and Louella Cable as examples of what was possible for women. Yet she firmly believed that militancy was women's least successful weapon in winning recognition and was generally counterproductive.[93]

Sears described herself as "very GI" in the way she did things, though this seems to refer chiefly to the fact that she did not drink much around those she worked with, which aroused great respect among the civilians and enlisted personnel. Whenever Sears or her sister was promoted, however, they would arrange to meet downtown for dinner and "wet down" the new stripe. On one occasion when Sears's father was in town, he took his two daughters, each in navy officer's uniform, to a top restaurant for lunch. To celebrate he ordered sparkling wine, which Sears did not disdain.[94]

The picture that emerges of Mary Sears at work at the Oceanographic Unit is one of a team player who fostered a congenial atmosphere conducive to the maximum effort they were all required to put forth. Some of her own stories reveal her sense of humor, which must have helped to lighten the tasks the group faced. Her favorite about the WAVES was an announcement that came over the loudspeaker one day while she was at the Bureau of Ships "waiting for Roger [Revelle] as usual." As with all navy announcements, this one ended with the customary refrain, "that is all." The full message, broadcast throughout the building, informed listeners that "WAVES officers will wear gloves to drill this afternoon. That is all." Even Sears's graduate school mentor, Henry Bigelow, had shared risqué jokes with her that he would not tell some of the more staid scientists at WHOI. Her sister Leila maintained that this sense of humor developed early, a prerequisite for living with their father.[95]

In the course of the war the work of Sears's oceanographic group continued to expand in volume and importance. Nevertheless, in November 1944, when WAVES finally received permission to serve in a few U.S. territories overseas, Sears was quick to apply for a position in oceanographic intelligence at Pearl Harbor. She applied again—again unsuccessfully—in August 1945. Although her adventurous spirit was undiminished, Sears was apparently too valuable to be released from Washington. In October 1945, when she agreed to stay on in the navy for another six to nine months, Sears was promoted to lieutenant commander.[96]

Sears's Oceanographic Unit made valuable contributions to amphibious warfare, to air-and-sea rescue, to mine warfare, and to the extension of oceanographic knowledge in general and especially in the fleet. At the end of a postwar report on her work, Mary Sears summed up what she had learned: "Military necessity does not wait for explorers and scientists to accumulate sufficient information." Nevertheless, even without such information, by her understanding of the factors that control conditions in the sea and by her skillful interpretation of the available data, Sears had been able to answer many of the questions submitted to her.[97]

It was both in recognition of this excellent work and because of the many evident peacetime applications of oceanographic research that plans for an expanded navy oceanographic program had been under discussion since November 1944. A meeting convened by Rear Admiral Bryan on 19 October 1945 to determine the future of oceanography in the Hydrographic Office was the culmination of a year's worth of analysis. In addition to the admiral there were three navy captains, four commanders (including Roger Revelle), one lieutenant commander, and five civilian Ph.D.'s present. Lt. Mary Sears was the only woman at the meeting and the lowest-ranking military person there. As a direct result of this meeting, on 1 February 1946 a permanent Oceanographic Division was established within Hydro, with Sears as the officer in charge.[98]

The new division's task was to "collect, codify, coordinate, and implement basic research required by the Navy Department, the War Department, the Coast Guard and other government agencies." While carrying on an extensive research program of its own, it would also act as the coordinating agency for oceanography throughout the country. Mary Sears stayed at Hydro after VJ Day to set up the new division and then to serve as its first chief from February 1946 until her retirement from the active navy on 4 June of that year. She later recorded sardonically that her high rank had been pushed through by her boss "on the understanding that she leave government service after the war."[99]

When Roger Revelle, Sears's mentor in the navy, was discharged at the end of the war, his citation, signed by Secretary of the Navy James Forrestal, praised "his technical knowledge and ingenuity." Forrestal noted that Revelle had "contributed materially to the successful prosecution of submarine, anti-submarine and amphibious warfare," and he was therefore authorized to wear the Commendation Ribbon.[100]

In a 1944 report the Hydrographer described the work of the Oceanographic Unit as "invaluable," noting also the testimony received to that effect from units of the fleet.[101] Sears pioneered the application of oceanographic intelligence to operational problems, and her influence on the new field was profound. A few years after the war, she was invited by a former colleague who had set up his own meteorological consulting firm to "drop down to Washington and see us all plodding in your footsteps."[102] The breadth of Mary Sears's contribution to the U.S. naval war effort is perhaps best summed up by CNO Adm. Chester Nimitz, who praised her "technical knowledge and administrative skill[, which] were instrumental in the selection, compilation, and publication of oceanographic data of great value to the armed forces of the United States." His letter of commendation, in the stock phrase of the times, noted that Sears's "performance of these duties was at all times exceptional, and beyond the high standard normally expected." Though reluctantly allowed into the navy by the back door, Sears had served it and her country well.[103]

On 3 June 1946, after picking up her Qualifications Jacket, Fitness Report, Health Record, and Dental Record, and returning or accounting for all library books to Miss Doris Friday, the redoubtable librarian, Lt. Cdr. Mary Sears, USNR(W) reported to Room 1065, Navy Department, for detachment from CNO. The next day, at the U.S. Navy Personnel Separation Unit (WR) in New York, she was officially separated from active naval service. For Lt. Cdr. Mary Sears, the war was over. On 22 June Dr. Mary Sears, planktonologist, sailed for Denmark to resume research on her beloved siphonophores.[104]

3

FLORENCE VAN STRATEN
meteorologist

As long as weather remains an important factor in naval operations, those naval establishments which fail to provide accurate, timely and comprehensive weather information, and those naval commanders who fail properly to use it when it is provided, need never fear losing their amateur status in the game of war. The amateurish conduct of war operations will be in direct proportion to the importance of weather in those operations regardless of the professional skills of the commander in other fields.[1]

The importance of weather in warfare was a lesson learned by all U.S. Navy commanders in the Pacific in World War II, but its significance had not diminished by the time this statement was used after the war to impress on budget oversight committees the importance of continuing to support, even in peacetime, the rapidly developing new science of the weather.

Aerology, the scientific study of the atmosphere, is the term used by the U.S. Navy for the more common term *meteorology,* or the study of weather. During World War II navy aerological units provided on-the-spot information for naval operations. Aerological officers, noncommissioned officers classified as aerographers, and enlisted aerographer's mates were assigned to major naval units afloat and to naval shore establishments. Aerologists can best be described as scientists of the weather, while aerographers are recorders of the weather. The rest of the navy generally referred to them collectively as rainmakers.[2]

The weather played some role in practically every major naval operation in World War II. The demand for weather information, vital to every phase of operations—planning, strategic, and tactical—for carrier strikes, amphibious landings, and naval engagements, could not be met by traditional sources; there were simply not enough meteorologists. The service of many weathermen overseas, moreover, left an even greater vacuum in the United States, which like other vacuums discussed in this book, was filled in part by women. By one estimate 10 percent of the military weather service during World War II, including all branches, was composed of women. One of the most successful of these women was Florence van Straten.[3]

Nothing in van Straten's early life indicated an interest in any of the sciences, nor would it have been possible to predict her lifelong career engaged in scientific research for the U.S. Navy. She was born in Darien, Connecticut, on 12 November 1913, but soon moved to New York City with her parents, recent immigrants from the Netherlands. Before emigrating to the United States, her mother, fluent in six languages, had had a brilliant career as a linguist, and she made sure her only child was bilingual in English and Dutch as well as being competent in French, German, Italian, and Spanish. Van Straten's father was a financial representative for Metro-Goldwyn-Mayer Pictures at their New York headquarters, but his job also took him abroad from time to time. The family lived in Nice, in the South of France, for one year during van Straten's secondary schooling, which improved her mastery of French. Back in the United States, she attended Girls High School in Brooklyn, where a combination of her own aptitude and her mother's coaching prepared her to graduate with straight As when she was only sixteen. As with Mary Sears, much of van Straten's later success was grounded in an excellent early education, the result of strong parental guidance and encouragement.[4]

While she excelled in all subjects at school, van Straten's greatest interest during the early years was in English; she knew from a very young age that she wanted to be a writer. Though not opposing this plan, her father also had some practical advice, which he summed up in a favorite riddle: "Why do writers live in garrets?" Van Straten knew the answer well: "Because they can't live on the first two or three stories." Owing to a sudden change in his family's fortunes when he was about to enter medical school, Mr. van Straten had had to go straight to work instead. Always mindful of this experience, he wanted to be sure that his daughter would be well prepared to support herself in case her writing did not pay. When he suggested taking a course in chemistry as a practical stopgap during her last year in high school, van Straten cheerfully agreed. Following the same thinking, she declared two majors—English and chemistry—when she registered at New York University that fall, never dreaming that anything other than writing would define the rest of her life.[5]

Van Straten's move toward a career in science was equally casual. At the beginning of her senior year in college, and still not quite nineteen, van Straten was asked to teach a freshman laboratory class in chemistry for a faculty member who had fallen ill. She taught the class so competently all year that at the end of it she was offered a teaching fellowship for the following year if she would accept her bachelor's degree in chemistry instead of English and enroll in the Ph.D. program in chemistry. It was a difficult decision for van Straten, but by then she was fascinated with the scientific method of inquiry and the search for objective truth; by comparison, fiction writing seemed subjective and ephemeral. She accepted the offer, graduating Phi Beta Kappa with a B.S. in chemistry in 1933. Although she pursued science thereafter, van Straten maintained a lifelong habit of writing: much of her writing was on scientific subjects, but she soon resumed writing fiction as well. As she acknowledged some years later: "The serious fiction writer and scientist each seeks truth in his own way. Though I am primarily a scientist, I believe art is another way of searching for the universal truth the scientist is trying to express. Truth must be a unified whole, not little compartmented sections labeled 'scientific truth,' 'religious truth,' 'artistic truth.'"[6]

Continuing her education at New York University, van Straten completed an M.S. in 1937 and a Ph.D. in chemistry in 1939, just as the war in Europe was about to begin. Part of her dissertation was published that same year as a paper written in collaboration with William F. Ehret: "The Reaction of Zinc with Copper Sulfate in Aqueous Solution." During this time and for the next three years, van Straten continued to live at home in Brooklyn while remaining a junior faculty member of the Chemistry

Department at NYU teaching inorganic chemistry and doing research in physical chemistry.[7]

When the Nazis overran the Netherlands in May 1940, van Straten and her parents must have felt profound sorrow, and while no record has been found of her motivation to join the U.S. Navy, concern for her parents' homeland might well have influenced her thinking. It is also at least plausible that in addition to the usual patriotic sentiments, she may have welcomed the chance for a change from the academic routine. Otherwise, even the demands of war did not offer van Straten much hope for a new assignment. There were almost no jobs for women chemists in industry, perhaps because, unlike engineering, there was quite a good supply: 395 female Ph.D.'s in all. Apparently, most of those women remained in their teaching jobs when the war broke out. Those who signed up for the National Roster of Scientific and Specialized Personnel probably expected to be called to war service, but very few were. Whether she assumed that or not, van Straten was among the very first women to join the WAVES, signing up on 22 October 1942 and attending the first formal indoctrination class at the Midshipmen's School at Smith College. Cdr. Howard T. "Shorty" Orville, in charge of the navy's Aerology Section in Washington, D.C., since 1940, had urged the navy to find female scientists and mathematicians for meteorological training as soon as possible. After completing indoctrination at Smith—sometimes scornfully referred to as the navy's "charm school"—van Straten was one of the first group of twenty-five new WAVES ensigns holding master's degrees or higher selected to take classes in meteorology at MIT.[8]

Weather watching in the United States had originated mainly in response to the needs of farmers. Weather science had always been of equal importance to ocean transportation, however, and by the nineteenth century steps were under way to learn more about the weather at sea. From the beginning, U.S. maritime meteorology was linked to the navy. Lt. Matthew Fontaine Maury, appointed superintendent of the navy's Depot of Charts and Instruments in Washington, D.C., in 1838, soon acquired the title "Pathfinder of the Seas" because of his widely used charts and sailing directions. Maury is often considered the founder of marine meteorology. In 1880 the U.S. Army's weather forecasting was put in the hands of the Signal Corps, by that time operating a network of 132 weather stations across the country. In 1890 Congress directed the army to transfer all its meteorological activities to a civilian weather bureau to be established in the Department of Agriculture, but the advent of aircraft, advances in communications, and the demands of war would soon bring meteorology back to the military. Yet, in the first years of the twentieth century it was the civilian U.S. Weather Bureau that dominated the weather scene.[9]

The Weather Bureau provided general weather information, forecasts, and storm warnings prepared in Washington. It also conducted research and trained personnel, since only two universities—Johns Hopkins and Harvard—offered courses in the field. Beginning in 1901, the Weather Bureau was the first U.S. government agency to adopt wireless telegraphy. The uses of radio to the military were clear, and in 1904 the government of President Theodore Roosevelt assigned wireless operations on the U.S. coasts to the navy, and in the interior to the army. From 1904 on, navy radio stations broadcast storm and hurricane warnings to ships at sea as a regular service, and in 1913 they began to broadcast daily weather bulletins from stations at Arlington, Virginia, and Key West, Florida. Radiotelegraphy greatly improved the accuracy of reports based on observations from ships at sea. Indeed, in an article she wrote for the *Scientific Monthly* in 1946, Lt. Cdr. Florence van Straten dated the birth of meteorology from the beginning of telegraphy.[10]

The advent of the air age added to the importance of meteorology. Pilots needed to know about cloud levels, wind direction and velocity, the location of severe air turbulence, altitudes and locations where ice might be expected to form on aircraft, and weather conditions at the flight destination. The development of military aviation generated even more interest in these questions. Just five years after they made their historic 1903 flight at Kitty Hawk, North Carolina, the Wright brothers sold a military aircraft to the Signal Corps. In 1911 the navy began buying Curtiss "hydroaeroplanes." Compared with other countries, however, the United States was slow to move into aviation, and the study of atmospheric influences on aeronautics was generally left to the Weather Bureau.[11]

World War I, which hastened European developments in aeronautics, proved that meteorological support for airships and aircraft was essential. Airships could function only under favorable weather conditions, and weather information was crucial not only for reconnaissance, but also to assist in aerial bombing, artillery spotting, and for defensive cover. By 1915 the British, French, and German armies had already created effective military weather services to provide forecasts for the battlefield, but the U.S. Army still lagged far behind them when it reached Europe in 1917. The

Signal Corps assumed weather service responsibilities again with the creation in August 1917 of its Meteorological and Aerological Service. Army weather observers were hastily trained at Weather Bureau field stations, and the first two hundred of them entered the system in the spring of 1918. By August there were thirty-seven domestic military weather stations in the United States, the largest, apart from Washington, being the contingent of twenty-two men at Aberdeen Proving Ground in Maryland who provided aerological data to improve long-range firing tables. Even apart from the traditional strategic issue of when to schedule major offensives, the weather factor had become very significant tactically. Antiaircraft gunners and long-range artillerymen firing at unseen targets needed accurate wind data, which was also crucial for gas warfare.[12]

The navy, too, quickly revived its meteorological capability to meet the demands of war. There was an urgent need for qualified officers to interpret weather reports at French coastal air stations used for antisubmarine patrols. In December 1917 the first six-week course in aerology was given to eight men by Prof. Alexander G. McAdie, director of Harvard's Blue Hill Meteorological Observatory. Eventually, the fifty-five-year-old McAdie was badgered by fellow Harvard man Franklin D. Roosevelt—at that time the acting secretary of the navy—into accepting a navy reserve commission as lieutenant commander to head up the navy's aerological program. The heavy-handed effort to force the reluctant McAdie into uniform was part of a pattern of clumsy military domination of war-related science that alienated civilian scientists, who remembered when the next war came around twenty years later. In France in 1918, meanwhile, McAdie and his graduates wrote *A Manual of Aerography for the United States Navy*, heralding the beginning of the modern U.S. Naval Weather Service.[13]

World War I stimulated important scientific advances in meteorology. Both sides during the war banned the broadcast of weather forecasts to avoid supplying information useful to the enemy, which in turn deprived Norway of data needed by its fishing and farming communities. Norwegian scientists seeking new methods of forecasting, led by hydrodynamicist Prof. Vilhelm Bjerknes, whose work in oceanography would influence Mary Sears in the interwar years, concentrated their efforts on the boundaries between great air currents of different temperature and humidity. Using the analogy of the wartime battlefields, these boundaries were called "fronts." Professor Bjerknes and his son Jacob pioneered the polar front theory and the air-mass method of weather analysis. Instead of just analyzing individual storms, as had been the practice before, they reshaped the science of meteorology by providing a general atmospheric model that could be used to forecast the weather. Van Straten compared the importance of this development for meteorologists to Isaac Newton's laws of motion for the physicist. The ideas of the Norwegian school of meteorology were quickly adopted in many places. The U.S. Weather Bureau, though, resisted the change and did not establish an air-mass analysis section until 1934; weather maps showing fronts like those we see today first began to appear in the United States in 1936.[14]

The U.S. Navy was much quicker than the Weather Bureau to adopt the new frontal and air-mass analysis concepts. This was largely the work of Francis W. "Reich" Reichelderfer, navy meteorologist, pilot, and balloonist, who after studying in Europe wrote a report dealing with the application of Norwegian methods to weather forecasting. His report became a standard technical manual used extensively by the army, navy, Weather Bureau, commercial airlines, and other industries having meteorological services. Between 1922 and 1928 Reichelderfer manned the navy's aerology desk, which had been transferred from the Bureau of Navigation (BuNav) to the Bureau of Aeronautics (BuAer) in 1921. He organized a course of training in aerology and established regular aerological units at all naval air stations. He encouraged the use of the new forecasting methods and techniques, and it was Reichelderfer who persuaded MIT to offer a full year's meteorological course in 1928 under Carl-Gustav Rossby, paving the way for van Straten's attendance there fifteen years later. In 1933 the California Institute of Technology (Cal Tech) set up a department of meteorology offering a graduate curriculum that, like MIT, taught the latest Norwegian-style thinking. Also, in an effort to improve the professional training of navy aerologists, Reichelderfer arranged to offer a two-year postgraduate course to a small number of officers. The first year's study was undertaken at Annapolis, and the second year was eventually handled at MIT.[15]

In spite of these efforts, navy aerology maintained only a precarious hold on existence between the wars. Meteorology was especially important to naval aviation because of the added danger of operations over water, takeoffs from water or from ships, and landings on water or on carriers, yet recruitment to scientific billets had dropped dramatically, further exacerbated by repeated manpower cuts during the Depression. An even more important impediment to progress in aerology was the effect of navy careerism. The Battleship Boys were as strong as ever in the immediate prewar years, and few foresaw the primacy of naval aviation that would quickly raise the demand for meteorologists. Rear Adm. Ernest J. King, the chief of BuAer, made this very clear in his comments to a congressional committee in May 1933: "In so far as there is any prospect of there being a corps of aerological officers, there is none whatsoever at present. If they want to continue to be naval officers, they will have to do some work aside from aerology. If you keep a man in aerology or in airships, or in the heavier-than-air line, he cannot get to the head of the [naval] service."[16] In 1934 the navy had twenty-four aerologists on its rolls, but the number had shrunk to eighteen by 1940 when Lt. Cdr. Wilbert M. "Red" Lockhart was sent from the navy's aerology desk in Washington to open the first navy weather central in San Francisco. His replacement at BuAer, Flight Division, and only the second officer in the navy to be designated an aerological engineering duty officer (aerology) and assigned to the Flight Division's Aerology Section, was Lt. Cdr. Howard T. Orville, a 1925 U.S. Naval Academy graduate. Orville had been a classmate of Lockhart's at the third postgraduate aerology course at MIT, which they began together in 1928. After World War II broke out in Europe, the navy's weather center at Anacostia and the weather center the air corps ran at adjoining Bolling Field were both moved next to the Weather Bureau's forecasting center at 24th and M Streets, N.W., in Washington to avoid duplication of effort. By then Reichelderfer had been running the Weather Bureau for two years, having resigned as the executive officer of the USS *Iowa* to take that job. Orville, meanwhile, remained as head of the Aerology Section for the duration, securing promotion to commander and then to captain. Reichelderfer's position was to have important consequences for navy aerology during World War II because it ensured a close cooperation between the military and civilian weather organizations.[17]

By tradition, navy aerology had worked closely with a variety of bureaus and offices of the navy as well as with the army, other governmental agencies, civilian universities and research institutes, commercial airlines, and the weather services of other countries. The Naval Observatory, for example, supplied advice on specifications and stocked and supplied naval aerological equipment. The Hydrographic Office made data available on certain aspects of the weather and cooperated in the dissemination of aerological information to the navy and in the preparation of aerological charts. As noted in chapter 2, this cooperation became even closer in wartime. The Scripps Institution of Oceanography under Prof. Harald Sverdrup, which provided courses in his techniques of sea and swell forecasting to navy oceanographers, also provided the same courses to aerological officers. The importance of cooperation was clearly illustrated by a complaint lodged with the Aerology Section in May 1944 by the acting chief of the U.S. Army Air Forces Weather Division. "Erroneous and misleading information is being disseminated on the effects of wind and ocean currents on life raft drift," wrote Col. Floyd B. Wood. "In one instance, the directions on ditching procedure given to pilots by weather officers would have seriously jeopardized their chances of reaching shore or would have greatly increased the difficulty of air-sea rescue missions." The colonel asked Aerology to review a memo he wished to distribute based on experiments on life-raft drift made by the Woods Hole Oceanographic Institution under the auspices of BuShips. He further noted that BuShips would prepare a complete manual on the subject as soon as the experiments on drift had been completed so that Aerology could bring its instructions into line with the latest oceanographic research.[18]

In further examples of cooperation, the National Bureau of Standards of the Department of Commerce conducted research and development for aerological equipment for BuAer, and the National Advisory Committee for Aeronautics (NACA) was deeply interested in problems involving the observation and forecasting of air and weather conditions affecting flight. The Aerology Section also maintained liaison with the Civil Aeronautics Authority (CAA), which was vitally interested in any developments in weather forecasting that would improve safety standards. Information did not pass only one way, moreover. In November 1943, for example, the Bureau of Aeronautics requested information from Pan American Airways on the best methods for seaplanes to ride swells during takeoff and landing, and received a detailed reply including diagrams. The Weather Bureau had long been a source of assistance on weather forecasting problems, and navy aerographers coordinated their forecasts with those put out by the civilian agency.[19]

Military-civilian cooperation had been somewhat formalized in 1940 when Reichelderfer created a committee to coordinate the activities of the Weather Bureau with the CAA and the War and Navy Departments. In April 1942 the descendant of that committee officially became the Joint Meteorological Committee (JMC), a working subcommittee for the Joint Chiefs of Staff, the same organization to which Mary Sears sent reports as head of the Oceanographic Unit at the Hydrographic Office. Orville was the BuAer member on the committee. On 16 October 1942, the Combined Meteorological Committee (CMC) was formed to coordinate weather matters affecting the United Nations—the Allies—and to provide all necessary strategic and tactical weather information to the Combined Chiefs of Staff. Among its other assignments, the JMC was responsible for preparing and maintaining a bibliography of meteorological intelligence reports for the Combined Chiefs.[20]

Before World War II the tiny field of meteorology was very much like a club, as was oceanography, in which all the members knew each other well. Harald Sverdrup, for example, had been a student of Vilhelm Bjerknes, and Rossby had been a colleague of Sverdrup and of Jacob Bjerknes, Vilhelm's son. This closeness helped to ensure wartime cooperation among the various interagency groups formed to deal with the national emergency. There was little rivalry between the Weather Bureau meteorologists and the few of the army air forces, the navy, and the universities. Again like oceanography during the war, common interests and personal friendships made it natural to seek informal solutions to common problems, transcending organizational boundaries.

This does not mean, of course, that there were never any problems. A 1944 memorandum to Howard Orville pointed out the delays that occurred because of the differing priorities of the army, the navy, and the Weather Bureau for meteorological information they all needed to share. The memo concluded that "the only satisfactory arrangement is to have a central agency responsible for compiling statistical weather data and that this information be equally available to all services having need for it." It suggested that an agency such as the Joint Meteorological Committee should control the priorities on the information so that the most important information would be given the highest priority. Centralization would also ensure that all the information would be collected in one place and eliminate the need to search the independent files of the various weather services. These concerns had already been raised in JMC discussions in October, and Reichelderfer had sent Orville and Col. H. H. Bassett of the army a photostat of Joint Memorandum No. 1, "Organization of the Meteorological Service for War Purposes," which outlined the policy the JMC followed when questions of priority arose.[21]

The real problems, of course, had begun on 7 December 1941 when the Japanese air attack on Pearl Harbor came under cover of frontal cloudiness, thereby giving the Japanese the element of surprise. Examination of a captured Japanese aeronautical meteorology manual later in the war led the British Air Ministry to form a low opinion of Japanese meteorological proficiency in general. Orville agreed that "the Japanese meteorological techniques . . . appear to be inferior." Nevertheless, he also acknowledged that their "military [commanders had] missed few opportunities to use weather in their operations to the fullest advantage."[22] After Pearl Harbor, weather played a critical role in America's extensive two-ocean naval operations, putting severe pressure on the navy's relatively small aerological service.

To meet this demand the navy trained a rapidly increasing number of aerological personnel. In 1939 only thirty-five men graduated from the Primary Aerographer's School at Lakehurst, New Jersey, and only nine men graduated from the advanced school there. Even before the United States entered the war, however, training had been greatly accelerated. In 1941 the basic aerography course was condensed to twelve weeks, and classes ran continuously with seventy-five men in each class. That year, six officers completed the regular three-year graduate course in aerology at MIT and were assigned to the fleet. Four officers went to Cal Tech for a course in applied aerology, eleven aerographers were given intensive training in synoptic forecasting at Lakehurst, and eighteen officers were assigned to an intensive postgraduate course at Annapolis. The Catalogue of Curricula for student officers at Annapolis for the academic year 1941–42 lists ten meteorology courses, including climatology, physical processes, dynamic principles, instruments, upper air analysis, and a seminar on oceanography. The objective of the weather map analysis course was "to impart to the students the technique of Norwegian methods of analysis on the weather map and the applications of these methods to weather forecasting."[23]

In 1943, when the Aerology Section became so large that it was transferred out of BuAer, 959 aerographer's mates (AerMs) trained at Lakehurst were assigned to aerological units. Sixty-five of the AerMs were Waves. More officers had been recruited as well. Twenty-five officers were commissioned from special university courses, 34 others were finishing the twelve-month aerological engineering course at Annapolis, and 80 more were ready to take their places starting in June. A total of 191 officers were enrolled in advanced classes at MIT, Cal Tech, NYU, and the University of Chicago. Among the 103 at MIT was Florence van Straten. Evidently, the education they received was thorough, even if compressed. Cdr. Columbus Iselin at Woods Hole Oceanographic Institution wrote to Carl-Gustav Rossby, who established the syllabus, that he was "much impressed by the quality of the men [sic] who have been trained by the army and the navy in meteorology. They were extremely well selected on the whole and well trained." But even these men and women were not enough to meet the demand. An additional thirty-eight experienced meteorologists were recruited from the Weather Bureau and from commercial airlines and given commissions. By August 1945 the Aerological Service comprised 1,318 officers and approximately five thousand enlisted personnel.[24]

Among the five thousand were several hundred enlisted Waves. Like their officers, who would become forecasters, the enlisted Waves were recruited early for training as weather observers. Sixty-five had already graduated as aerographer's mates (third class) from the weather school at Lakehurst NAS in June 1943, and a number of them were later among the few Waves with assignments outside the continental United States, serving at Pearl Harbor and in Argentia, Newfoundland.[25]

If Mary Sears had difficulty making a career in oceanography before the war, jobs for women were even scarcer in meteorology. For a long time between the wars there were only two graduate meteorology programs in the United States, the one at MIT inspired by the navy and the other at Cal Tech. The Guggenheim Foundation supported both programs, and both were adjuncts to the aeronautical engineering departments, but before 1950 only MIT admitted women. Furthermore, only one woman, Margaret Whitcomb, had graduated from MIT's meteorology program by 1940. However, she soon married, and in a theme characteristic of those times and increasingly familiar in this book, she appears never to have used her training professionally. Only one other woman graduated in meteorology from MIT during the war years: Karen Gleim received her M.S. in 1942, but it has proved impossible to ascertain whether or not she ever worked in the field.[26]

The first American woman to earn a degree in meteorology and then go on to work in the field attended a newer program. In 1938 New York University's College of Engineering started a master's degree program in meteorology, again with support from the Guggenheim Foundation. Fern

Kirkman, a 1937 graduate of Hunter College in New York City (where Mina Rees was at that time a professor of mathematics), had enrolled in NYU's engineering program and subsequently shifted to the new Department of Meteorology. In 1939 Kirkman became the first woman in the United States to earn a master's degree in meteorology. She then went to work as a forecaster for American Export Airlines at Floyd Bennett Field on Long Island. Kirkman hoped eventually to work for the U.S. Weather Bureau, although records indicate that there were no women meteorologists on the staff in 1938.[27]

The situation was somewhat better for women scientists in Germany during the prewar years, and for meteorologists in particular. By the mid-1930s at least seven women had received degrees in meteorology from German universities. The strength of meteorology in Germany is indicated by the facts that Vilhelm Bjerknes was at the University of Leipzig until World War I, and that even during World War II a prerequisite for undertaking a Ph.D. in meteorology at the University of Chicago was a facility in reading German. The language would have been no problem for van Straten, of course, even though she already had a Ph.D. and did not need another.[28]

In Germany, the number of women medical doctors and the number of professional places available for them increased steadily in the 1930s, from 5 percent in 1930 to 7.6 percent in 1939. Unlike the situation in the United States, moreover, 42 percent of German women physicians were married, and of those, 70 percent were mothers. Nazi ideology notwithstanding, the shortage of suitable male candidates in the professions in the 1930s—in part the result of the losses of the Great War—provided opportunities for women even in occupations not considered suitable for them. In the technical and scientific professions, long a male preserve, women were increasingly employed because of the lack of men. According to one study, women chemists, physicists, engineers, and biologists found employment in German industry and research without difficulty in the interwar years.[29]

The six or seven German women who had had meteorological training before the war worked in the climatology section of the Reichswetterdienst (German weather service) during the conflict, but not as forecasters. The thousand or so female noncommissioned officers and privates from the Nachrichten Dienst (Signal Corps) of the Luftwaffe who were working in the Reichswetterdienst at the end of the war were working in communications, coding, and decoding, and not on weather observing. In Japan, women had never been permitted to pursue scientific careers, and their contribution to the scientific war was therefore minimal. It seems highly unlikely that women were recruited into the Japanese weather service, either as observers or as forecasters.[30]

As in other scientific fields, the Allies made better use of women in weather forecasting than did the Axis countries. In England, some fifty of the nearly two thousand forecasters trained during the war were women from the Women's Auxiliary Air Force (WAAF), whose training was similar to that of the Waves in the United States. After officer training they took a three-month course at the British Meteorological Office and then spent another three months of supervised training at outstations. Eventually they took over weather forecasting at all Royal Air Force training bases in England. A number of women served as meteorologists in the Russian weather service as well, although little is known about them and it is unclear how many there were. One or two specific cases of Russian women forecasters at bomber and fighter escort bases in the Ukraine have been recorded, but this is a subject that still needs investigation.[31]

In the United States, even the pool of male meteorologists was small before the war. A 1940 census counted 377 weather forecasters in the whole country: 150 in the Weather Bureau, 94 working for commercial airlines, 62 in the U.S. Army Air Corps, only 46 in the navy, and the remaining 25 teaching and doing research in educational institutions. By the fall of 1942 the army air forces had increased the number of weather officers to 450 and were projecting a need for as many as 10,000 by early 1945. The challenge to meet that need was very similar to the challenge faced in the search for oceanographers: how to train scientists from other fields in the finer points of weather forecasting as fast as possible. The solution was similar as well: recruit college students in math, sciences, and engineering and train them in meteorology. This effort was largely successful. By 2 September 1945—VJ Day—5,924 weather officers had graduated from five civilian universities: the University of Chicago, UCLA, Cal Tech, MIT, and NYU. In addition, the air corps ran its own training center at Grand Rapids, Michigan. Of the more than six thousand forecasters trained, about one hundred were women, some of them Waves and some from a joint Weather Bureau/Civilian Aeronautics Administration program.[32]

As early as June 1941 the Weather Bureau had recognized the coming need to hire and train women to fill jobs for which they would not have been eligible in the past. "Surveys have demonstrated," the bureau announced in a circular, "that women can satisfactorily perform almost all kinds of work that men can perform." Advertisements were placed in major newspapers offering scholarships for women recruited into meteorology. Applicants had to have two years of college and one year of physics and one of mathematics, including calculus. Women who had completed civilian pilot training were designated Civil Aeronautics Administration (CAA) trainees, and those without were Weather Bureau trainees. By VJ Day more than half of the bureau's weather observers were female. Generally they worked as junior observers taking surface and upper air observations, and the bureau could not have continued to function without them.[33]

Among those who undertook officer meteorological training was Lois Coots, a pilot and a premed student at Marietta College in Ohio, who accepted a full Civil Aeronautics Administration scholarship to study at NYU. She began the program in the fall of 1942—just as van Straten was leaving NYU to join the WAVES—the only woman in a class of two hundred. Joanne Gerould Simpson also entered the field through the Civil Aeronautics Administration program. She was one of the few who stayed in meteorology after the war, eventually becoming a leading researcher. Simpson was trained at the University of Chicago campus, where 7 of the approximately 215 CAA students were women. After graduating from the Chicago training program in May 1943 Simpson joined the NYU faculty to teach in the cadet program. The wartime recruitment did not lead to a permanent change in the profession. In 1948 there were only four Weather Bureau women (and only twenty women altogether) on the roster of sixteen hundred professional members of the American Meteorological Society.[34]

A total of 242 members of the Women's Army Corps (WAC) performed wartime weather duties for the army. In the spring of 1944 the first all-WAC weather observing station was established at Kelly Field, Texas, soon followed by two others. The results were mixed, however. Whereas the WACs did a good job of chart maintenance, map spotting, and record keeping, all-WAC units were criticized for being unable to function in severe weather. The solution adopted was to assign one male observer per shift, which seems to have solved the problem, or at least ended the reports of problems. Most of these WACs were enlisted weather observers, though in April 1944 ten WACs joined sixty men in a class for enlisted forecasters. That September, five of the WACs graduated, but by then there were enough forecasters in the pipeline and the experiment was discontinued. Some WACs were also assigned to weather squadrons overseas, but only as clerical workers, although one WAC officer served as a weather equipment specialist in Hawaii.[35]

Among the civilian women who were involved in weather services, the most significant was probably Frances L. Whedon. Mrs. Whedon had earned a bachelor's degree in physics and aeronautical engineering at MIT in 1924. Hired by the Army Signal Corps in February 1942, she quickly became the indispensable mainstay of the Signal Corps' meteorological office, essentially running the section until she herself became section chief in 1947. After spending fourteen years in the Signal Corps, Whedon became the staff meteorologist for the army's Office of Research and Development before retiring in 1971.[36]

In large part because of the influence of Howard Orville, described as a "likeable, low-key person," the navy did a much better job than the army of utilizing the professional skills of its weather women. Orville urged that women be assigned to aerological engineering training, and as noted earlier, Florence van Straten was among the first group of twenty-five women sent to MIT for a nine-month training program. In all, sixty-three Waves received meteorological training at MIT during the war, another twenty or so went to UCLA, and twenty-one were trained at the University of Chicago. About one hundred Waves thus received forecaster training.[37]

The "cadet" training for candidates with the high educational attainments previously noted was supervised by the University Meteorological Committee, which consisted of representatives from each of the five universities involved, from the AAF Training Center at Grand Rapids, and from the army air forces, the navy, and the Weather Bureau. The committee was headed by noted meteorologist Carl-Gustav Rossby, whom Reichelderfer had taken with him to the Weather Bureau, and who tried to maintain a certain uniformity among the schools with regard to requirements, course content, and instructional materials. The program was for three eleven-week terms, with a week's recess between each term. Four hours in the morning were devoted to lectures, while the afternoons were consumed with four hours of synoptic laboratories where the students learned how to draw charts showing the large-scale distribution of meteorological conditions. The rigorous program usually included a weekly two- to three-hour exam, and overall the attrition rate was close to

25 percent. At MIT, twenty-two of the twenty-five Waves in the original class with van Straten survived. Had she not already had a Ph.D., the nine-month course would have earned for van Straten two and a half years of graduate credit toward a Ph.D. in aerological engineering, a testament to the intellectual caliber of the course.[38]

After graduation in September 1943, most of the women, who now held the rank of ensign, went to the West Coast for two months of supervised forecasting duty for naval aviation. This included forecasting for lighter-than-air blimps, which patrolled the Pacific coastal waters and were particularly sensitive to strong winds. Finally, the Waves, at this point usually promoted to lieutenant (j.g.), were assigned as forecasters to the growing network of navy air stations around the country. Among the duties they drew was forecasting for local and cross-country flights at NAS Hutchinson, Kansas, where four-engine bomber pilots were trained. A WAVES officer was assigned to the Naval Air Facility, Columbus, Ohio, which was shared with commercial airlines and a civilian airport. The WAVES forecaster at Astoria, Oregon, was one of only two forecasters, and she pulled a twenty-four-hour shift every other day. For all their importance to naval air, there was still reluctance in the navy to have women aerologists as senior ranking officers. On completion of the cadet program the male officers were sent immediately to their permanent assignments without the two-month supervised period, and at least one WAVES officer noted that a man a few months her junior was designated the officer in charge when she reached her permanent assignment.[39]

Enlisted Waves were also recruited to aerology. A booklet prepared by the navy to familiarize enlisted Waves with specialization opportunities before their classification interviews described the aerographer's mate as the navy's "Weather Man." Aerographer's mates were trained to take readings from scientific instruments such as barometers to measure air pressure, thermometers to measure temperature, psychrometers to measure relative humidity, and anemometers to measure surface wind speed and direction. Clinometers, hand-held instruments for measuring angle of inclination, were used together with a vertical beam of light at a known distance to figure the visibility ceiling at night, although by the end of the war they had been replaced by ceilometers that used reflected light beams for the same purpose. Van Straten noted that the single most vital meteorological need was measuring the humidity of the air. The normal method was to stretch a fine, blond, human hair between two posts. With changes

WAVES aerographers with balloon and theodolite, November 1943
National Archives photo no. 80-G-150554

in humidity the hair stretched and shrank and a pen fastened to one of the posts recorded the changes. During the war, the navy had a drawer full of letters from patriotic citizens offering hair for meteorological use. "Oddly enough," van Straten recalled, "it was usually someone else's tresses that were sacrificed, 'my wife's,' 'my daughter's,' and so on."[40]

AerMs were also responsible for keeping weather instruments clean and in good working order. Their duties included taking observations of the upper atmosphere, making accurate hourly weather observations, and recording the data in the monthly aerological record. For most of the war, wind velocities aloft were measured by releasing a hydrogen- or helium-filled balloon into the atmosphere and tracking it optically by means of an instrument called a theodolite, which measured the azimuth and elevation, from which drift could be calculated given the altitude. Temperatures and humidity aloft were measured by taking aerograph soundings by plane or by radiosonde. The radiosonde was essentially a radio transmitter whose transmitting frequency varied with the temperature and the humidity, the number of signals transmitted being controlled by the pressure. The instrument was balloon-borne, and about 10 percent were recovered by attaching parachutes to the gear. Such soundings were used to compute ballistic densities for antiaircraft and surface firing. Aerographer's mates also helped to prepare charts on which to base weather predictions. The qualifications for aerographer's mate training included a high school diploma and high school mathematics, with physics a plus. A college background with work in meteorology, astronomy, geography, geology, or physical science was regarded by classification interviewers as "highly desirable," an indication of the high level of education of many enlisted Waves.[41]

WAVES AerMs were assigned to naval air stations, weather centrals, and other weather activities, at first only within the continental United States. They had to be familiar with standard weather codes in order to exchange encrypted weather information with other weather units, the network of such activities being part of the strength of navy aerology. Whether they were male or female, station aerological officers had the same duties. They were responsible for the requisitioning, installation, and maintenance of aerological equipment. During flying hours they had to supervise a continuous watch and ensure that observations were made and recorded in the prescribed manner. They supervised pilot balloon (pibal) observations of winds aloft and the taking of plane and radio-sonde soundings.[42]

WAVES AerMs were also responsible for maintaining self-recording instruments in continuous operation and for organizing regular reception of weather broadcasts. They had to see to the preparation of weather maps at least twice daily, more often if weather reports were available, and they had to prepare weather advisories and outlooks and issue them to designated units. Each day aerological officers filled out weather bulletins providing the latest weather reports from other locations, thirty-six-hour local forecasts by twelve-hour periods, and records of verification of forecast.[43]

The creation of an increasing number of weather centrals avoided the duplication of much of the weather work and reduced the number of radiosonde observations that had to be made in any given area. The idea of weather centrals came from the synoptic weather forecasting technique. Overlapping or contradictory local forecasts could be avoided if many widely dispersed observations were collected at one central location, which then prepared and issued synoptic forecasts for the entire area. In a summary of the "Navy Aerological Service," which he wrote in December 1943, Orville described the navy weather central as a "large and completely staffed aerological unit, whose primary function is collecting, analyzing, and disseminating weather information and forecasts for the fleet." Commander Lockhart had established the first weather central in San Francisco in October 1940 to collect and disseminate weather information under wartime conditions and to collaborate with the Pacific Fleet in exchanging weather information. In March 1941 the second weather central was set up in Washington, D.C., at the headquarters of the Weather Bureau, to supply weather reports and weather map data to the Atlantic Fleet. Additional weather centrals were soon established at Cavite in the Philippines and at Ford Island at Pearl Harbor, and in 1942 U.S. involvement in increased naval activities in the worldwide theater of operations brought about the creation of still more weather centrals.[44]

While Waves took over much of the navy's weather work at home, the men saw duty overseas as aerologists and aerographers with the fleet or at distant weather stations. The total number of navy aerological units rose rapidly as the number of bases and vessels with such units mushroomed. In 1942 practically all vessels larger than destroyers received aerological units, and by the end of the war essentially all combatant vessels had an aerological detachment onboard, although sometimes this was just a single weather observer. In 1943 there were 251 aerological stations on ships and 207 onshore, and the majority of them were gathering information for advance operations. By the end of the war more than 1,500 aerological units were in operation. Aerological officers making regular radiosonde observations were aboard thirteen aircraft carriers, eight light carriers, sixteen escort carriers, nine aircraft tenders, ten AGC-class amphibious command or communications headquarters ships, and one battleship, for a total of fifty-seven vessels. By war's end there were also aerology units onboard forty-two weather ships.[45]

Accurate knowledge of the weather was especially necessary at sea for making decisions of importance to the fleet such as refueling, avoiding storms, and launching air offensives. Weather had to be taken into consideration for all small boat operations—especially amphibious landings —aircraft operations, gunnery practice, and, of course, action with the enemy. Major naval vessels to which aircraft were assigned had weather specialists responsible for making observations and forecasts on which the safety of the ship, the aircraft, and the pilots depended.[46]

In 1943 special weather ship operations were added to the services provided by weather centrals. The Coast Guard had undertaken weather reporting and observation in 1939, and in early 1941 five cutters were already serving as Weather Patrol vessels operating out of Boston. On 1 November 1941, President Roosevelt placed the Coast Guard under the jurisdiction of the navy for the duration of the war emergency, and their North Atlantic Weather Patrol work continued after the outbreak of war a month later, but under the navy's operational control. The Coast Guard had a tradition of operating weather ships for the Weather Bureau, with Weather Bureau instruments and observers, and they now had aerographer's mates aboard, many of them former Weather Bureau men. The first navy weather ships that began operations in the northern Pacific also had the full support of the Weather Bureau. Increase in the volume of military and naval traffic between San Francisco and Hawaii in particular required an increase in the number of weather ships in the eastern North Pacific to a total of seven by January 1944.[47]

In August 1943, just before van Straten finished her course at MIT, the navy's aerological function had grown so large that it was divided in two. With the creation of a Deputy Chief of Naval Operations for Air,

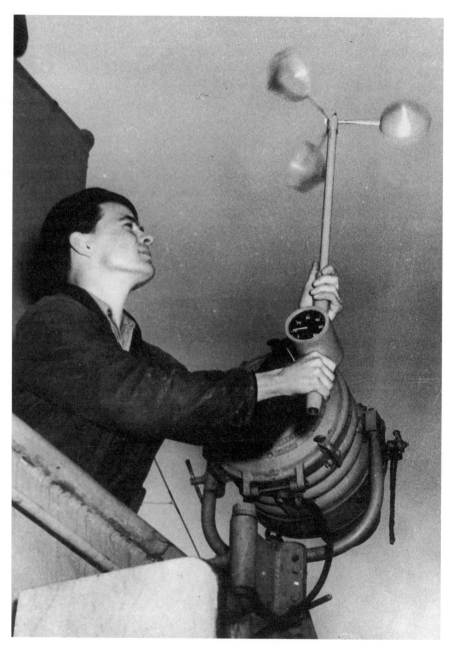

Coast Guardsman with anemometer on weather patrol duty in North Atlantic
U.S. Coast Guard

several of the most important policy and operating units of BuAer were transferred to the Office of the Chief of Naval Operations. The Aerology Section was transferred along with the rest of the Flight Division, in which it became section Op-34-E. Orville, by then promoted to captain, took most of his BuAer staff with him to run the Naval Weather Service from a new desk in the Office of the DCNO(Air). After that, all operations, policy, and planning matters concerning aerology and the administration of all aerological and weather matters were assigned to DCNO(Air), although the change was not profound since the activities under way were continued without interruption. Left behind in BuAer was the Aerological Equipment Section, which logically remained in the Aircraft Maintenance Branch where it continued to handle aerological equipment and material as it had done before.[48]

At that point, the Aerology Section consisted of eleven officers. Under Orville's command were two lieutenant commanders, two lieutenants, four lieutenants (j.g.), and two ensigns, none of them Waves, plus seven civilian employees, all female. Also under Orville's supervision, and headed by a lieutenant commander, was Weather Central Washington, which had ten officers, none of them women, thirty-three aerographer's mates, and one chief. The weather central provided for the collection, analysis, and dissemination of weather information to the Atlantic Fleet and Commander in Chief, U.S. Fleet (COMINCH).[49]

After the transfer of Flight Division and its Aerology Section, instructions for the aerological service of the navy were issued by the CNO. The primary functions of the service continued to be the preparation and dissemination of weather advisories for naval operations, the preparation of recommendations for aerological operating plans and policies, and cooperation with other government agencies to improve the weather service. Among the secondary services were regular observation of weather at the scene of operations, collection and tabulation of weather observations and their exchange with other aerological activities, preparation of climatological summaries for the various operating areas, and compilation of historical aerological data. The Aerology Section was also charged with preparing analyses of the strategic and tactical influence of weather on naval and amphibious operations. Van Straten described her experiences preparing these analyses in her 1966 book *Weather or Not*. Finally, the Aerology Section was supposed to encourage development of the naval aerological service by sponsoring research in all aerological fields, which was the area of responsibility van Straten moved into in 1945.[50]

World War II, sometimes called the physicists' war, made great scientific demands on the young science of meteorology. The influx of new people—chemists (like van Straten), physicists, geologists, and engineers hastily put into uniform and trained in a new profession—brought fresh concepts and new knowledge to help meet the pressing demands. The work at the central office also reflected the change in climatology brought about by military needs. Long-range weather forecasts had become an essential ingredient in advanced military planning, and Orville's office had to supply estimates of the climatological odds of different kinds of weather for any given area. Instead of presenting general weather averages for each geographic region, the normal peacetime practice, climatology was now used to help provide solutions to very specific problems. These problems might be complex, involving all aspects of an amphibious invasion, or they might be single-purpose issues, like how to design a weapon to enable it to withstand jungle humidity. Often, as Mary Sears also found out, these questions involved geographic regions for which very little information was available, and yet answers had to be given. And to answer them Orville drew on many of the same resources used by Sears.[51]

The many strands in the development of wartime science were intertwined, braiding together concurrent advances and strengthening the whole. For example, John Mauchly, a physicist, had initially been inspired to begin his work on the first functioning electronic computer in the United States—ENIAC—in order to run numbers for his weather studies. In October 1944 Roger Revelle wrote from BuShips to Harald Sverdrup about the Hydrographic Office publication of the *Manual on Breakers and Surf, Principles of Forecasting*, which was based largely on Dr. Sverdrup's principles. In the letter Revelle also mentioned that Lts. John Crowell and Charles Bates of the army air forces would not be assigned to the Scripps Institution, as had been planned, because they had been ordered instead to wave forecasting in the China-Burma-India theater. Revelle's letter can be found in the files of the Aerology Section because a copy was sent to Orville. Another copy was sent to the Hydrographer, attention Lt. Mary Sears. There was, in fact, considerable correspondence between Sears and Orville, mostly to do with surf codes and forecasting, much of it generated by Sears's position as secretary to the Subcommittee on Oceanography of the Joint Meteorological Committee. In fact, a very small group of scientists was working on weather and oceanographic problems, which was surely an advantage to the women involved because their professional reputations could override any hesitancy about their gender.[52]

In a 1946 *Scientific Monthly* article, van Straten pointed out some important accomplishments of navy aerology—for example, working with oceanographers to forecast sea, swell, and surf conditions before each amphibious landing. In April 1945 four men with sea and swell training were sent to the Seaplane Facility Project in the Central Pacific Area. Their job, routine but vital nevertheless, was forecasting for air logistics. World War II was the first war dependent to a great extent on air supply, and flying efficiency had to be maximized. If, to cite a van Straten example, a transport plane flying to Europe via Stephenville, Newfoundland, could not arrive before 3:00 P.M. when fog with zero-zero conditions was forecast, then the plane had to be held back. If the forecast was wrong, this caused an unacceptable loss of time. War operating conditions left little slack between the cost of erring on the side of caution and the perhaps fatal cost of making a wrong forecast. The pressure on forecasters was intense.[53]

A lesser-known but very important project undertaken by naval aerology was to give thousands of pilots a practical operational knowledge of weather by producing a series of aerology training films and preparing a number of well-illustrated booklets, a set of which was given to each pilot. The success of the project was demonstrated by the fact that many of the Allied nations also used the same booklets and films in an effort to reduce plane losses due to accident.[54]

Women were beginning to play a significant role in navy aerology by December 1943. The weather central in Washington was requesting WAVES aerographer's mates to fill vacancies left by men who had been transferred. By then, too, the Navy Weather Central Communications Board, which was attached to the Aerology Section, consisted of one male lieutenant (j.g.), one male ensign, and nine WAVES ensigns. When van Straten arrived in Washington from Ohio that same month, WAVES ensigns M. Loitski and Helena C. Hendrickson had joined the Aerology Section, as had Lt. (j.g.) Rosana J. Roebuck and Lt. (j.g.) Mary E. Brown. By August 1944 at least one other WAVES officer, Lt. (j.g.) H. Alber, had been added. Other Waves who were not aerologists also contributed to the activities of the weather central by decrypting intercepted Japanese weather transmissions. Working in shifts around the clock at Arlington Hall, these Waves "turned out lots and lots of weather in the South Pacific." On the other hand, Rosana Roebuck and Mary Brown, who had been with van Straten in the first group of MIT aerologists, were among those in the weather central who had aerological duties. Helena Hendrickson, who had also been in that pioneer group, was with van Straten in the operational analysis section. At least four of the WAVES officers of the first graduating class of twenty-two thus ended up serving under Captain Orville in Washington.[55]

Before reporting to Orville in Washington, van Straten had been sent to the Daniel Guggenheim Airship Institute to do research on gust velocity at the request of the inspector of naval aircraft at the Goodyear Aircraft Corporation in Akron, Ohio. Her six-week investigation involved analyzing data collected by the institute in an attempt to find the factors influencing gustiness. She discovered a "number of gross errors" in the previous method of handling the problem, mostly due to elementary procedural mistakes such as using base data from an area that had completely different weather. She noted that "the methods by which these calculations were made should have been questioned immediately." Not content merely to criticize, however, van Straten used the results of her analysis to set up an improved procedure for forecasting the maximum gust velocity. The stability of the atmosphere near the surface of the earth was of major importance to lighter-than-air craft, and van Straten's analysis and accompanying graphs were sent on to Commander Orville and to the lighter-than-air naval air station at Lakehurst, New Jersey, for comment. Not only did she point out the serious flaws in previous calculations carried out by meteorologists at the Guggenheim Institute, van Straten also pointed out that she had been carrying the burden of her investigations essentially alone, with no assistance from the staff of the institute. That being the case, she suggested that "this research could be carried out at least as well by one Aerological Officer and one Aerographer's Mate working at any one of the Naval Air Stations." Her suggestion was forwarded to Orville with the recommendation to cancel the contract with the institute and carry the work forward at a naval air station.[56]

In her first sortie as an aerologist, van Straten had proved that she was a competent researcher, a good analyst, and a problem solver. She had also

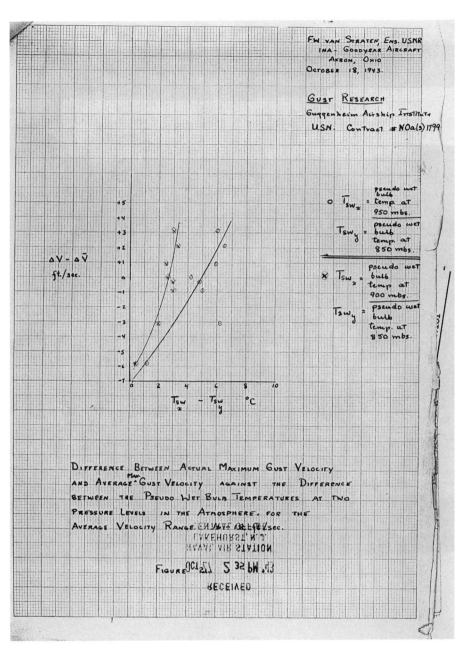

Ens. Florence van Straten's Gust Research at Goodyear, October 1943
National Archives, box 141, Aerology Branch, RG 38

shown herself to be tough-minded and not afraid to challenge authority. A tall, slim, and somewhat reserved woman, van Straten had a quick mind and a broad store of information. Her neat, careful signature was to become a fixture on charts, graphs, letters, and reports from the Aerology Section for the remainder of the war. But Flossie, as her friends called her, was not all facts and figures. She had a great sense of humor, and those who knew her remember that she was very good company in any setting. Perhaps because of her doctorate in chemistry, van Straten's navy experience was rather different from that of many other WAVES aerologists. After a brief time in Akron, instead of being posted to an air station she was sent to Washington, where she remained until 1946, first in the Operational Analysis Section and then in the Research and Development Section.[57]

In December 1943 Orville wrote a memorandum briefly summarizing the navy aerological service. In it he seemed to suggest that one of his duties was to remind commanders of the importance of the weather factor. "For long-range planning," he wrote, "and in order that weather considerations will not be overlooked in military operations, the aerological service prepares complete weather summaries for strategic areas. These weather summaries are used by military commanders so that the effects of weather on operations will not be overlooked," he repeated, "and in order that full advantage may be taken of existing weather conditions." Orville was also responsible for the preparation of recommendations concerning operating plans, policy, procedures, and other aerological matters requiring the attention of the CNO. The recommendations derived from "a constant analysis of the strategic and tactical influences of weather upon naval, air and amphibious operations." Producing these analyses occupied van Straten for most of 1944.[58]

According to van Straten, Howard Orville believed that weather information was vital to all aspects of naval operations and could cite innumerable examples in which the outcome of military and naval engagements had depended on the elements. He would describe the Greek defeat of the Persians in the waters around Salamis in 480 B.C., the winds that destroyed the Spanish Armada on its way to invade England in 1588, and the weather factors involved in the great World War I naval clash at Jutland in 1916 to support his contention. However, he had little confidence that World War II naval commanders had been taught to consider weather as a weapon to be used against the enemy. It was his idea, therefore, to prepare a series of reports of the early engagements of the war to show how weather had been used to good advantage or had been ignored at great cost. He intended that the analysis should be rigorous and that praise or blame should be unflinchingly assigned to friend and foe alike. Knowing the risk such a critique might pose to his career, Orville was nevertheless determined to proceed, spare no feelings, and distribute the reports to every American naval commander.[59]

Apparently Captain Orville succeeded in selling the idea to his boss. On 18 January 1944, Vice Adm. John S. McCain, deputy chief of naval operations (air), wrote the following foreword, which was subsequently printed at the beginning of each report:

> This is one of a series of pamphlets dealing with the weather aspects of Naval and Amphibious Warfare. The data on which these studies are based are taken from official documents and reports submitted to the Navy Department. The material has been collated and presented in a semi-technical form with particular attention given to the operational aspects of weather.
>
> During the preparation of this study, it was found that weather data submitted by the various commands were occasionally at variance. An effort has been made to reconcile these differences in order to provide an accurate account of the sequence of weather conditions as forecast for the Force Commander, to describe the actual weather conditions observed during the operation, and to give a practical explanation of these weather conditions.
>
> It is hoped that these studies will afford a clear view of the use of weather information during the planning, strategical, and tactical phases of the operation, and that they will form a basis for a better understanding of the applications of weather information in future operations.
>
> The primary objective of these analyses is to assist those officers who are charged with the responsibility for the planning and execution of similar operations.[60]

Between them, van Straten, her MIT classmate Helena Hendrickson, and another aerologist produced a number of studies under such titles as "Weather and Amphibious Warfare" and "Weather and Naval Warfare," as well as the confidential pamphlets of the Aerology and Naval Warfare series. "Under Captain Orville we did every engagement up to the D-day invasion," van Straten recalled in 1982. "We came a cropper with that one because the navy and the army fought World War II ½ re[garding] who actually gave the forecast." All the reports were put together from war diaries and battle reports, and were full of quotations from each, vividly demonstrating the participants' views recorded at the time, the actions taken, the orders given, and an analysis of the consequences.[61]

One of van Straten's early reports analyzed Vice Adm. William F. "Bull" Halsey's 31 January 1942 hit-and-run raid on the Marshall and Gilbert Islands, which marked the first offensive action of U.S. naval forces. Two U.S. Navy task forces were involved in the attack, one approaching from the north and one from the south, subjecting Kwajalein, Maloelap, Wotje, Jaluit, Mili, and Makin Atolls to simultaneous air attack. Aided by the cloudless sky and unlimited visibility, the planes from the northern task force were able to bomb targets all morning, but by early afternoon the same unlimited visibility had enabled Japanese planes to locate the northern carrier and begin to bomb it just as it was recovering its last raiding planes. Given the superior speed of the Japanese planes, it seemed impossible for the task force to escape, but Halsey's aerological officer on the carrier *Enterprise* had the answer. His weather map showed a cold front extending southwestward from a depression about 150 miles north of Midway Island presenting a natural smokescreen pointing toward Pearl Harbor. By steaming north at high speed into the frontal zone and then adjusting speed to the movement of the front, the task force managed to hide in the light showers, low ceiling, and reduced visibility of the thirty-mile-wide front. They could hear the Japanese planes overhead, but were so effectively hidden that they were never found. Once out of range of Japanese air patrols the task force emerged from the front and steamed for Pearl Harbor.[62]

"Needless to say," van Straten wrote later, "the task force commander received a great big plus for his canny use of the weather." As she herself had only a stripe and a half (as a lieutenant [j.g.]), she favored giving the credit to the lowly weather officer, but "the navy does not operate that way. The admiral received the plaudits."[63]

The action surrounding the 5 November 1942 attack on the large Japanese air base at Rabaul, on the Pacific island of New Britain in the Solomons, provided another example of the kind of tasks aerologists performed for the navy. This was an operation of necessity; it was required to protect army landings on the neighboring island of Bougainville from attack by Japanese planes based on Rabaul, and therefore it had not been planned to coincide with favorable weather. The weather map indicated the location of an intertropical front close to the area from which the U.S. Navy planes were to be launched. Observations made by the shipboard aerologist confirmed the position of the front. He also noted, however, that a wave disturbance had formed along the front near the launching point, causing a circulation of winds toward the east, north of the front, and toward the west, south of the front. Steaming west toward Rabaul the task force stayed to the north of the front heading into the wind to launch its aircraft without deviating from course. The task force hid from enemy scouts in the frontal clouds while the air group found Rabaul to the west of the frontal disturbance in perfectly clear skies and dropped their bomb loads. The task force then cut south through the front, reversing its base course 180 degrees. The American ships found the easterly winds in time to recover their planes, again heading into the wind without having to deviate from their course or lose any time in leaving the danger zone.[64]

Everyone engaged in this action referred to the almost incredible assistance of the weather as the result of having an "angel riding on the yardarm." Van Straten saw that although the action, on its own, had relatively little military significance, it represented an almost classic textbook case of using the weather as an ally. The aerological unit onboard had successfully fulfilled the primary mission of operating units on the spot, which was to "tell commanders the best time, from the weather point of view, at which to launch an attack," and the best location to retrieve.[65]

In her report on the Battle of the Coral Sea (4–8 May 1942), van Straten demonstrated how for the first few days the American forces made good use of bad weather by hiding in an equatorial front. They sank the Japanese carrier *Shoho* in ten minutes ("Scratch one flattop," famously signaled the successful dive-bomber pilot), and many Japanese planes were shot down and six more were lost when they mistakenly landed on the U.S. carrier *Lexington* in the poor visibility. Obscured by the weather front, the U.S. forces successfully damaged another Japanese carrier while losing only one tanker and one destroyer themselves, which as ordered had stayed away from the combat area and were therefore under clear skies. Then, inexplicably to van Straten, during the last days of the engagement the U.S. ships left the shelter of the cloud band and the Japanese moved into it. At that point the *Lexington* was sunk by Japanese planes. In the "lessons learned" department, van Straten assigned the task force commander both "verbal pats on the back as well as blows to another anatomical feature."[66]

The report concluded: "It is clear that during this engagement the most advantageous position was obtained by the forces operating within a frontal zone. . . . The strategic and tactical importance of holding this modern version of the 'weather gauge' is adequately demonstrated in this and other battles and engagements and cannot be overemphasized."[67]

Analyzing the landings on Guadalcanal in the Solomon Islands in August 1942, van Straten found that they had been well timed to coincide with the movement of a cold front from Australia toward the Solomons. Because the Japanese had air superiority the U.S. forces needed a combination of bad weather conditions that would prevent the Japanese from flying during the long approach of the task force and calm seas for the landings. The invasion forces followed the storm front northeast, emerging from behind it to land just as the bad weather moved on. Apparently the Japanese, grounded by the driving wind and rain, did not realize how narrow the storm band was and did not expect such a rapid clearing. They were caught completely by surprise, and although the island was hotly contested for the next three months, the two days of grace resulting from the initial surprise eventually enabled the American forces to prevail. In a standard, nonmeteorological account of Guadalcanal, a history of the U.S. Marine Corps gives credit not to good or bad aerological planning, but to good fortune, stating laconically that the landing was "blessed by bad weather and Japanese inattention."[68]

Nor was the use of weather as an ally restricted to the Tropics. In the invasion of Attu in the Aleutians in May 1943, U.S. forces used weather to advantage in the northern latitudes. For most of the year the Aleutians have extremely stormy weather, and for the rest of the time they are fogbound. The invasion was planned to coincide with the fog, and the invasion forces arrived off Attu and landed troops and equipment undetected by the Japanese entrenched in the surrounding hills. The first the Japanese knew of the invasion was when the big guns of the U.S. warships opened up on their positions.[69]

As the Coral Sea analysis demonstrates, not all the reports concerned successes. On 17 December 1944, a fast carrier task force of Admiral Halsey's Third Fleet engaged in the Philippines operation was caught in a savage typhoon with winds between ninety and one hundred knots, zero visibility, and mountainous seas. Three destroyers were lost, and analysts generally blamed Halsey and his aerological-navigation officer, Cdr. George F. Kosco.[70] Van Straten and the Operational Analysis Section issued many other reports, both positive and negative, including "The Battle of Midway" (issued March 1944), "Operations of the Seventh Amphibious Force" (issued August 1944), "The Occupation of the Marshall Islands" (issued November 1944), and "The Assault Landings on Leyte Islands" (issued December 1944).[71]

Van Straten herself described these and many other specific examples of the war work of navy aerology. She noted, for instance, that it was Lt. Cdr. Richard C. Steere, a former Olympic fencer while at Annapolis, who, as the aerologist for the Western Naval Task Force, advised Rear Adm. H. K. Hewitt and Maj. Gen. George S. Patton two days ahead of time that in spite of an apparently unfavorable weather prospect, Operation Torch's landings in North Africa should proceed as scheduled on 8 November 1942. Addressing a congratulatory message to the December 1943 graduates of the UCLA naval engineering course, the CNO, too, applauded the early successes of navy aerology: "The skillful forecasting of weather conditions has been an important factor in the conduct of many campaigns in the present war. Our successes in the Solomon Islands, North Africa, Sicily, and the Aleutians were due in no small part to the competence of navy aerological officers." Moreover, it was the forecast of the position of the equatorial front that season that determined in what order and when the Gilberts and the Marshalls would be attacked: the Gilberts in November 1943 and the Marshalls in February 1944.[72]

Since weather patterns change little from year to year, climatology proved a valuable aid in the prosecution of the war. This was demonstrated in September 1944 when aerologists worked feverishly to assemble data relevant to the invasion of Okinawa. Summaries were prepared on the number of days per month suitable for high-altitude bombing, for low-level bombing, and for the use of incendiary bombs. Facts were collected about sea and surf conditions by month and according to wind direction. The aerologists even calculated the probability that one day of rain would follow another. All of this information was factored into the decision-making process.[73]

Where did van Straten get the information on which she based her reports? One of the most useful sources was the monthly data submitted by all aerography units. Filled out by aerographer's mates, these reports were supposed to provide "a description of significant and unusual weather phenomena observed." In an effort to encourage submission of such weather reports, which were sometimes not forthcoming, the Aerology

Section published an article in the June 1943 BuAer newsletter: "You Give Us the Weather Today and We'll Forecast It for You Tomorrow."[74] The Aerology Section also received information directly from beachmasters via the Office of the Commander, Amphibious Forces, U.S. Pacific Fleet. "Although it is recognized that there will be many errors in these reports, which were made by relatively inexperienced personnel under trying combat conditions," wrote Adm. Richmond Kelly Turner, commander, Amphibious Forces Pacific, "it is believed that a careful analysis will reveal some very useful information." There can hardly be more convincing evidence than that of the value placed by combat commanders on aerological information. Admiral Turner's June 1945 letter to the Aerology Section accompanied surf reports for Iwo Jima and Okinawa, two of the most bitterly contested islands in the whole Central Pacific campaign.[75]

At first, van Straten enjoyed her work in the Operational Analysis Section, "digging out the facts of the various engagements from the war diaries and reconstructing the action and the weather." However, as the American forces recovered their strength and built up their numbers, engagements became more complicated and less clear-cut with respect to weather effects. It seemed to her that rather than brainpower it was now mostly "numbers and overwhelming strength [that] usually carried the day." There was another problem with her job, too: Captain Orville. For all his early earnestness she sensed that he had succumbed to the temptation posed by an admiral's broad stripes. He seemed to show increasing reluctance to blame senior officers for blunders. "At any rate," van Straten wrote, "the kudos were made more fulsome and the boos were so revised as to become all but inaudible." When she finally challenged him, he was very understanding and she always retained for him the greatest respect and admiration. "Flossie was a fairly positive person," remarked one meteorologist who knew them both, "and she got along very well with Captain Orville." Nevertheless, she wanted a change from operational analysis, and when he asked her what job she would like, she told him "research and development." "OK, report to the R and D section tomorrow," was his response. And she did.[76]

Van Straten's duties with Research and Development appear to have been quite varied. Much of her work—which generally went out over Orville's signature—dealt with expediting the exchange of technical information among numerous agencies. In January and again in March 1945, for example, van Straten was in communication, both by telephone and by mail, with the forecast branch of the weather division of the army air forces regarding verification of the accuracy of temperature forecasts for northern Europe. She helped a representative of TWA at the Lockheed Air Terminal in Burbank, California, obtain requested material on pressure pattern flying and sent out pamphlets on upper-air trajectories and weather forecasting, plus copies of constant pressure tables. Much of this work was the sort of routine communication that clogs up all bureaucracies. The records indicate that the male officers in the Aerology Section were also fulfilling the same routine functions, and there is nothing to differentiate van Straten's duties from theirs. Documentary evidence frequently demonstrates only the result without showing the research that must have gone into arriving at given conclusions or finding and assessing requested data or equipment.[77]

On 23 January 1945, van Straten wrote a detailed memorandum addressed to Captain Orville reporting on the visit of two American aerological officers to the Soviet Hydrometeorological Service. The main objective of the Soviet observatory they visited was to investigate weather phenomena of interest to aviation by use of free and captive balloons. The observatory scientists were also concerned with investigating and testing the accuracy and adequacy of meteorological instruments for making observations for ballistic, antiaircraft, barrage balloon, and artillery control. Van Straten pointed out in her report that the observatory operated under the principle that balloons that travel with the air mass are the most accurate means for upper air determination. She also noted the use of equipment furnished by the British to conduct radio-bearing observations (radar wind sounding, or rawin) in poor visibility. Van Straten's report gives no further details other than a diagram illustrating the Soviet device for determining cloud height, which she characterized as notable for its "extreme simplicity."[78]

Perhaps van Straten's most important task in Research and Development was to delineate fleet requirements for new meteorological equipment and systems. Much of her correspondence concerned such things as radiosonde receivers and washers, valves, and safety devices for a hydrogen generator to be sent to the Pacific Fleet. In June she wrote to BuAer —where the supply function of Aerology had remained after the other functions were transferred to CNO—regarding types of anemographs suitable for recording hurricane-force winds. Van Straten discussed in detail temporary expedients that could be used by the new storm warning centers in the Caribbean until their equipment was in place and measures to ensure proper training in the use of the new instruments once they were delivered. She also expedited the supply of additional equipment, including radiosonde ground receivers, for weather patrol vessels being outfitted in the Charleston and Philadelphia Navy Yards.[79]

Another of van Straten's duties was to act as Orville's envoy to professional seminars and conferences, writing synopses of what was relevant to Aerology from each session. She also attended meetings and seminars at the Weather Bureau and wrote summaries of the information presented. In February 1945 she reported on the "Detailed Study of Coastal Stratus" presented by a scientist from UCLA, and in April she attended a seminar at the Weather Bureau on "Research in the Technical Investigation Section." She reported back on a session about a system for avoiding errors introduced on synoptic maps by a correction to sea level pressure. Van Straten was clearly unimpressed with the procedure. After describing it in some detail she noted that "the prognostic possibilities are merely guessed at and the ultimate significance can as yet not be determined." She also found the method "laborious and time-consuming," and concluded: "It is difficult to see that a short period forecast could be prepared in sufficient time by this method."[80]

The following month, van Straten, now promoted to lieutenant, attended a meeting at the Weather Bureau on "Stream Flow Forecasting." Her report was brief. She summarized the method as "a statistical study of the relationship between the nature and extent of precipitation in the vicinity of stream basins permitting the establishment of a forecasting system whereby the amount of water in a stream during the warm season can be predicted during the cold." "The application of this work to navy problems is not immediately apparent," she concluded in typically forthright language.[81] On another occasion van Straten commented on proposals made by the Committee for Improvement of Cloud Forecasting at a conference on "Far Eastern Weather." She maintained that "any well-developed network of stations reporting weather must rely to such a large extent on unskilled observers that great credence can only be given to cloud reports." The reason for this, according to van Straten, was that "the untrained man is more likely to report clouds correctly than any other meteorological element." On another of the committee's proposals van Straten merely commented: "Army, Navy and Weather Bureau 5-day groups now work on this plan, I believe. . . . No purple hearts yet."[82]

Van Straten's position in the navy meant that she was often privy to the latest technological developments, for example, the immediate postwar plans for the facsimile program. Many of these technological innovations were first developed or implemented by the military, which must have made an appealing environment for scientists working in the war effort, perhaps for some counterbalancing the lack of free time in which to pursue independent research. The navy was particularly successful in attracting the support of many of the country's top scientists during the war, and—as the chapter of this book on Mina Rees suggests—it found a way after the war to continue supporting scientific research without scaring off even the most sensitive scientists.[83]

Wartime advances in meteorology and computing made it possible for navy aerology to fulfill its numerous tasks. Often as far as a year ahead of any major action, climatological records were assembled for use by the Joint Chiefs of Staff for tactical and strategic planning. With punch-card technology every possible interpretation of the data available could be presented to the strategists who had to make decisions about the course of the war. One forum for the presentation of climatological and other aerological reports was the Joint Army-Navy Intelligence Studies (JANIS), which included a "Climate and Meteorology" chapter prepared by the navy for most Pacific areas and by the army for others. The Aerology Section prepared the sections on naval operations, amphibious operations, and climatic elements, as well as the summary of chapters, the general description, and the bibliography. Until July 1944, whenever special weather studies were required for strategic planning by the Joint War Plans Committee of the Joint Chiefs of Staff, the Joint Meteorological Committee assigned it to the navy or the army depending on which was thought to have primary interest. In addition to JANIS and special climatic reports for strategic purposes, the Aerology Section prepared forty-six climatological surveys during the course of the war. Only seven of these had been completed before van Straten arrived in Washington, and the annual number rose to a peak of twenty-seven in 1945.[84]

During the 1940s weather forecasters generally felt confident making a forecast twenty-four hours in advance, and possibly even for the following thirty-six hours, although confidence in its accuracy diminished as the length of time grew. Anything longer than thirty-six hours was usually euphemistically termed an "outlook." Yet for military operations, thirty-six hours was generally not long enough; it took more advance notice than that to bring together the elements of a major offensive. As a result, the army, navy, and Weather Bureau each created long-range weather units working together to study weather patterns and statistical correlations in order to provide five-day forecasts. This work was facilitated by their joint location in the old Weather Bureau building. BuAer also invested modest sums to support research on the same problem at MIT.[85]

Another element in the development of improved meteorology during the war was the extension of weather networks. The accuracy of weather forecasts depends to a large extent on the density of the reporting network, and the war saw a great increase in the number of weather stations. The navy, army, Weather Bureau, and Pan American Weather Services together provided weather stations that "practically encompassed the globe," in Orville's words. They were also established in many new areas and in areas that had been only lightly covered before. The Aleutian Islands and Greenland each received a share of new weather stations, and as each Pacific atoll was taken, weather stations were established there. Aerologists sometimes learned of successful invasions several days before news of such actions was released to the public because they would start to receive weather reports from a latitude and longitude that covered territory previously in Japanese hands. Indeed, aerologists sometimes landed not long after the first assault troops and set up their anemometers, wind vanes, and barometers before the beachheads were secured. One report from Lt. Cdr. H. R. Carson, who landed on Guadalcanal with three aerographer's mates on 1 November 1942, noted that they arrived at Henderson Field as it was being shelled by a Japanese fieldpiece. Three more AerMs arrived by ship with all the equipment on the eleventh. "The Japanese greeted them with the usual bombing raid about noon; high altitude and dive bombers were combined for this occasion."[86]

Some aerologists spent time behind Japanese lines. When weather information was needed from enemy-occupied territory, aerologists would be sneaked in on submarines or PT boats and then extracted with the data. Dozens of weather stations were also established on the Asiatic mainland with the sometimes-lukewarm cooperation of the Russians and the Chinese. Altogether the navy established some thirty weather stations in China, some of which were retained until 1947. Two top-secret U.S. Navy weather stations (Expedition Moko) were established in Russian

Siberia in September 1945, although both were terminated three months later at the Soviets' request. All such stations were absolutely necessary for planning operations in the western Pacific because of the normal flow of weather systems from west to east.[87]

The development of automatic weather stations was among the wartime advances in meteorology that promised to be of continuing use in peacetime. Automatic weather stations designed for use either on land or on buoys at sea were deployed in remote areas like islands, atolls, and Arctic wastes where it was impracticable to establish manned stations. Generally, they could operate for three months without attention. The data recorded by their weather-measuring instruments could be accessed by radio, the series of dashes they transmitted translating into barometric pressure, wind direction and velocity, temperature, and amount of precipitation. Van Straten, though, referred to automatic weather stations as "a noble concept which did not work out very well." Something always went wrong: they froze in the Arctic and disappeared in the tropical jungles. To van Straten's knowledge, none ever became fully operational, although one was spotted a decade later serving as a shiny shrine on a South Pacific island. Eventually, the largest floating automatic weather station was the NOMAD. "With pride or shame I must confess," wrote van Straten, looking back, "that I am responsible for the acronym: *n*avy *o*ceanographic *m*eteorological *a*utomatic *d*evice."[88]

Aircraft were increasingly assigned to weather-gathering missions, and weather reconnaissance squadrons extended even further the spread of the wartime weather net. U.S. vessels were scattered all over the Pacific Ocean, making typhoons a major concern, yet the course of those violent tropical storms was usually erratic. The only solution was to attempt to find every storm and track it, and reconnaissance squadrons were detailed to do just that. Because of the destructive force of the storms it was important to locate them in their early stages. For this purpose typhoon warning service units were set up in the Pacific and hurricane warning service units were established in the Atlantic and Caribbean. Scout planes swept the oceans in search of storms; weather-reporting units on ships or islands sent in reports; and, increasingly, seismographic stations sent in reports from directional microseisms, minor vibrations indicating the presence and location of a storm. Once a storm was located, a weather plane flew through the 150-knot winds forming its circumference into the calm center, or eye, from where the plane could radio back its position.

As long as the plane remained in the eye the cyclone or hurricane could be effectively tracked. Later, land-based, shipborne, and airborne radar became available to assist in tracking typhoons and hurricanes.[89]

Many historians consider radar the single most important new technology to emerge in World War II, in part because it had so many different applications to the scientific war on land, in the air, and at sea. Meteorology was no exception. Radar extended the reach and improved the accuracy of weather forecasting. One of the most important ways it accomplished this was through radar wind soundings, or "rawins." The great pressure systems, identified by Bjerknes, that determine the weather are moved around by the upper air currents. In order to predict where these pressure systems are headed it is necessary to know the wind velocity and direction at five thousand, ten thousand, and twenty thousand feet. Until World War II the only way to accomplish this was by using pilot balloons and theodolites. Then, with the advent of radar, it was found that a reflector attached to the balloon could be picked up and tracked by radar, no matter what the weather. Moreover, a transponder suspended from the balloon could pick up and amplify the original radar pulse, which made it possible to continue tracking the balloon to far greater altitudes than ever before. In addition, radar gave an accurate reading for range as well as for elevation and azimuth, and it worked under all weather conditions, a great improvement on earlier observations.[90]

When she was transferred from Operational Analysis to Research and Development, van Straten became very involved with using radar for weather detection and analysis. A major application of radar to weather forecasting was discovered as a side effect of the development of the plan-position-indicator (PPI) for tracking approaching ships and aircraft. The Aerology Section had been receiving many complaints from ship commanders that enemy aircraft being tracked by radar on PPI scopes would merge into an almost static blob on the screen and disappear. It turned out that precipitating clouds give a fairly solid radar echo. Planes were taking shelter in clouds and disappearing both visually and on the radar screen. While this was an annoyance to the radar operators, it was a wonderful discovery for aerology because it meant that the aerologist's vision could be extended by a hundred or more miles to see weather patterns developing at a distance. Among other things van Straten worked on the identification of weather information on radar screens.[91]

Radar was still a rudimentary technology, however, and its effectiveness depended a great deal on the intuitive skill and experience of the operator. Normally, surface search radar had a range of thirty to forty miles before the curved surface of the earth dropped away from the straight radar beam. On occasion, however, warm moist air could bend the radar beam back to earth, and in those conditions echoes might be received from a great distance. Unless the operator was very careful, he could not always distinguish between a target at normal range and one reflected from a great distance. "At least once during World War II," van Straten recorded, "a U.S. Navy task force opened fire with its 16-inch guns on units of the Japanese fleet that were 400 miles away."[92]

The limit of radar's range to the optical horizon was countered by equipping all weather reconnaissance planes with airborne radar suitable for storm detection. With the development and spread of this technology it was no longer necessary to fly into the eye of a storm, which was clearly visible on radarscopes as an echo-free circle in the spiral of storm clouds. The ability to locate storms had a further positive use. To launch and recover planes from an aircraft carrier the ship must head into the wind, and the combined speed of wind and ship must exceed a certain minimum speed in knots. One of the means to accomplish this in an otherwise calm area was to identify a thunderstorm on the radarscope, steam to it, and circle around it. The higher winds associated with the thunderstorm might be enough to allow takeoff or recovery of planes.[93]

Van Straten was far from deskbound in pursuit of information to make her weather reports. While conducting research on fog she flew in light and heavy planes, in DC-3s, B-25s, and B-17s. Once, illegally ensconced in the nose bubble of a B-17 during landing, she witnessed a sight few airmen had seen. From her position she could see nothing of the plane except the cockpit overhead. Below, the ground rushed up to meet her, threatening to crush her fragile bubble. After that, she understood why safety regulations forbade occupation of the nose bubble except when the plane was fully airborne.[94]

While conducting research on infrared radiation, van Straten had another experience that was unusual for a Wave. Work was being done on the use of infrared for IFF (identification friend or foe), but little was known about the effect of weather on it. Van Straten's interest was to find out if the change in intensity noted in infrared beams according to the weather could be used to measure the thickness of the atmospheric obstruction. She helped to design a project to test her hypothesis and secured the use of a vessel. The navy would give her only a patrol craft escort (PCE), however, the smallest vessel still called a ship and not a boat. Since it was illegal for Waves to go to sea on any but passenger ships, van Straten assumed that her boss would conduct the experiment. Instead, having ascertained that she was keen to go, he arranged to confuse the Bureau of Personnel by adept use of the words *confidential* and *secret* to get her the necessary travel orders. The captain of the PCE agreed, and van Straten, armed with a piece of paper declaring she was an officer and a gentleman, went to Lewes, Delaware, to join the ship. As she went up the gangplank the loudspeaker blared, "Now hear this! WAVES officer aboard. Observe all proper precautions."[95]

Although van Straten outranked the captain of the ship, she freely admitted to being "strictly a landlubber type." Knowing she could not impress them with her nautical skills, after tasting the first effort of the seaman drafted to replace the absent cook, she took over cooking the main daily meal. As the ranking officer onboard, she noted that she had probably made some sort of history that would never be recorded in any navy document.[96]

Since van Straten's equipment could be operated only in the dark, the PCE traveled up and down the coast at night looking for good sources of infrared radiation. Van Straten, the captain, the watch officer, and the civilian engineer in charge of the equipment huddled on the open bridge drinking coffee while the anchor detail below had to spend the night alternately letting the anchor down and pulling it up again. Van Straten's sense of humor comes out in her account of the progress of the seamen's conversation:

> Early in the evening, their language, which came through loud and clear to us on the bridge, was quite moderate considering their labors. An occasional "hell" or "damn" was used for seasoning. The captain would apologize for the profanity and remind me that I knew what men were like. As the hours wore on, these expletives became more frequent and were joined by more resounding Anglo-Saxon words, together with their derivatives: verbs, adjectives, and nouns coming from the same four-letter roots. These the captain did not hear although the next "hell" or "damn" would be accorded a better-than-average apology.

The experimental project came to an abrupt end on the third night when the equipment unexpectedly burned out. Van Straten was convinced by her positive results, but she was never able to pursue the idea further.[97]

After VE Day began a slow rollback of aerological units which accelerated rapidly after VJ Day. By 1 April 1946, about half the aerological units had been deactivated and more than half of the aerological officers demobilized. By 1947 the peacetime numbers had stabilized with the closing of thirteen bases in the Pacific, and only about 240 aerological officers remained with the service. Most of the weather centrals were retained as a permanent part of the Navy Aerological Service. In June 1947 the Joint Hurricane Weather Center was established in Miami, Florida, where the officer in charge of Navy Weather Central, Miami, served as the navy's liaison. Similarly, the Joint Meteorological Committee approved the joint Weather Directorate, Alaskan Command, with a navy captain serving as the first director. Most navy weather ships were decommissioned and the Coast Guard replaced navy vessels with the assistance of the Weather Bureau.[98]

WAVES aerological engineers continued to work in the field after the war, although rumors that the WAVES program was to be eliminated caused some of them to seek discharge and look for jobs elsewhere. One who left in 1946 was Mary White Lockhart, who took a job at the Thunderstorm Project under her former professor, Horace Byers, at the University of Chicago. She returned to active duty in the naval reserve when the Berlin Airlift got under way in 1948 and stayed in until the navy reduced its forces after the Korean War. Eventually, Lockhart became a technical writer in the computer field. Dorothy Bradbury, another aerological engineer trained at the University of Chicago, also requested a discharge in 1946, and after pursuing her original goal of an advanced degree in mathematics found she missed meteorology too much to continue in mathematics. Again with the assistance of Professor Byers, she returned to the University of Chicago, where she worked on analyses of the jet stream and obtained her M.S. in 1951. Bradbury remained at the University of Chicago as a research scientist until her retirement in 1974 making important contributions in synoptic and mesoscale meteorology.[99]

Navy training in a specialized field had a profound influence on many more navy women than the three profiled in this book. Helena Hendrickson, for example, left the navy at the end of the war and then entered the air force. She retired as a lieutenant colonel after twenty years. Florence Coyne McDonald, who had been in the second WAVES class of aerologists at MIT, completed her twenty years as a reservist and achieved the rank of commander. Mary Ellen Thomas, a member of the third class at MIT, got out of the navy and became a geophysical sciences curriculum specialist at Lakehurst. She retained her reserve status and is thought to have advanced to captain, USNR. Laura E. Wintersteen was the only woman to attend the Advanced Aerological Engineering School at Monterey, California. Although she admitted the very difficult circumstances, "it did assure my selection to lcdr. (4th time around)." "The limitations provided by the USN selections were difficult to surmount," she wrote. "Though phases of life were exceedingly difficult, the work was very rewarding," she concluded.[100]

As in many other fields, some women who wished to continue working in meteorology after the war were discouraged from doing so. In August 1945 Dr. Reichelderfer, chief of the Weather Bureau, sent a memorandum to Captain Orville for publication in the Aerology Section's newsletter. The article announced postwar opportunities for employment in the Weather Bureau, and Reichelderfer explained to Orville that he wanted "to plan our reemployment program in a way that will place returning veterans as far as possible according to merit and qualifications." To some women this seemed to say that veteran status, coupled with experience in the field, would preempt their jobs. It must be added that many women, conscious of the sacrifices the men had made, saw some justice in this.[101]

In 1946, by then a lieutenant commander, van Straten switched from the active to the inactive naval reserve. For the next sixteen years she continued to work for the Naval Weather Service as a civilian atmospheric physicist, heading the technical requirements section from 1948 to 1962. On the information sheet she filled out for the American Meteorological Society, van Straten described her field of specialization as "application of environmental factors to military operations."[102] In her article "Meteorology Grows Up," van Straten evaluated the progress made in meteorology during the war and noted that, while important, it was almost all concerned with data collection. This was true of the vastly increased numbers of climatological records and their correlation for long-range forecasting, the information derived from aircraft reconnaissance, and the data derived from new radar techniques. What had been missing was a way to solve

Cdr. Florence van
Straten, USNR(W)
*National Archives photo
no. 80-G-1035471*

problems that had as many variables as atmospheric physics. Van Straten
knew where the solution lay: with the new "electronic calculators." The
first task was to develop the fundamental equations that determined the
circulation of the atmosphere. The navy was already working on that,
according to van Straten, sponsoring fundamental research on the physics
of the atmosphere involving such problems as vertical motion and heat
exchange. "Had we the proper equations to impress on the machine," she
noted, "we would need only to feed in the synoptic data and take out the
weather forecast for one, two or five days." This was a forward-looking
view of the future, particularly characteristic of van Straten's strategic
grasp of the new field, because at the time she was writing there was only
one functioning general-purpose electronic calculator in the United States
—ENIAC. The next chapter deals with the advent of these new "calculators," which, with radar, may have been the most important scientific and
technological developments of World War II.[103]

As well as looking resolutely forward, van Straten also had a broad
appreciation of the distance already traveled by navy meteorology. When

the navy published its World War II Administrative History of the Bureau of Aeronautics in 1957, Mapheus Smith, the author of the volume that included the Aerology Section, acknowledged in his foreword "the able assistance of Dr. Florence W. van Straten of the Aerology Branch, Flight Service Division, Deputy Chief of Naval Operations (Air)." What van Straten really enjoyed, however, was seeing tangible results from her work. There were few scientists available to the Naval Weather Service after the war as experienced as she and as able to convert knowledge of atmospheric conditions into practical scientific procedures. All her wartime experience had involved analyzing the effects of weather conditions and evaluating equipment and practices in order to determine what worked best. With her incisive mind and no-nonsense approach, van Straten continued to perform a valuable service to navy aerology. Eventually, she noted, she "became a sort of troubleshooter for the navy," dealing with problems all the way from fog to radioactive fallout.[104]

4

GRACE MURRAY HOPPER
computer scientist

It was seventeen degrees below zero on 6 January 1996 when the Bath Iron Works Corporation in Maine launched *Hopper*, the eleventh *Arleigh Burke*–class destroyer, DDG 70. True to its namesake, the ship surged purposefully ahead in spite of the temperature and the stiff wind, a tug pulling it out into the Kennebec River to begin the trip to Portland for its fitting out. Grace Murray Hopper, for whom the ship was named, was well known for her combative personality and her unorthodoxy. She loved to point out, paraphrasing Benjamin Franklin, that "ships in port are safe but that's not what ships are for," and she urged whomever would listen to sail forth and attempt mighty deeds. She herself had done no less: one of the first women to achieve the rank of rear admiral, she was also a mathematician and a pioneer in data processing. Her *New York Times* obituary described her as "a legendary figure."[1]

Hopper had a long and very distinguished civilian career, first as a professor of mathematics and later as a computer scientist in several major corporations. After World War II she moved into commercial computing, entering the new field on the ground floor.

The pivotal point in Hopper's life, however, and the catalyst for all her later successes, was her service in the U.S. Navy during World War II. It was the navy that introduced her to the emerging world of computing, pushing her into the field that was to absorb the rest of her life. When she was asked thirty years later how she became interested in computing, Hopper replied, "I was ordered to the first computer in the United States by the United States Navy, and I reported to the Mark I computer." Before that, she said, "there were no computers so I didn't know anything about it. I was a college professor teaching mathematics."[2]

Born on 9 December 1906, Grace Brewster Murray was the oldest of three children. She was raised in New York City and spent her summers in the family cottage on Lake Wentworth in Wolfeboro, New Hampshire. Perhaps because her father, a successful insurance broker, lost both legs to hardening of the arteries when his children were young, he instilled in them the notion that they must learn to support themselves. To this end he wanted his two daughters to have the same educational opportunities as his son, a rare notion in those days. Hopper's maternal grandfather was the senior civil engineer of New York City, and she recalled with pleasure going with him on surveying jobs, holding the red-and-white pole as he laid out the streets of Pelham. He had encouraged his own daughter to pursue her interest in mathematics, which she passed on to her children. All three of them later excelled in the subject. Throughout her life Hopper was also a persistent tinkerer with a passion to find out how things worked. As far as possible her family indulged her, even when her youthful zeal for disassembling gadgets such as clocks and irons exceeded her ability to reassemble them.[3]

During the summers, especially, the Murray children led vigorous outdoor lives. They were encouraged to be hardy and independent, whether this involved climbing to precarious heights in trees or sailing on the lake. Once, when Hopper was about to abandon a fast-sinking sail-canoe that was rapidly taking on water, her mother, who was watching from shore, firmly admonished her through a megaphone to remember her great-grandfather the admiral. Instead of letting her little craft sink Hopper tipped it over and towed it safely ashore. With such influence and encouragement from their parents it is hardly surprising that all three children were high achievers. At Wolfeboro they learned how to sew, how to plant and grow things in the garden, and how to cook as well. They were also "mavericks," in Hopper's word. "We were always supposed to have new ideas." When asked if the women in the family were particularly encouraged to compete, Hopper answered, "No. But if we had a good idea, it was evaluated and we were patted on the back if it was a good one."[4]

In 1924 Hopper went to Vassar, a women's college in Poughkeepsie, New York. Like other leading feminist institutions of the day, Vassar had originally modeled its curriculum on that of Harvard and Yale, and four of the original eight professors had taught science. One of the most frequent reasons for wanting a Vassar education given by women who graduated before World War I was the desire for a career. Among postwar graduates, however, it was much more common to hear that Vassar's popularity among their friends was a deciding factor. This reflected both a pronounced shift away from the gains made by the suffrage movement in the first two decades of the century and a slackening of interest in the employment opportunities opened up by World War I. In Hopper's freshman year, Vassar followed the postwar trend in women's education away from pioneering efforts at equality with men's colleges, introducing instead subjects aimed at preparing women for marriage and children. That very year the college created a School of Euthenics offering courses such as "Husband and Wife," "Motherhood," and "The Family as an Economic Unit" that were designed "to raise motherhood to a profession worthy of [women's] finest talents and greatest intellectual gifts." Hopper's sister, Mary, who followed her to Vassar in 1926, took a double major in economics and child studies.

For women, interwar academics was thus increasingly viewed as preparation not for an independent career, but to serve a higher, domestic, calling. The Depression further hastened this drift away from the goal of equality in education and economic opportunity between women and men, while widespread unemployment fostered the notion that working women were selfishly taking jobs away from men on whom families depended for support.[5]

Disregarding the trend toward domesticity, Hopper graduated from Vassar with honors in mathematics and physics in 1928 and then went on to earn an M.A. in mathematics from Yale University two years later. Her father had gone to Yale and her younger brother was in the undergraduate class of 1932. He, too, like his elder sister, graduated Phi Beta Kappa, but with a major in economics. Hopper had thought about studying engineering in college but knew "there was no place for women in engineering at that time." Therefore, she continued in mathematics, and in 1934 she was awarded a Ph.D. in mathematics at Yale, a rare accomplishment, especially for a woman. Between 1862 and 1937 only 1,279 doctorates in mathematics were awarded in the entire country, and Yale awarded only 7 between 1934 and 1937. Hopper was the only woman who received one. During the 1930s the percentage of women earning doctorates actually declined, especially in male-dominated fields such as the sciences and mathematics. The only other woman going through a doctoral program in math at the same time as Hopper was a nun.[6]

With a distinguished degree in hand, Hopper nevertheless had little choice but to enter the traditional female profession of teaching. It should also be noted, however, that most men with Ph.D.'s in mathematics took the same route. In 1930 only 15 percent of all math Ph.D.'s were in non-academic employment. Even here, though, women were losing ground; in the 1930s the percentage of female college teachers fell 6 percent to 26.5 percent, the decline affecting private and all-female schools as well as public coeducational ones. According to Hopper, most of her Vassar class-mates had had no interests or career goals other than getting married. If they expected to work at all it was assumed they would become school-teachers. Of those with graduate degrees Hopper knew of a few women actuaries and one or two who worked in laboratories, but women employed outside academics were rare.[7]

The situation of women in Europe was similar. In Germany during the 1930s the proportion of women in the teaching profession remained fairly stable, with women representing 68 percent of the staffs of girls' senior schools in 1939. This was true in spite of the removal of a number of women from teaching on political or racial grounds and heavy govern-ment pressure for teachers to be actively involved in activities supporting National Socialist principles. The favorable position of women in teach-ing was not maintained at the university level, however, where the percent-age of women dropped from a high of 1 percent in 1930 to 0.8 percent by 1936. In the technical universities there were even fewer women lecturers. Government control of education and science in Germany during the 1930s, however, did not seem to close doors to professional women much more than economic and social forces closed them in the United States in the same years. The greater difference emerged in the official attitude toward mobilizing women once the war began.[8]

With few other options open, then, between 1931 and 1943, Hopper worked her way from instructor to associate professor of mathematics at her alma mater, Vassar College. In 1930 she had married Vincent Foster Hopper, a professor of comparative literature at New York University, and for a number of years she commuted in her model-A Ford between Poughkeepsie and Manhattan. Although Hopper later maintained that dual careers such as theirs were not uncommon, 82 percent of the respondents to a 1936 Gallup poll believed that wives of men who were employed —double-earners—should not work. During the difficult Depression years, moreover, bills were introduced in almost all states to restrict the employment of married women. Hopper's strong character made her generally impervious to social pressures, but perhaps they added to the strain of an already difficult commuter marriage. At any rate she and her husband were separated in 1941 and divorced in 1945, although she kept her married name.[9]

World War II brought an end to Hopper's academic life, and perhaps offered escape from her unsatisfactory marriage as well. When the Japanese attacked Pearl Harbor the only women in the U.S. Navy, or in any other military service, were nurses, but on 30 July 1942 Congress authorized the establishment of the Women's Reserve U.S. Navy. Hopper was eager to join but had to fight to be admitted. At age thirty-five she was considered old for enlistment. To make matters even worse, she weighed only 105 pounds, 16 pounds under the navy weight guidelines for her height of five feet six inches. The most significant impediment, however, was her profession. Mathematics was crucial to the war effort; teaching mathematics was classified as an essential occupation, and Hopper would have to apply for a release. She persevered, however, later explaining that she had wanted to serve the war effort more directly than just by teaching. Since her maternal great-grandfather, whom she remembered meeting, had been a Civil War rear admiral who fought at Mobile Bay and Vicksburg, she "naturally . . . went navy."[10]

Hopper's determination to serve in the navy, like the same decision made by Mary Sears and Florence van Straten, begs an explanation. In her case the answer was family history. In World War II, as Hopper put it, "we were all in . . . everybody was in something." One of her cousins was a navy nurse, and her brother served in the army air forces until 1946, when he returned to his job as vice president of the Bankers Trust Company. Hopper's father served on the Selective Service Board, and her mother served on the Ration Board. Hopper's sister, who could not join the military because of her two young sons, ran the nursery at the General Electric plant in Bloomfield, New Jersey, for all the women who were making fuses for bombs.[11]

When Hopper first applied to the navy, however, the admissions board seemed unimpressed by her nautical forebear. Disappointed, she spent the summer of 1943 in New York City teaching mathematics at Barnard to women enrolled in the special defense courses created to prepare them for war work in laboratories. Finally, the navy gave her a waiver for the weight requirement and she obtained a leave of absence from Vassar and a release from mathematics. Her marital status was not an impediment because she had no children. In December 1943, having just turned thirty-seven, Hopper was sworn in to the U.S. Naval Reserve. She was sent to the Northampton Midshipmen's School for women at Smith College, where she had sixty days' training: "thirty days to learn how to take orders, and thirty days to learn how to give orders, and you were a naval officer." The midshipmen were divided into the "campus battalion" and the "hotel battalion," the latter so named because the women lived in the Northampton Inn. Hopper was in the hotel battalion. After graduating first in her class in June 1944 and accepting a commission as a lieutenant (j.g.), Hopper was sent directly to the navy's Bureau of Ships Computation Project at Harvard University.[12]

Although the rapidly expanding data management needs of World War II accelerated the development of modern digital computers, especially in Britain and the United States, few of the machines were operational until after the conflict ended. A notable exception in America was the brainchild of Howard Aiken, the culmination of a project he began in 1937 as a communication engineering graduate student at Harvard. Frustrated by the tedious and time-consuming mathematical calculations required for his doctoral dissertation on the theory of space charge conduction, Aiken designed a mechanism to perform such calculations automatically. Engineers at Thomas Watson's International Business Machines (IBM) built Aiken's machine under his guidance but using many of their own patented parts. The device that emerged from this collaboration, the Automatic Sequence Controlled Calculator (ASCC), or Harvard Mark I, was the first functional, large-scale, automatically sequenced, general-purpose digital computer to be produced in America.[13] The press called it

Lt. Grace M. Hopper,
USNR(W)
*Courtesy Mary Murray
Westcote*

a "Robot Brain," but Aiken, by then a professor of physics and applied
mathematics at Harvard, called it "just a lazy man's dream."[14]

When the Mark I was finally completed at the IBM facilities in Endicott, New York, in 1944, Watson of IBM gave it to Harvard as a gift. It
was installed that spring at the university but was immediately leased for
the duration of the war by the U.S. Navy, which was desperate for gunnery and ballistics calculations. Aiken, a naval reserve officer, was put in
charge of the Mark I for the BuShips Computation Project at the Harvard
Computation Laboratory.[15]

The uneasy alliance of academic, business, and military interests held
together by Howard Aiken was responsible for the development and early
use of the Mark I. The magnitude of his accomplishment will become
clearer in chapter 5 when we examine the difficulties encountered by the
National Defense Research Committee as it tried to fulfill its mandate to
coordinate government and academic scientific interests. Similarly, Mina
Rees's postwar work at the Office of Naval Research was not restricted by

civilian industrial imperatives. For a time, Aiken and patriotism were able to hold together the competing professional agendas, and the Mark I successfully carried out a strenuous schedule of important calculations for the navy and for other military projects. After the war, however, the centrifugal interests of each group reasserted themselves, obscuring the lab's wartime achievements.

What Watson may not have understood when he gave the Mark I to Harvard was that the university with which he wished to become associated had a tradition of indifference toward what it viewed as the "applied" sciences. As the *Encyclopedia of Computer Science and Engineering* diplomatically explains with regard to Howard Aiken's interest in computer technologies, "Harvard was not the most likely environment to get support for this type of research." At an institution where pure theory was emphasized, Aiken was on the academic fringe, "a real outsider and upstart," according to Harvard professor of the history of science I. Bernard Cohen. Indeed, there was so much institutional resistance at Harvard to the application-oriented science of computers that Aiken was always forced to struggle for funding.[16]

Harvard also aggravated Aiken's situation by snubbing Thomas Watson—at least in Watson's eyes—during the opening ceremony for the Mark I computer. Watson struck back by severely curtailing IBM's contribution to Aiken's project, setting off a bitter competition between the two men that lasted for years. With halfhearted support from Harvard and IBM, only Aiken's relationship with the navy assured the survival of the lab in its early days. Hopper thought the project might never have been funded at all had it not been for the war.[17]

The importance of the Mark I's computing ability to the navy was indicated by the presence of senior naval officers at its inauguration at Harvard on 7 August 1944. Among them were Rear Adm. Edward L. Cochrane, the chief of the Bureau of Ships; Rear Adm. A. H. Van Keuren, the director of the Naval Research Laboratory (NRL); and Rear Adm. Julius A. Furer, the navy's coordinator of research and development.[18] Admiral Furer, in particular, was a strong advocate of scientific development. Holding his position as coordinator from 13 December 1941 until his retirement after VE Day, he worked closely and well with the civilian scientific authorities, maintaining a smooth mechanism for liaison.[19]

After the inauguration the *Boston Daily Globe* ran a photograph of the "World's Greatest Calculator," noting that it was invented by

IBM ASCC—Harvard Mark I
Courtesy IBM Archives

Cdr. Howard H. Aiken, U.S. Naval Reserve. The "Algebra Machine," as the *New York Times* called the Mark I, was a trailblazer in a new and rapidly developing discipline.[20]

The computing machine taken over by BuShips in 1944 was in many ways unique. It was enormous, some fifty feet long, eight feet tall, and eight feet deep, filling an entire room. It had more than 750,000 parts, used 530 miles of wire, and weighed about five tons. A four-horsepower electric motor and a driveshaft that extended the length of the machine drove all the mechanical parts by a system of gears and chains, and more than a thousand ball bearings kept its components moving.[21] Many sorts of electromechanical desk calculators were then in common use, and IBM punch-card machines were numerous, but the Mark I was "clearly not of the same species," according to Richard M. Bloch, a Harvard mathematics graduate who wrote many of the machine's early programs. Indeed, the Mark I, built to exploit the ideas of nineteenth-century British inventor Charles Babbage, was a rare creature, an electromechanical digital computer destined to dominate the field for only a few years, briefly bridging the gap between calculators and electronic computers.[22]

Howard Aiken described the Mark I as a "general arithmetic machine capable of addition, subtraction, multiplication, division, and the transfer of numbers."[23] Most impressive were its speed of computation and its automatic functioning enabling it to proceed through a series of arithmetic operations without human intervention. Automatic sequence control was accomplished according to programmed instructions fed into the machine on punched paper tape, while the output was handled either by punched cards or by two electric typewriters.

The multiple-purpose capabilities of the Mark I—the fact that it could be set to accomplish a wide range of different types of numerical calculations—set it apart from other contemporary computing devices. For Aiken—who always wanted practical results—flexibility, accuracy, and reliability were even more important than speed, although he estimated that the Mark I was nearly a hundred times more productive than a manually operated calculator. It attained its accuracy by representing numbers to twenty-three significant digits, and it ran twenty-four hours a day, functioning 90 to 95 percent of the time with few interruptions for fifteen years.[24]

Aiken was well aware of ongoing experimental work using vacuum tubes to replace relatively slow mechanical relays, but he believed it was better to sacrifice some speed for a device that could be put to use immediately. A postwar history of wartime computing developments by George Stibitz bears him out: "Electronic equipment held great promise in the high speed computing field but it appeared that the established techniques . . . [of] relays would permit earlier completion of large scale computing equipment."[25] Hopper agreed, noting that tubes were not reliable enough until at least two years after Aiken started work. She further observed that Aiken's concepts were so far ahead of the material resources then available that they were later transferred to electronics as soon as suitable equipment was produced.[26]

The BuShips contract for the Computation Project, which was to last until "six months after the cessation of present hostilities," was part of a pattern of increased military and government involvement in industry and academe.[27] As war threatened, intellectual resources all over the country —especially scientific and mathematical resources—had been enlisted to tackle the challenge of a vast technological expansion. Various agencies appeared under the Office of Emergency Management to mobilize and direct engineering and scientific talent. In June 1940 the National Defense

Research Committee was established for this purpose; it was joined a year later by the Office of Scientific Research and Development (OSRD). As head first of NDRC and then of OSRD, Vannevar Bush, formerly of the Massachusetts Institute of Technology, directed more than thirty thousand people working on such projects as radar, fire-control mechanisms, proximity fuses, and the atomic bomb. At first, both the navy and the army opposed the control of wartime scientific research by a civilian organization, even though each service was represented on the committee.[28] It was clear to one British scientific observer that in the beginning "the Navy Dept. and Research Laboratory [NRL] were jealous, or in danger of feeling jealous, of Dr. Bush and his committee," even though Bush had been a faithful member of the naval reserve for years.[29]

The traditional navy suspicion of academic laboratories receded once it became clear that this war, unlike previous ones, might be won by technical and scientific advances made during the course of the war itself. As a result, most navy bureaus worked rather smoothly with the civilian scientific structure. This cooperation was facilitated by the number of scientists—civilians and former civilians temporarily in uniform—who were involved in war-related research in academic and corporate as well as in military laboratories. Howard Engstrom, for example, who had taught Hopper at Yale (and who, like Bush, was a longtime member of the naval reserve), was made a captain and headed a special research group of top mathematicians, engineers, and physicists from all over the country charged with applying mathematics to cryptanalysis. Exemplifying the wartime mixing of science and technology, the group influenced both the building and the operation of the navy's first coding and decoding machines.[30]

Many academic and corporate applied science facilities were under some form of supervision by both NDRC and the navy (or the army).[31] This was certainly true in the case of the Harvard Computation Lab. While Howard Aiken technically reported directly to Cdr. David Ferrier of the nearby Harvard Radio Research Laboratory, and to Cdr. Eugene Smith at BuShips, he also received instructions from NDRC's Applied Mathematics Panel on projects assigned to his lab.[32] The situation was at times confusing, but hardly unique during the war. Such mixtures of civilian and military authority occurred in research facilities all over the country, including at other Harvard laboratories. Nor was the Computation Lab the only case in which the navy took over a whole structure. In

1942 the Naval Computing Machinery Laboratory was formed at National Cash Register's (NCR) plant in Dayton, Ohio. Eventually, the navy took over all of NCR's cryptanalytic work.[33] But at the Computation Lab—an entirely naval reserve outfit—civilian and military leadership were fused in the person of Howard Aiken; the navy put him in command of his own laboratory. Also, perhaps because of the small number of people involved and the innovative nature of the work, which few outsiders understood, Aiken was essentially autonomous locally, running his nominally navy facility in his own idiosyncratic way.

The complex, interlocking structure of the Mark I research program exemplifies the American scientific war effort. By contrast with Germany, Britain, and Japan, American science benefited from a late entry into the war. Vannevar Bush had time to create an organization capable of connecting a wide variety of military and civilian resources in the solution of problems whose component parts were farmed out to many separate and otherwise unconnected entities. The navy's Computation Lab became one of those entities, running calculations whose results formed part of the answers to many different kinds of technical military questions.[34]

Of course, Aiken's lab was not the only one addressing the country's computing needs. During World War II, the United States manufactured approximately 45 percent of all armaments produced by all parties engaged in that conflict. Scientists and technicians worked at a feverish rate on the design, testing, modification, and analysis of these weapons, and their efforts required extensive numerical calculations. Trained specialists —usually women called "computers"—produced many of the numbers using desk calculators. Wartime pressure, however, generated government contracts to create better and faster methods of computation. The rapid speed of progress in the field was due in part to solid groundwork laid down earlier.[35]

Between the two world wars the growth of large businesses had already sparked efforts to come to grips with modern calculation and record-keeping needs. Work on improved calculators progressed in industrial as well as academic laboratories, and one or two early computer designs were produced. By 1930, Dr. Bush and his colleagues at MIT had developed a "differential analyzer"—a general-purpose, automatic analog computer, driven by electric motors, that could be set to work on most problems involving differential equations. Copies of the analyzer were eventually widely used in the war effort, especially to create firing and bombing tables. Similar, but simpler, analog machines were also used during the war for radar and gunnery.[36]

While Aiken was working on the ASCC/Mark I at IBM, George R. Stibitz was engaged in a similar effort at Bell Telephone Laboratories (BTL). On 8 January 1940, Dr. Stibitz put into operation a digital device called a "partially automatic computer" capable of performing addition, subtraction, multiplication, and division of complex numbers. By the mid-1940s BTL had completed machines roughly comparable to the Mark I in overall performance. At the same time, at Iowa State College, mathematician John V. Atanasoff was working on a device that some consider the first electronic digital computer, but it never became operational.[37]

In October 1943 the navy's ballistics center at Dahlgren, Virginia, expressed interest in George Stibitz's relay device for computing solutions to the differential equations necessary for ballistics tables. Before committing to having BTL construct a computer, however, the navy asked OSRD's Applied Mathematics Panel (AMP) to "conduct a survey of the present possibilities in the field of step-by-step analyzer design and construction to see whether or not an adequate and sufficiently flexible analyzer can be designed and built at this time."[38] The head of AMP, Warren Weaver—who had taught Howard Aiken calculus years earlier and who knew of his nearly completed machine at Harvard—directed that it be included in the survey. Very likely, the navy-initiated survey of computational equipment, and the attention this focused on the Mark I, combined to spur the navy's takeover of the Harvard machine.[39] Moreover, the survey won Aiken the Dahlgren contract too, and the navy agreed to pay $250,000 "for a machine like the Harvard machine."[40]

Overseas, advanced computer developments were also in progress, accelerated by the war. In Germany in 1938, six years before the Mark I began operating, engineer Konrad Zuse completed his Zuse 1, an electro-mechanical relay computer. By 1943 he had completed the Zuse Z3, which was probably the first fully functional general-purpose digital computer and was used—though too late to affect the outcome of the war—in the German aircraft industry and in the engineering of V2 rockets. In Britain, impending war brought a rush of computer developments focusing on code-breaking applications. The "Colossus" series of machines, produced by mathematician Alan M. Turing and others for cryptanalysis, was certainly one of the most important computer developments of the war. The first Colossus, an electronic protocomputer, became operational in January 1944 just at the time the Mark I was being installed at Harvard.[41]

While the true record of the Computation Lab's contribution to the war was obscured at the time by the secrecy of the work itself, the glamorous combination of Harvard cachet and navy war service was apparently too appealing to succumb to censorship. The lab was so widely publicized during the war through print and pictures in newspapers and magazines that Aiken received requests for computing help from private individuals all over the country, even requests from schoolchildren for information for class projects. Indeed, the Mark I became something of a poster girl, and her creator, Commander Aiken, a symbol of navy scientific accomplishment.[42]

Aiken and his mathematicians were anomalies among academic and even service laboratories in that they were almost all in uniform, which suited them well in their navy propaganda role. In early 1945, all eight scientists on Aiken's staff, including Grace Hopper, were temporary naval reserve officers. Not all scientists engaged in war work were so willing to espouse military discipline. In a much more characteristic and well-known case, Maj. Gen. Leslie R. Groves, the director of the Manhattan Project, asked the scientists under his care at Los Alamos National Laboratory to wear uniforms and adhere to military rank. He was scornfully refused by the laboratory's director, J. Robert Oppenheimer, on behalf of the scientists working there. At the Harvard Lab, however, even the eight technicians were navy enlisted men, and there were only six civilian support staff.[43]

OSRD maintained a "Reserved List of Scientific and Technical Research Workers" to eliminate conflicts with the Selective Service. The minimum basis for inclusion in the list was "that the man is using his training and experience at a job for which he is specifically trained and on which he must use his analytical brain power."[44] Interestingly, all the male scientists at the Computation Lab clearly qualified for exemption from the draft on occupational grounds; the two women were exempt by gender; and Howard Aiken, who was forty-one when the United States entered the war, would have been exempt from military service because of his age. Yet they were all in the navy by choice, not only surrendering personal freedom but suffering considerable loss of pay.[45]

The unusual voluntary military status of the Harvard staff is even more surprising considering the intense competition for scientists among the services and with OSRD/NDRC. Moving from one agency to another increased the scientists' chances of avoiding the draft and maintaining civilian status, and "pirating" scientists was common. Once the war began, the navy moved to secure the services of eminent scientists. Columbia University astronomer Wallace Eckert, with his IBM machines, was recruited for secret work at the Naval Observatory in Washington; he worked directly for the navy but as a civilian. In 1942 John Atanasoff left Iowa State College to join the staff of the Naval Ordnance Laboratory (NOL), and he, too, remained a civilian.[46] In June 1944 the navy tried, unsuccessfully, to lure physicist John W. Mauchly away from the University of Pennsylvania's Moore School of Electrical Engineering to work at NOL. He was told that "the Laboratory's need for men with the proper qualifications is urgent,"[47] but he declined the offer, even though he was only thirty-six (a year younger than Grace Hopper) and would have been allowed to remain a civilian.

The U.S. Army also recognized the importance of civilians and civilian facilities to serve its scientific war needs and recruited a formidable group of scientists at academic and industrial laboratories. One of the most productive of these collaborations was between John Mauchly and J. Presper Eckert at the University of Pennsylvania's Moore School and the Army Ordnance Ballistic Research Laboratory at Aberdeen Proving Ground, Maryland, resulting in the Electronic Numerical Integrator and Computer (ENIAC), designed for ballistics analysis. The Moore School also carried out war research for the Army Signal Corps, the Navy Bureau of Ordnance, and OSRD. In 1944–45 it spent $350,000 on such projects as rockets, radar, the aerodynamics of projectiles, and antiaircraft fire control. More than one hundred employees of the Moore School were working on war projects by April 1945.[48]

In all, Harvard University took on more than one hundred research contracts during the war, totaling $33.5 million. OSRD contracts employed 1,759 people, mostly civilians, while 69 additional personnel were engaged in non-OSRD work. Projects ranged in size from the 808-person Radio Research Laboratory, which occupied a whole wing of the biology building, to 454 at the Underwater Sound Laboratory, to a lone researcher working in his own office. The Computation Laboratory was one of Harvard's smallest contracts in terms of personnel; and those personnel were drawn into the navy more or less by serendipity.[49]

Aiken, "a gray-eyed six-foot blond Viking from Wisconsin," was an assistant professor at Harvard University in mid-1941. The basic design of his computer was complete by then, and the machine was under construction at IBM. Nevertheless, Aiken volunteered for the U.S. Naval Reserve, took up a commission as a lieutenant commander, and went to teach magnetic mine technology in Yorktown, Virginia. While at the Mine Warfare School Aiken made many trips to Washington, D.C., most probably to advertise his machine and arrange for its use by the navy. In the meantime, however, he needed someone to act as his deputy on the project and as liaison with IBM. In typically abrupt fashion, Aiken recruited and hired Robert V. D. Campbell on the basis of a brief interview while changing trains at Grand Central Station during the Christmas vacation of 1941. Campbell, a graduate student in the Harvard Physics Department, turned out to be an excellent choice. For the next two years, in addition to keeping up with his own academic career, he worked closely with engineers at IBM on Aiken's machine. Aiken assigned Campbell to see the Mark I to completion and to get it to run without error. His main tasks were to check circuit diagrams and to develop programs to test each component of the machine as it was built. There was no precedent for much of what he was doing nor any training; a notable characteristic of those who worked on the Mark I was their ability to innovate.[50]

In January 1944, with Aiken still stuck in Yorktown, the Mark I was disassembled at Endicott, transferred to Harvard, and set up in the old battery room in the basement of the Cruft Laboratory by a team of IBM technicians. On one of his trips to Washington Aiken had visited Rear Admiral Van Keuren at NRL in Anacostia, where much of the navy's research on radar, radio, and sonar was conducted. Later, Aiken had been given a tour of the facility by Richard Bloch, a young naval reserve ensign. In 1941, as an undergraduate at Harvard College, Bloch had volunteered for the navy's V7 program, which committed him to officer training on graduation. When Aiken found that Bloch was a recent mathematics honors graduate of Harvard, he invited him to return to his alma mater to work at the newly created Computation Lab. It did not take much to persuade Bloch to fulfill the rest of his navy obligation at Harvard, though how NRL was induced to relinquish him is not known.[51]

Finally, in June 1944, Aiken was promoted to commander and sent to run the BuShips Computation Laboratory at Harvard. It is not clear how Aiken managed to obtain this transfer, nor who authorized it. In an interview given years later, Aiken said that one day he received a phone call at Yorktown from a "high ranking naval officer" who wanted to know why he was not personally running his calculator. He replied that he was just following orders. Within hours those orders were changed and Aiken was on his way back to Cambridge to become, as he put it, "the only man in the world who was ever commanding officer of a computer."[52]

Although the Mark I technically belonged to Harvard, during the war its use was devoted exclusively to the navy, which paid for its operation, including the salaries of the Computation Lab personnel and even an eight-hundred-dollar monthly rent to Harvard. This outside funding set the lab apart from the rest of the university, leading to independence and a certain isolation. Tucked away in a basement among the ivory towers, Aiken's Computation Lab was guarded night and day by navy armed guards.[53]

Aiken's little staff grew quickly. When Dick Bloch had moved up from the NRL in March, Aiken had indicated that he should help get the machine operational as soon as possible. Bloch had never taken an engineering course and had to teach himself on the job. In addition, his particular assignment was to learn how to develop sets of operational instructions for the Mark I to execute. These operational instructions were written in a machine code, and Hopper recalled that they referred to Bloch's task as "coding." The word *programming* came over from England later, and Hopper continued to believe that the word *coding* more accurately described what they were actually doing; *programming* should have been reserved for a higher level, she thought.[54]

On 2 July 1944, Grace Hopper reported for duty. After hunting around the campus for several hours, Hopper finally located the lab and gained admittance. Aiken snapped at her for being late and then said: "That's a computing engine. I would be delighted to have the coefficients for the interpolation of the arc tangent by next Thursday."[55] Aiken knew, of course, that Hopper was there because of her mathematics background and not because she knew anything about computers. Twenty-one-year-old Ens. Ruth A. Brendel arrived at the laboratory soon after Hopper. She had been an instructor in mathematics at the University of Buffalo and had joined the navy because she thought her technical skills could make a contribution to the war effort. The navy sent both women to Harvard in answer to a direct request from the Computation Lab for Waves for scientific billets.[56]

Aiken cared only about getting the job done, and if the only people available with the requisite skill to do it were women, that was fine with him. Indeed, he was equally critical of all his mentees, male or female, and young and inexperienced Ruth Brendel often found his harshness almost impossible to take. Many times Brendel determined to seek a transfer, but Hopper was always there to talk her out of it. Brendel described the older woman as an almost perfect mentor who shielded her from Aiken and made her life at the lab bearable.[57]

In June 1944, just before Hopper arrived at the lab, Bob Campbell, Aiken's deputy, joined the navy, too, and became an ensign junior even to young Dick Bloch. Although Campbell believes that Aiken probably wanted him to join the navy, he had not pressured him to do so; nevertheless, Campbell thought the idea rather intriguing, so he signed on. Rank was generally not an issue at the lab; Aiken ran a tight operation as far as computing went, but he was interested in performance, not hierarchy. Those present in the early days, like Campbell, remember that "even though it was a navy organization[,] . . . Aiken didn't stand on ceremony very much, and it was quite informal."[58] One petty officer recalls that "personal relations [at the lab] were atypical for a navy unit."[59]

The navy provided enlisted men as well as officers to work at the lab. One report states that a number of the former were IBM technicians who were "drafted en masse into the navy" while working on the Mark I at Endicott.[60] Delo A. Calvin, who was one of the enlisted men in the Computation Lab, questions this statement. In February 1944, Calvin was inducted into the naval reserve while he was working as a customer engineer for IBM in Florida. In July he was sent to Harvard. He and three other petty officers who had had three or four years' experience repairing IBM equipment were given the rating of "specialist-I" (for IBM) and were assigned to the Mark I as machine operators. They installed the coded program tape, installed or changed the functional tapes, changed the specified values, set switches, and physically controlled the machine's operation. Another petty officer, John Hourihan, came not from IBM training but via the navy's Class A Electrician's Mate School. He believes he was selected through the Bureau of Personnel based on requirements set up by Aiken. Today the specialists-I would be known as data processors (DPs) and data systems technicians (DSs).[61]

Years later, when asked whom she had enjoyed most of the many brilliant people she had worked for in her long career, Grace Hopper chose Howard Aiken. He "always said you could make any mistake in the world

Harvard Computation Laboratory Staff, August 1944. *Top row, second from left,
Delo Calvin. Bottom row, from left,* Bloch, Arnold, Aiken, Hopper, Campbell
*Grace Hopper Collection, Archives Center, National Museum of American History,
Smithsonian Institution*

once as long as you didn't make it twice," she recalled. Hopper thought
Aiken an "excellent leader" who kept the group moving forward at a
formidable pace while maintaining high standards, both teaching and
challenging his young staff. She said nothing about Aiken being likable or
having a pleasant personality. Even those most devoted to Aiken, like Dick
Bloch, described him as a "tough hombre."[62] Bob Hawkins, a technician
who worked for Aiken for more than ten years, "got along with him fine,"
but nevertheless added that "he was a hard man."[63] Numerous anecdotes
about Aiken support this view. At a Harvard faculty meeting years later,
according to legend, someone mentioned that Aiken was not present
because he had gone to the dentist. "To have his teeth sharpened I sup-
pose," was the quick response. Prof. Bernard Cohen, who knew Aiken
well, wrote that "only such a man could have made a reluctant Harvard
become a center for the new science and art of computing."[64]

Everyone in the Computation Lab compulsively worked long hours
(though in theory operating in three shifts), personnel and machine alike

Cdr. Howard Aiken and Lt. Grace Hopper with the Mark I, 1944
*Grace Hopper Collection, Archives Center, National Museum of American History,
Smithsonian Institution*

pushing to the limit to help end the war by winning it. Hopper and most of the rest of the staff lived in rented rooms a quick walk away. Cooped up day after day listening to the Mark I's constant clicking (some thought it sounded like a giant sewing machine, others like knitting needles), the staff formed a close fraternity and relieved the pressure by "great kidding around." Aiken was constantly attentive, in his office at all hours with the door open and his back to the machine; if it stopped he was out in a flash to see what was wrong, quickly pitching in wherever necessary to help get it going again. "Howard was only at peace with the world when the Mark I was producing numbers," Dick Bloch later recalled.[65]

And produce numbers it did. Dick Bloch wrote that Bob Campbell "was really responsible for getting the machine into productive operation," but Campbell called Bloch "the primary force as far as I'm concerned." Bloch became so skilled at programming that Hopper used to call him the Mozart of computers. He was the only person she knew who could write a program, flawlessly, in ink.[66] When problems were brought to the Computation Lab, even by other mathematicians, they had to be prepared for the machine using a code book put together by Aiken and Campbell that covered all the better-known numerical processes. The operator, usually one of the enlisted men, would punch the appropriate code holes in the paper tape to feed the problem to the machine. Once a function was coded in paper-tape form, the tape was preserved so that it could be used again. Gradually, a tape library was assembled, which greatly speeded the work of the programmers. Thus began the concept of programming, central to Aiken's understanding of computing.[67]

Bob Hawkins, originally recruited by Aiken from the Cruft machine shop, was largely responsible for keeping the machine going. He did a good job—eventually it was running for 730 hours a month, or 168-hour weeks. Hawkins had to test and maintain the 3,304 mechanical relays and 2,200 counters, the typewriters, the two card feeds, and the cardpunch. He also became very adept at solving all sorts of glitches that might stop the machine. "You've got to have scotch tape to run a machine like that," he explained. If you find an error in the punched paper tape which holds the code for the machine, "you plug the [erroneous] hole up with a piece of scotch tape and then you duplicate the tape and start off again."[68]

The Computation Lab completed twenty-three reports for BuShips in less than two years. By 1 January 1946, when the project was transferred to the Bureau of Ordnance, the staff had grown to almost forty.

Most of the reports were purely technical, often in the form of laboratory records, and many did not even mention the practical use to which the computations would be put. The projects were so secret that even the coders usually identified them only by letters of the alphabet. During the war BuShips had the final word on the use of the Mark I, and even the Applied Mathematics Panel had to request permission to assign specific problems to it. The machine was much more powerful than almost everything else then available to the navy and the nation, and it ran only those calculations regarded as essential to the war effort.[69]

The first problem Hopper remembered working on at the lab was the one Aiken thrust on her the very first day: finding the interpolation coefficients for applications of the arc tangent series. This was a fairly elementary problem except that it had to be computed to twenty-three digits for the Mark I. The numbers would be used to compute rocket trajectories. Instead of shooting only inert objects (projectiles) the navy was now firing self-propelled missiles (rockets), for which there were no firing tables. A similar early problem was to figure fire-control calculations for 5-inch .38-caliber antiaircraft guns. The completed solution accommodated input variables including target bearing, elevation and range, the ship's angle of pitch and roll, drift angle, time of flight, and residual projectile velocity. High-capacity projectiles had been developed so much faster than the corresponding range tables that in 1942 the navy was already some five hundred tables behind. The advent of proximity fuses also meant extensive recomputation of existing tables. Until the Mark I became operational, the navy had to rely on what Hopper described as "acres of girls down at Aberdeen [Proving Ground] using hand-driven calculators" to create such tables.[70] Another problem Hopper worked on concerned magnetic mines located by conducting sweeps with a dipole dragged behind a minesweeper. The sweeper had to know the range of the dipole for an effective sweep, and Hopper made those calculations, in three dimensions, on the Mark I.[71]

When she was asked years later about her first days at work at Harvard and how she learned to program the Mark I, Hopper's reply was as straightforward as her approach to the problem must have been. "Well they gave me a code book and told me to do it," she said. "We were all in the navy," she would often say later, and "we didn't have time to react or think or anything. We just had to go ahead and do things."[72] She and her colleagues in the Computation Lab were involved in an ongoing experiment that required continual adaptation and development throughout the course of the war. "Mark I was new, a pioneer"; Hopper wrote some years later, "programs were improved or invalidated as changes were made in the computer's internal circuits to increase its efficiency."[73]

The very early programming was actually extremely basic according to Hopper. Programmers had to tell the computer exactly what to do, step by step. They instructed it to get a particular number and add it to another number and put the answer in a particular place. Then they might tell it to pick up a new number and multiply it by another number and place it in another place. All of the mathematical processes had to be broken down into very small steps of addition, subtraction, multiplication, or division and put into a sequence; this is still the essence of programming today. After figuring out how to write the machine instructions, Hopper then punched them on tape, put the tape in the computer, and hoped it would run. "But it was wartime, and there was never enough time to organize and systematize the information," she remembered.[74]

One of the major challenges Hopper and her fellow programmers faced was that the Mark I had only seventy-two words of storage to handle a range of computations that included some extremely large and complex partial differential equations and statistical problems. Working within such tight parameters at the top speed demanded by the war required an intense focus of energy and intellect. It was a challenge Hopper found fascinating, and one that she thought might well defeat the "so-called sophisticated programmers" of more recent times.[75]

Hopper was not particularly interested in hardware and had relatively little to do with it. Instead, she quickly focused on methods to speed the process of writing coding instructions to run individual problems. Like Aiken, Hopper claimed to be "lazy as all get out. I never want to do anything over again."[76] She was always looking for shortcuts, which in the early days meant assembling collections of subroutines. Similar work putting together a library of mathematical subroutines was also being undertaken in England at the same time, although Hopper was not aware of it, largely because of security restrictions. Compartmentalization was the norm at the Harvard lab, with Bloch, Campbell, and Hopper doing the bulk of the programming. Normally, in a research lab the workload would be distributed among teams, but there were not enough personnel to have teams at the Computation Lab, so they worked on their own problems individually. "You didn't go after anything else unless you had an actual need to know," Hopper explained. Besides, "you were too busy trying to get the problem you had at the moment on and get the results out to think of anything else or go after anything else."[77]

And yet, in the midst of this frantic activity Hopper developed the seeds of what was later to become her famous work on a universal computer language. The inspiration, as she candidly admitted, was her own difficulty in writing loops (codes that would instruct the machine to repeat the required operation a specified number of times). If she wanted to do something twelve times, for example, Hopper found that she usually ended up doing it eleven or thirteen times because she could not remember whether she had started with a zero or a one. Then, too, there was the problem of copying. When she worked out a useful little piece of code for a specific problem, Hopper wrote it down in her notebook so that it could be used again. An example of this was the code she wrote for a problem involving the roll of a ship. Because a ship cannot roll more than 90 degrees either way, there was no need to compute the angle for anything greater. So Hopper wrote a little piece of code within those parameters and filed it away in her notebook. Soon, both she and Bloch had built up collections of small subroutines that they could reuse and borrow from each other. Yet, each time they reused a subroutine it had to be copied into the new program.[78]

At this point Hopper recognized two weaknesses to which all programmers were subject—especially late in the day—that injected a good deal of error into the programming process. The first was that they could not copy correctly, and the second was that they had trouble with addition. Frequently in the process of copying, the letter *B* had the annoying habit of turning up as the number 13, and mistakes caused by inversion (e.g., writing 839 for 893) were common. Such mistakes, compounded by not infrequent elementary errors of addition, could turn the best subroutine, and the program into which it was inserted, into a guaranteed failure. As long as subroutines had to be copied into other programs by fallible humans, such program-stopping errors would persist. It was perfectly clear to Hopper that the engine sitting nearby was an expert at both copying and adding, so her solution was to make the computer do the work. She believed a whole library of subroutines could be stored and the computer could be instructed to pull one out and establish the desired parameters, making a new program out of pieces of previous programs. The process would both save time and cut down on copying errors. Eventually, after the war, this insight led to her work on compilers at Univac.[79]

Aiken kept tight control of the work at the lab, and it was he who handed out job assignments. Hopper was busy computing the extent of influence of the antimine dipole one day when Aiken put her to work (against her wishes) writing a manual. Handicapped by her lack of an engineering background, she took copious notes from Dick Bloch at the lab or over late dinners at the Coach Grill in Harvard Square. She had to understand all the basic circuits of the Mark I so that she could explain its coding procedures and the plugging instructions.[80] Despite Hopper's success, Aiken, ever practical, was convinced that an engineering education was the most useful for the new field of computing. When a scientist from the Aberdeen Proving Ground visited the Computation Lab in March 1945, Aiken impressed on him very forcefully that he should seek "not mathematicians but engineers" for his Ballistics Research Laboratory. In fact, an interest in both engineering and science was not uncommon among computer pioneers. John Mauchly, for example, started out as an engineering student at Johns Hopkins University and then switched to physics.[81]

Aiken's view reflects the blurring of the boundaries between science and technology that characterized much of wartime science. Everything was done at such a fast pace, and there were so many new developments, that few could afford the luxury of specializing. People just pitched in wherever they were needed, often working directly on machines and devices while at the same time helping to construct their theoretical framework. Although Hopper had a degree in theoretical mathematics, all the work she did at Harvard involved applied mathematics. She did a formidable job in putting together a 561-page manual that gave a full and detailed description of the Mark I: all its parts, with which she had become intimately familiar, and all its circuits, as well as how to program it. The manual eventually became the first in a series of thirty-five volumes: the *Annals of the Computation Laboratory of Harvard University*. Published over the next sixteen years and consisting of detailed technical notes and mathematical results of the lab's operations, the *Annals* represent the core of Aiken's contribution to computing and constitute an impressive legacy.

Another early Computation Lab problem run for BuShips involved solving ten simultaneous algebraic equations for a multiple correlation. The purpose of the calculation was to determine the correlation of key mechanical properties of steel with varying quantities of small uncontrollable impurities, and the results affected the many uses to which steel was put during the war, especially in ship construction. The Mark I also worked on the theory of coupled antennas, evaluated the accuracy of experimental fire-control computers designed and built by the NRL, ran numbers for the MIT Radiation Lab that could not be handled by MIT's own differential analyzer, worked on calculations for a new type of lens for the army air forces, and calculated the effective ranges of magnetic and acoustic mines.[82]

By October 1944 Aiken's lab was undertaking computations for the Bureau of Ordnance on spherically and cylindrically symmetric underwater blast problems. The problems, dealing with the pressure increases that occur in convergent detonations, were carried out in conjunction with Jan Schilt's computing section at Columbia University and overseen by AMP, to whom regular reports were submitted. At first it had been thought possible to carry out all the computations on Columbia's IBM punch-card equipment, but the volume of material was too extensive. A numerical computing scheme set up to perform the calculations seemed suitable for the Mark I. Aiken agreed, and BuOrd sought permission from BuShips to use the Mark I.[83]

Perhaps the largest problem run by Aiken—problem *J*—was the compilation of tables of Bessel functions requested by Bernard Salzberg at the NRL. Bessel functions are important in applications as diverse as radio wave propagation, heat flow, and frequency modulation. The production of Bessel tables became a huge baseload project at the Computation Lab, lasting at least five years; it was run whenever there was no problem of higher urgency, especially at night. Dick Bloch did most of the computing for this project. The electric typewriters produced such clear results that the tables could be printed directly in a photo-offset process—avoiding retyping and eliminating one of Aiken's chief concerns, inaccuracy. Eventually Bessel and other functions filled twenty volumes of the *Annals of the Computation Laboratory*.[84] The Computation Lab also computed tables of Hankel functions. These had been requested by NRL but were also used by other naval research activities such as NOL, the U.S. Navy Radio and Sound Laboratory, and the David Taylor Model Basin to solve problems of radio wave propagation and radiation, underwater sound propagation, and the like.[85] In March 1945 Philip M. Morse, an MIT physicist who headed the Anti-submarine Warfare Operational Research Group, suggested that the Mark I might be used on the tables of Mathieu functions he needed urgently to complete one of his studies.[86] Morse's group had firmly established in the navy the new field of operational research, which had been instrumental in, among other things, the defeat of the German U-boats.

Despite these many successes, there were those during the war who doubted the value of calculating mathematical tables. Mina Rees, by then serving as a technical aide to AMP, was a strong supporter of such calculations. She explained that "it is seldom possible to justify in advance the computation of extensive and fundamental tables in terms of military necessity; yet those tables when they have been computed are found to be of wide and important usefulness, both for military and for other research."[87] This was one of many occasions when Rees's wartime activities intersected those of the other improbable warriors.

By the time the Mark I was fully operational, Bob Campbell was already absorbed in helping Aiken design the Mark II for the navy, and it was Campbell who wrote the original prospectus. The computations required by the new guided missiles were too complex for the limited storage capacity of the Mark I; they needed the ninety-six-word storage of the Mark II. Thus the Mark II was a wartime crash program built within urgent time limits using the most readily available pieces of equipment. Nevertheless, it had certain unique features: it was a dual processor with the capacity to act as two separate machines, and design improvements had made it ten times faster than the Mark I.[88] Until the Mark II went into operation at Dahlgren in 1948, the work there of computing range tables was done under contract by MIT with a mixture of old and new differential analyzers, IBM equipment, and "a battery of [human] computers."[89]

When in August 1944 the celebrated mathematician John von Neumann, from the Institute for Advanced Study at Princeton, made his first visit to the Computation Lab, he "didn't know a computer from a tomato basket," quipped Dick Bloch. Hopper confirmed this, explaining that von Neumann would appear at the lab at intervals for needed calculations and would "go over and peer at the printouts on the typewriters."[90] After the war von Neumann went on to do impressive work in computer design, but he got his first experience with computers at the Computation Lab.

By October 1944 von Neumann had reported to AMP that Aiken had started work on his nonlinear partial differential equations and had assigned a member of his own staff, Ensign Bloch, to it.[91] In what he describes as "proper navy tradition," Bloch did not press von Neumann for information about the project, although he knew that von Neumann's work on spherical shock waves came from the Los Alamos National Laboratory in New Mexico and correctly assumed that it dealt with atomic fission.[92] Von Neumann was wrestling with the difficult implosion problem for detonating plutonium, which involved lengthy mathematical calculations. The numbers run on the Mark I were necessary to complete his work and resulted in the plutonium bomb that exploded at Alamogordo, New Mexico, on 16 July 1945—the first atomic detonation—and the "Fat Man" device dropped on Nagasaki, Japan, on 9 August 1945. This was certainly the most dramatic role played by the Mark I in the war effort.[93]

In November 1944, after only six months of operating the Mark I for the navy, Aiken was already complaining that "we are at present so much occupied with the problems submitted us in connection with the war effort that we cannot take the time to publish a suitable scientific article dealing with the calculator."[94] There was no time to look ahead, either; their only concern was winning the war. Many of the new scientific developments generated by the war passed through the Computation Lab, and the personnel there were very much involved in the rapid changes in planes, missiles, guided missiles, and new types of depth bombs, among many other things. Hopper recalled that it was normal to be at work two or three days at a time when there was a project on, just grabbing a nap on the desk and never even getting home to bed. Once, she recalled, she had been at the lab for three consecutive days and nights, so even though there was a hurricane blowing she was determined to leave. She, Brendel, and Aiken's secretary, Ruth Knowlton, linked arms and ventured out into the storm, grabbing at trees and lampposts for support as they laughed in giddy exhaustion. On other occasions, though, there was time to go out for lunch, and Brendel recalls that Hopper invariably ordered a double Manhattan to drink. Aiken, however, seemed to live at the lab all the time. He often went home late in the evening only to reappear after three or four hours' sleep. All he wanted was to see results coming out of the machine; "are we making numbers, are we making numbers?" was his constant wartime refrain.[95]

The electronic ENIAC, intended to fill the army's pressing computation needs, produced no numbers for the war effort. Hopper pointed out that Mauchly's original idea when he started work on ENIAC, like Aiken's impulse to develop the Mark I, was to shorten the length of time and effort in the computations he needed for his own studies, in this case of weather forecasting. Mauchly's project, too, would probably not have received funding without the war. In spite of erroneous statements to the contrary in popular works on the history of computing, ENIAC did not produce usable results until 1946. Until then it was not even clear that vacuum tubes could be used effectively in computers.[96] In July 1945 Capt. Herman Goldstine, a University of Chicago mathematician serving as army liaison with the Moore School, asked the Chief of Ordnance for any reports issued by Aiken on the navy's Harvard IBM machine. "I feel it would be a great help to us," Goldstine wrote, "if we could see the methods that he used to handle this problem."[97] By then the Mark I had already been operating for a year.

Why, then, did ENIAC win the battle for historic recognition? In two articles in November 1996, the *Wall Street Journal*—reflecting a widespread view—asserted that ENIAC was the first "computer" even though it did not begin operation until 1946, almost two years after the Mark I and well after the end of the war.[98] While it is true that ENIAC was electronic (using vacuum tubes), and was therefore much faster than the electromechanical decimal counter system of the Mark I, it is not clear that speed is the defining requirement for a computer. ENIAC, for example, was designed primarily to solve trajectory problems; unlike the Mark I, it could not be readily used as a general-purpose computer. According to Hopper an even more important distinction was that at that time ENIAC was not programmed. "It was put together with patch cords like punch card machinery, but Mark I was actually programmed."[99] ENIAC "went from an adder to a storage to a multiplier, and so on and it was all done by plug wires." To that extent, Hopper pointed out, "I had a slight head start on programming because I started in '44 on Mark I."[100] Experts still disagree, on these and a number of other technical grounds, about which was the first "true" computer, and the issue remains unresolved for them—if not for the *Wall Street Journal*.[101]

Nevertheless, the pervasiveness of the ENIAC myth has been allowed to bury the Mark I, in part because some consider the Mark I "a technological dead end."[102] But this view ignores one of Aiken's most important contributions: the Mark I's programming system provided by punched tapes (today's software) was the first step toward fully automatic program execution and was much more like systems now in use than anything in ENIAC or its contemporaries. The Mark I programmers created what were essentially the earliest digital computer programs—subroutines stored on paper tape. By contrast, ENIAC had an unwieldy programming system of external plugs which could take a day or more to set.[103]

A biographer of Thomas Watson—quite possibly biased—describes the Mark I as "a lumbering giant of primitivism and obsolescence" and claims that it was "of little value."[104] Yet during the war the only functioning alternatives to the Mark I were analog machines like Vannevar Bush's differential analyzer and manual calculators. Douglas R. Hartree, a British professor of mathematical physics who was an authority on computers and very familiar with both the Mark I and ENIAC, elegantly disposed of the idea of competition between them. He regarded each, he wrote in 1949, "as being outstanding steps in the development of automatic general-purpose machines, the one as the first practical realization of such a machine and the other as the first electronic digital machine."[105] Nevertheless, the publicity surrounding ENIAC and the corresponding neglect of the World War II history of the Harvard Computation Laboratory accounts in part for the relative ignorance about that phase of Hopper's life as compared with the extensive coverage of her later years.

In 1946 Aiken, discharged from the navy, resumed his academic career at Harvard as a full professor and director of the Computation Lab. Each of his staff reverted to civilian status and left the lab, which became a civilian organization for the first time since the Mark I had taken up residence in February 1944. The switch to civilian life created funding problems for Aiken. After his Mark II computer for the navy's ballistic center at the Dahlgren Proving Ground was completed in 1948, the navy no longer needed to finance the Mark I. Aiken was able to secure a contract with the air force for 50 percent of his funding and with the Atomic Energy Commission for the other 50 percent, but the continuing federal connection inhibited integration of his lab with the research needs of the rest of the university and reinforced Aiken's reputation as an outsider.[106]

Even after he completed the electronic Mark III and Mark IV, Aiken found that some of his contemporaries still viewed him as a conservative, especially after he abandoned machine design altogether in favor of program development, which seemed of only peripheral significance. A more persuasive argument has been made by Hopper, along with others well qualified to judge, that Aiken was actually ahead of his time in recognizing the importance of software. This seems to have been largely forgotten, however, as have Aiken's many other postwar contributions to the science of computing. Aiken understood the need to program the quickly growing number of computers, and at Harvard he introduced academic courses in computer science a decade before such courses existed in most other universities. He also organized successful international conferences to encourage open discussion of computers and computing.[107]

After the war, when collaboration with the government was no longer a patriotic duty, Harvard's distaste for government-sponsored, and especially military, research projects reasserted itself. The university also frowned on Aiken's close ties with industry, and ultimately the continual struggle for funding drove Aiken to retire from the university at the minimum age in 1961.[108]

None of Aiken's little band of scientists remained at Harvard for long after the war. Although some of them went on to careers in the field to which Aiken had introduced them, making contributions that reflected his inspiration and rigorous training, they did not stay to form a solid phalanx of scholarship that might have buttressed Aiken's reputation within university circles. Both Bob Campbell and Dick Bloch entered the world of industry, at first helping Raytheon to establish its computer project, which at one point was staffed almost completely by Harvard Computation Lab alumni. Ruth Brendel returned to teaching mathematics, and Specialist-I Delo Calvin returned to IBM.

Grace Hopper was an exception. Although offered a full professorship to return to Vassar, she turned it down because, as she said, she liked computers better. She stayed on at the lab for another three years as a research fellow under navy contract working on the Mark II and then on the electronic Mark III. Most of all, Hopper wanted to remain in the navy, but although she asked for a transfer to the regular navy, she was two years over the cutoff age of thirty-eight and was turned down. She continued to serve in the naval reserve, however, switching to inactive duty in 1946. She attended monthly reserve meetings, went on training duty every summer, and took the necessary correspondence courses, advancing in rank to lieutenant commander and then commander.[109]

During the immediate postwar years Hopper's name became known in the fast-growing computer community through a number of publications resulting from her wartime work at the lab. As Aiken had noted, there was little time to write for publication during the war, and security issues prevented the normal free exchange of scientific information. In 1946, with the lifting of those restrictions, Aiken and Hopper coauthored three articles on "The Automatic Sequence Controlled Calculator" based on the operations manual for the Mark I. The original manual, though essentially written by Hopper, had also listed Aiken as coauthor. After the war, Aiken traveled extensively at home and abroad lecturing on computing and maintaining a high visibility. Unlike most scientists, however, throughout his whole career he wrote very little for publication. Hopper, on the other hand, was a prolific author.[110]

Hopper could not remain at the Computation Lab after 1949. Since no one was appointed to the Harvard faculty for more than three years without being promoted or given tenure, and—according to Hopper—no women were being promoted, she had to begin job hunting. She had no interest in returning to teaching full time and was determined to stay in computing in spite of its unpredictable future.

In the late 1940s, even many of those involved in the design and construction of electronic computers thought their use was limited to providing mathematical solutions for scientific projects. That being so, a very small number of computers would satisfy the world's need. Originally, moreover, most computers were built at universities under government contract, like the Whirlwind I at MIT. Commercial development was in its infancy; few investors saw computing as a developing market, and capital was hard to secure. The Association for Computing Machinery (ACM) had just been formed in 1947, and there were no journals, periodicals, or other institutional resources to nurture the new industry. Nevertheless, Hopper was already looking ahead to possible commercial applications for computers. Leaving the secure world of academia after five years at Harvard, she gambled that there was a future in commercial computing and plunged into the new business of computing; her wartime navy experience provided the key.[111]

There were still opportunities for women in the workplace in the immediate postwar years—even in an industry that later became exceptionally male dominated—because many of the veterans returned to college before looking for jobs. The GI Bill of 1944 made it possible for almost 15 percent of Americans to be in college in 1948, up from 10 percent in the prewar years. Therefore, women in the computer field initially had an advantage over men. Many of them were already experienced, having been drawn in on the ground floor during the war when the demand for mathematicians exceeded the available supply from the usual male sources. Although the gender-neutral environment of the pioneering days soon faded and the promise of a field accessible to female talent failed to evolve,

Hopper's early training under Aiken gave her a decided edge. "Everybody knew everybody that was at Harvard," she explained, "we were the original group."[112]

After looking around and interviewing with practically everyone in the field, Hopper narrowed the choice to working for John Mauchly, who had established the Eckert-Mauchly Computer Corporation (EMCC) in Philadelphia, or Howard Engstrom at Engineering Research Associates (ERA) based in St. Paul, Minnesota. Hopper was drawn to ERA because Engstrom had been one of her professors at Yale and because of the navy connection. During the war Engstrom and a talented group of academics-turned-naval-officers had spearheaded the navy's cryptanalysis effort. With the advent of peace the navy did not want to see the group broken up and helped find the money to start ERA. In the end, however, in June 1949, Hopper joined EMCC—the world's first computer company—founded by Eckert and Mauchly when they left the Moore School (and ENIAC) shortly after the war. Her decision was based in part on her desire to remain close to her family on the East Coast, and in part because she believed Mauchly's Universal Automatic Computer (UNIVAC) would be operating long before any computer produced by ERA. Interviewed thirty years later, Hopper noted with her usual self-deprecating humor that her decision was probably not all that important in the long run. The companies ended up together anyway because Remington Rand bought them both. Hopper neglected to add that the initial takeover at Eckert-Mauchly was caused by inept business practices and the failure of the company. Remington Rand bought EMCC in 1950, and in 1955 Rand merged with the Sperry Corporation. Hopper remained with the company through all these changes until her retirement from Sperry in 1971.[113]

Hopper joined EMCC as a senior mathematician at the company's new location in a former knitting mill, where she became a member of a small software group working directly for John Mauchly. EMCC had just finished building BINAC, a binary automatic computer, and was about to begin work on the first mass-produced commercially available computer, UNIVAC I. By the time Hopper appeared, some engineers were already leaving; BINAC had been built at a loss, and the company was in serious financial difficulties. Hopper liked to explain about those days that they had a pact at Eckert-Mauchly: if UNIVAC failed they would throw it out one side of the building where there was a junkyard and would themselves jump out the other side where there was a graveyard. As it happened, however, they did not need to jump right away; a number of UNIVACs were completed, which in itself spelled success by the standards of the time. Even in 1953 Hopper still believed that "at the present stage of the computer industry, two or more large-scale computers alike constitute mass-production." The first UNIVACs went to the U.S. Census Bureau, the navy's David Taylor Model Basin, and the U.S. Army Map Service. According to Hopper, the brilliance of John Mauchly's instruction code was responsible for making UNIVAC the first machine that really did data processing.[114]

In later years Hopper pointed out that when she joined Eckert-Mauchly, Frances E. "Betty" Holberton was already there working as a programmer. During the war Holberton had been one of the hundreds of women recruited from colleges across the country to help the war effort by working as "computers" on ballistics firing tables at Aberdeen. There she was chosen to be one of six women to work on ENIAC. With little instruction and no manual to follow, they had to figure out how to program problems into the machine and make it produce the correct solutions. Guided by block diagrams, wiring schematics, and consultations with engineers, their tasks involved a typical wartime mix of science and technology. In fact, Holberton and the five other women were doing pioneering work comparable to that of Bloch, Campbell, and Hopper at Harvard, though just too late to affect the war effort. Nevertheless, their work is another important example of women's contribution to scientific and technical developments during World War II, and they were responsible to a considerable degree for the success of the ENIAC project. A number of them, including Holberton, moved to EMCC with Eckert and Mauchly and went on to distinguished careers as programmers.[115]

At EMCC Hopper once again landed in an organization that was "singularly unprejudiced" against women, flexible, and willing to employ anyone who was qualified.[116] Hopper particularly acknowledged her debt to Holberton, "a very, very brilliant woman" who "taught me how to use flow charts [for computer programs] and everything under the sun."[117] She also credited Holberton with being the first person to use a computer to write a program with her "Merge-Sort Generator." This was a "tremendous piece of work," according to Hopper, because nothing like it had ever been done before, and Hopper regretted that Holberton never received due credit.[118] For Hopper herself it was far different. After working closely with Mauchly and Holberton to develop an instruction code for UNIVAC, she began the work that was to make her justly famous: first in the invention of the compiler, and later in the creation of COBOL.

Hopper's career gamble paid off. The 1950s saw dynamic developments in computing with rapid changes in hardware, increasing interest in software, and a growing differentiation between the two. It was a very different world from the circumscribed atmosphere of the wartime Computation Lab. Science was once again more open, even in the cold war atmosphere, and computing was stimulated by a broad international exchange of ideas. As it moved out of academic laboratories, however, computing also became subject to the highly competitive forces of the marketplace. Hopper took her place in the vanguard of this great growth, quick to pick up on the latest changes, at times responding, at times leading. While little in her Vassar or Harvard Computation Lab experience would suggest an aptitude for the hurly-burly of business, she turned out to be a superb publicist and a persuasive salesperson. She used those skills to the full for the next thirty years, both in industry and finally, once more, in the navy.

In 1951 Hopper started working on a compiler for UNIVAC. This was in effect a library of subroutines that the computer itself could put together into a program. Hopper had brought with her from Harvard a whole notebook of subroutines and was looking for a method of linking them together. The compiler would tell the computer how to do that, greatly simplifying program writing and avoiding many of the errors that occurred from copying. As with so many of her later accomplishments in computing, Hopper looked back to her training at Harvard as the source of her inspiration. "Heretofore, the compilation of a sequence of instructions for a digital computer has been 90 percent a programmer's job," she explained. "The idea of a 'library' of proven and tested standard subroutines was first proposed by Professor Howard H. Aiken of Harvard in 1944, but the realization of this concept was delayed." "Stated bluntly," she continued, "the compiling routine is the programmer, and performs all those services necessary to the production of a finished program."[119] People told Hopper that computers could only do arithmetic and that it was obvious that they could not write programs, but, ignoring them, she sat down and wrote a machine code that could do just that. Her first compiler, the A-o, was ready in 1952, and she reported on it at the Association for Computing Machinery meeting at the Mellon Institute that May. Her claim that she could make a computer do anything she could completely define was met with great skepticism, but of course she was right.[120]

By 1953, Hopper explained how far computers had progressed in their new role as programmers:

> With some specialized knowledge of more advanced topics, UNIVAC, at present, has a well grounded mathematical education fully equivalent to that of a college sophomore, and it does not forget and it does not make mistakes. It is progressing well in its further studies and soon its undergraduate course will be completed. It seems inevitable that it will present itself as a candidate for a graduate degree.[121]

By 1955 Hopper and her staff had completed the A-2 compiler, the first to see extensive commercial use.

In the meantime, the number of computers was growing rapidly in the United States and abroad, just as Hopper had expected, and they were beginning to be used for a variety of purposes. In England, a computer was designed and built for the Lyons Tea Company, while in the U.S. presidential election of 1952 a UNIVAC I (now under Remington Rand) electrified the nation when it correctly predicted Dwight Eisenhower's landslide victory with only 7 percent of the votes counted. The Metropolitan Life Insurance Company used UNIVAC to compute premium notices for all its policy writers, and computers began to be used for data files and payrolls. Computer companies proliferated, many not lasting very long, and IBM, too, finally moved away from its punch-card machines and started producing computers for business use.[122]

Defense needs, and particularly the demands of the navy, remained a major influence on the development of computing, and contacts established during the war continued to define the players in the game. Eugene Smith, who had been navy liaison to the Computation Lab for the Bureau of Ships, stayed with the bureau as a civilian after the war and urged the navy to expand its computer use, especially in shipyards. Hopper also pointed out that Mina Rees, heading the mathematics branch of the Office of Naval Research (ONR), "was very largely responsible for turning up the money after the end of the war to continue the work on computers."[123] During the war, Rees, then with the Applied Mathematics Panel, had helped to organize many of the navy's computer contracts—including those with the Harvard Computation Lab. Rees and Gene Smith knew each other well, and Hopper worked closely with both. Beginning in 1951, BuShips sponsored a series of seminars in Washington to gather the latest information on computer developments. Hopper helped organize the seminars and acted as director of ceremonies.

Although there was always a scramble among computer companies for government contracts, when clients such as Metropolitan Life, Prudential, and Aetna; some big banks; and manufacturing companies like U.S. Steel, Westinghouse, and Du Pont began to show profits from computer data processing, everybody began to climb aboard. Each of the first computers had been a "tailor-made job," as Hopper put it, and "they could not trade instructions without a human being as translator."[124] With the expansion of computing and the spread of computers to the private sector, the key to selling computers was to make them easier to program. The early compilers were a first effort at simplification, but more was needed. Since it would be impossible to teach everyone how to write computer code, there would have to be an interface that would accept what Hopper called "people-oriented" data that the computer itself could then translate into machine code. A number of people were working on the development of computer languages, among the very first of which was a formula translator developed at MIT, the ancestor of FORTRAN, a language still in use today.[125]

Hopper knew from her navy contacts and her summer reserve service that most of the people doing data processing for the navy were totally untrained in the use of symbols. As she characterized it, "they wouldn't know a cosine if they met one walking down the street in broad daylight."[126] Determined to make data processing accessible to word-oriented people, Hopper hit on the idea of writing in English instead of in symbols. She reasoned that the computer could be made to translate letters of the alphabet into machine code, and her success in accomplishing this feat was her most original contribution to computing. At the time, however, no one thought computer programs could be written in English, and although Hopper had been working on the idea on her own since late 1953, she did not actually get support to go ahead with the project until January 1955. "When you have a good idea," she loved to tell audiences, "and you've tried it and you know it's going to work, go ahead and do it—because it is much easier to apologize later than it is to get permission." What Hopper eventually produced, working with little institutional encouragement, was a B-0 compiler, a data-processing compiler later known as FLOWMATIC. By the end of 1956 Hopper had built a little pilot model, a program that translated instructions written in English into codes that could be read by computers. This experimental compiler could take only twenty statements, but that was enough to run a program and prove the worth of the concept. Apart from a slight difference in terminology, this was the pattern compilers followed thereafter.[127]

It was a startling concept—to think of using a compiler to write programs—and selling the idea met the usual resistance to change that Hopper spent most of her career opposing. During these years Hopper developed formidable skill at what she called the "marketing game." She later referred to introducing the compiler as the biggest selling job that she had ever been through. One of her best ideas was outlined in an office memo called "Layette for a Computer." Hopper had the notion that the company was "delivering" a computer, so they also had to deliver a layette to go with the baby: this was the compiler, or what later became known as the software. When she could not persuade management in her own company to believe in the efficacy of her compiler she went out and sold it directly to their customers.[128] At first nobody understood how much time an English-language compiler could save. When a programmer at E. I. Du Pont got caught one night with a report due for management the next day, he turned in desperation to the compiler that had been languishing unused. It worked, he completed the report, and he got a raise. "Then everybody started to use the compiler," noted Hopper. "It's a wonderful thing what a raise will do." Once she had the customers on her side, the money to develop the project came flowing in.[129]

Hopper was never shy about her accomplishments, though she was supremely unsentimental about them. She used to say that if she hadn't written the first compiler somebody else would have within five years because the need was there. Her thrust was always to simplify and to demystify. She reserved some of her most cutting remarks for those who insisted that only an expert in writing machine code could run a computer; she had no time for programmers who saw themselves as high priests standing between computers and the public. Some of the most strident opposition at Univac came from a young man who was working on building up a tremendous library of input-output routines, which Hopper thought was just "nuts." Her FLOWMATIC system made it unnecessary to write the input-output because the compiler knew how to write the whole thing. It was particularly galling to Hopper that there was a tendency in the company to prefer the young man's system to Hopper's because he was the first person to graduate from Harvard with a degree in computer science. Hopper's mentor, Howard Aiken, was now turning out professionals who were competing with his original wartime protégés.[130]

By 1957 there were three major computer languages being used in American computers: APT (Automatically Programmed Tools); IBM's FORTRAN, used mostly by scientists and academics; and Hopper's FLOWMATIC. It was obvious to some in both industry and the military that this proliferation posed a danger of massive confusion, and Hopper was closely involved in the move to systematize the use of one language. Through her navy associates she helped to inspire a meeting at the Pentagon that year which included representatives from all the computer manufacturers, all the government agencies that had computers, and all the big users such as Westinghouse, Du Pont, and U.S. Steel. At the meeting there was general agreement that in principle there should be only one data-processing language and that it should be English. At that time IBM still did not have its English-language compiler up and running, but FLOW-MATIC had been running for two years already and was operational in all navy shipyards. The 1958 FLOWMATIC manual thus became the basis of the new committee-generated language, COBOL, and Grace Hopper's compiler was at the heart of the new universal computer language. When COBOL was ready for testing it was run on UNIVAC II first. The next day it was taken over to Radio Corporation of America and run on the RCA 501 machine, proving that one data-processing language could be run on machines produced by different manufacturers.[131]

Hopper was always generous in her praise of the many women who contributed to these early successes in computing, freely acknowledging her debt to Betty Holberton, Mina Rees, and many others.[132] Perhaps in part because she believed that she and the others had all made it on their own, her attitude toward the women's movement was unwaveringly practical and generally unsympathetic. She made her sentiments clear in articles and especially in interviews.

When she was seventy-six years old and still working full time, Hopper was asked if there were any career goals she had not been able to achieve because she was a woman. "Back in those days you didn't have career objectives. You had a job and you did a job," she replied. She believed women could get on as well as men if they did a good job. "It's competitive," she would say. "I wouldn't want to get a job because I was a woman.

I want to get a job because I do it better." Her advice to women was "estimate your guy and give him what he needs to advance his purpose . . . being belligerent doesn't get you anywhere." The whole issue to her was one of marketing. "Marketing is not necessarily aggression. You have to be pretty smooth to do a good marketing job. . . . Avoid the confrontations. Make it easy. Make it slide in." When asked about unequal pay for men and women, Hopper denied ever experiencing that problem. "You get the bull if you do the job," was her answer. She firmly believed there was no inherent difference in women's and men's abilities in math and science and saw the wide disparity in jobs as the result of lack of encouragement in school and at home. "The first time a gal has a problem with her algebra, her father is apt to say, 'Well, girls can't understand that.'"[133]

Hopper acknowledged that computing had been equally open to women and men when she went into it, but when pressed she agreed that later it was much harder to break into established corporations like General Electric or Westinghouse. Her own success, due in part to the academic rigor and sturdy independence of her upbringing, may have made her impatient with those who sometimes faced more opposition with less preparation than she had. She was optimistic, however, about the future for women while recognizing that change was bound to be slower than many would wish. As recently as 1969 she had, after all, been awarded the Data Processing Management Association's Computer Sciences "Man-of-the-Year Award."[134]

Hopper considered her service in the navy the most important honor and responsibility of her life, even though the navy was slow to admit women. When they finally decided to let women in, Hopper maintained, "they went the whole way." Navy women were never auxiliaries as army women initially were, and Hopper believed that women in the navy were given the same opportunities as men and that rank or rating determined salary.[135]

It is almost inevitable that someone with as long and productive a career as Hopper's should become the stuff of legend. One of the most persistent stories about her involves the etymology of the term *bug* in the computer world. Hopper enjoyed telling audiences about the time when a computer at the Harvard Computation Lab was balking and she examined all the circuits until she found a two-inch moth jamming up the works. She removed the moth with tweezers and it was taped into the logbook— and there it can be seen today, along with Hopper's other papers, in the

Smithsonian Institution's National Museum of American History. Next to the moth is the notation "first actual case of a bug being found," which many have taken to mean that Hopper was responsible for the origin of the term. Hopper herself cheerfully perpetuated, even if she did not exactly invent, this interpretation, and the tale of the bug was one of her stock stories in articles and speeches. She usually ended by noting that after that, whenever anything went wrong with a computer they would say it had a bug in it, although she knew very well that the term had actually been in use for a long time. On 3 January 1992 the *New York Times* added to the luster of the story by noting in its obituary of Grace Hopper that she was "known for coining the term 'bug' . . . to refer to mysterious computer failures."[136]

Though Hopper loved a good story and was not above polishing it up a bit, she was straightforward about her own abilities. In a 1979 interview she was typically frank:

> To me, I guess basically when you come down to it, I have never done anything that's intellectually great. Everything I have done has been based on common sense. If I was going to copy subroutines out of a notebook I might as well let the computer do it. . . . It's basically common sense in everything I did—no mathematical genius, no theory.[137]

It is important in the fast-developing computer field to keep up-to-date with changes. Hopper was keen to be at the forefront of her profession, never satisfied with the status quo. It was her ability to sustain this eager probing with undiminished energy, even through her seventies, that set her apart. In her office she had a famous clock that ran counterclockwise. She kept it to remind her, and anyone else intrepid enough to ask, that the normal way of doing things was not the only way and was probably not even the best way. In later years Hopper became the perfect publicist for the navy's computerization because her genius lay in making accessible this highly technical and increasingly vital field. Even her technical reports were models of spare prose, clarity of structure, and logical purpose. They were filled with apt examples, making them readily understandable to the nonexpert. She passionately believed in the broad applications of computers and made it her business to see that they became increasingly easy to use. Everyone who uses a personal computer owes her a debt of thanks.

5

MINA SPIEGEL REES

science administrator

" F or scientific research on new weapons, as for the armed services as a whole—the battle is the pay off."[1] When James P. Baxter III, historian and president of Williams College, wrote those words to Warren Weaver, mathematician and director for the natural sciences of the Rockefeller Foundation, it was September 1944. World War II had made combatants of many intellectuals, even if they fought only with their brains and pens and slide rules.

Among the many other citizens called to serve the war was Mina Spiegel Rees. Rees's lifetime spanned most of the twentieth century. The only one of our four improbable warriors who did not join the navy, she was the oldest and lived the longest. She was born in Cleveland, Ohio, on 2 August 1902. Her mother, Alice Louise Stackhouse, had emigrated from England at the age of twelve, and her father was from Pennsylvania. Her parents had been living in Pennsylvania before moving to Ohio with the Berkshire Life Insurance Company, where Mina's father was a salesman. Highly regarded by the company, according to his daughter, Moses Rees was transferred back to the East Coast for good when Mina was two, settling with his young family in the Bronx, in New York City. They lived in an apartment on Trinity Avenue at 161st Street in what Rees described as a lovely middle-class area; maybe it was even upper middle class across the street, where there were private homes. Her family was definitely not upper middle class, however, and money was always tight with five children to raise. Mina was the youngest of the five; the oldest, her only sister, was nine years older, and in between were three brothers. Although Rees recalled that everybody in the family was very bright, none of them had much education. She did not believe that her mother had gone beyond elementary school, and while her three brothers all started high school, only the youngest finished and went on to get a college degree.[2]

Interviewed when she was eighty-one years old, Rees still had vivid memories of growing up in the Bronx. She went to P.S. 10, the local elementary school, where she was very happy and very successful, always getting straight As. Her father was so proud of her grades that he framed her report cards, but it is clear that she did not receive the kind of intellectual stimulation at home that was such an advantage to Sears, Hopper, and van Straten. When Rees was in eighth grade, a teacher suggested that she take the competitive admission exam for Hunter High School, an administrative unit of Hunter College and one of the most academically prestigious schools in New York City. Rees passed the exam and at Hunter, too, was extremely successful. In addition to excelling academically, she was also a natural leader who was elected class president every year. In her senior year she also served as president of the student council. At Hunter most of her teachers were women with degrees from very good colleges. Rees received what she called a classical education with a rigorous curriculum of required courses. She had to study Latin, four years of either French or German, four years of mathematics, and four years each of English, physics, chemistry, and biology. "It was the kind of education that nobody has now," she remarked sadly in 1983.[3]

From Hunter High School, Rees was admitted to Hunter College, a public women's college in Manhattan that she was very happy to be able to attend because the tuition was free. After her freshman year Rees got a job as a part-time faculty member at the college teaching a course called "transit," which turned out to be trigonometry. She prepared herself by taking a summer course in surveying at Teacher's College, Columbia University, and for the next three years earned half the salary of a regular instructor. Like Grace Hopper, Rees, too, showed a talent for mathematics from an early age. "I'm sure that in high school I was already addicted to math. I think it goes back even to elementary school," she recalled. "I just got great fun out of everything we did; it just seemed like the most interesting thing in my life." In college Rees also became absorbed in art and art history, and formed a lifelong habit of visiting art galleries and shows. In addition, she was deeply drawn to study law, and for a time considered pursuing a career in history, but she never succeeded in changing majors. "I think what happened really," she later concluded, "was that I didn't want to leave my math so I didn't choose to."[4]

Unlike Sears, van Straten, or Hopper, no family member influenced Rees's decisions or her choice of career. "They didn't have the slightest opinion on the subject," she once told an interviewer. "They never would have thought of intervening."[5] She knew she would have to earn a living just as her brothers did, and that meant being a teacher. "There's a fact," she said (as Hopper, less than four years her junior, would recognize, too), "that a woman had no options at that time, except to be a teacher." Hunter, moreover, was oriented toward teaching, most of its graduates entering that profession. Rees was also impressed by one of her professors at Hunter who had a Ph.D. in mathematics. She knew that there were few women Ph.D.'s in mathematics at that time, and that among the few math doctoral programs open to women were the ones at the University of Chicago and at Harvard under the Radcliffe name.[6]

After graduating summa cum laude—and Phi Beta Kappa—from Hunter College in 1923, Rees entered graduate school at Columbia to study for her master's degree in mathematics. Her specialty was linear algebra, but she also studied law. Both Hunter High School and Hunter College had been for women only when Rees was there; at Columbia, Rees was in class with almost all men. That did not seem odd to her, however, as she had grown up in a home with three older brothers and had learned to hold her own with males. For the next two years she taught at Hunter High School in the mornings and attended classes in the afternoons.[7]

When she had finished a number of the graduate mathematics courses and was beginning to think about a thesis, information was conveyed to Rees—not officially, of course—that the mathematics faculty at Columbia was not interested in having a woman get her Ph.D. there. She later admitted it was "a really traumatic affair" for her, and "the only episode that raised a question [in her mind] about the appropriateness of mathematics as a field for women." In the face of the perceived hostility she switched to Teacher's College at Columbia to take the rest of the courses necessary

Mina Rees in 1919
*Mina Rees Collection,
City University of New
York Graduate School and
University Center Archives*

for her M.A., which she received in 1925. By then she already knew that she wanted to study under the eminent mathematician Leonard E. Dickson at the University of Chicago for her Ph.D. Until she could save the money to go there she returned to Hunter College as an instructor in mathematics, where she was employed, off and on, for the next thirty-five years.[8]

In the meantime Rees had also moved out of the family home. Her mother was passionately against the consumption of alcohol, and by then Rees was having friends over who wanted to drink. With her petite frame and penchant for wearing dresses rather than tailored suits, Rees may not have looked like a typical mathematician, but neither was she a shrinking violet. She enjoyed a lively social life, and there were altogether too many constraints for a twenty-four-year-old in the family home. As a Hunter colleague remembered many years later, Rees was "a beguiling companion, the life of the party," and since she was already teaching she could afford a place of her own.[9]

By 1929 Rees had earned a sabbatical from Hunter College and was at the University of Chicago working on her Ph.D. Everyone was very aware of the Depression, of course, but the immediate impact on many young women involved fashion. Skirts, which had been above the knee, suddenly went down to mid-calf, but no one could afford to buy new clothes. There was a waiting list to use the one sewing machine in Rees's graduate dorm, as each student tried to make at least one new dress for parties. Rees enjoyed clothes, sewing, and parties, and she took her turn at the machine with the others. However, she also had a single-minded determination to become a great mathematician. She later suggested that it was not lack of ability that prevented more women from pursuing ambitious careers in mathematics but social influences. "The 'eye on marriage' is the background thing," she maintained. "In my family that wasn't present. There was absolutely no parental pressure for me to marry. . . . That was not typical of American society, I think." And, she continued, "it may be that in our society a woman must sacrifice too much if she wants a career that's offbeat. It didn't seem like a sacrifice to me because I had plenty of men friends, and I wasn't prepared to get married; that wasn't what I wanted to do."[10]

Of the few women with doctorates in math, most were teaching in women's colleges in the East, but there was one woman in mathematics on the Chicago faculty: Prof. Sophie Breckenridge. A University of Chicago graduate who had been appointed during the Great War when the men were away, Breckenridge had managed to retain her tenured position when they returned. She was head of the graduate dorm, where she expected all women working on advanced degrees to live, and Rees was grateful for her mentoring. Rees later maintained that she did not feel like a pioneer at Chicago because other famous women scholars there had already broken the ground for her generation. The chair of the English Department was a woman, for example, and she seemed to attract most of the female graduate students. Rees knew of no women on the history or social sciences faculties, however, and the science departments were typically male. Of the women who graduated with Ph.D.'s when Rees did, she recalled that most went on to have careers, generally teaching in women's colleges. Rees took less than two years to get her doctorate. She wrote her dissertation in the field of division algebras under the supervision of Professor Dickson while she was still doing coursework, and she graduated in 1931.[11]

With her Ph.D. in hand Rees returned to teach mathematics at Hunter College, and there she remained for the next twelve years, working her way from assistant to associate professor. She thoroughly enjoyed teaching and was very good at it, especially at required mathematics. She also remained a leader and an activist—for example, chairing the Hunter delegation to the combined faculty committee in the fight for tenure, which they won. During those years Rees also kept up with new developments in mathematics, and not just in her specialty. She was active in the American Mathematical Society, sitting on its major committees and getting to know mathematicians from all over the country. This gave her an overview of what was going on in the discipline and made her one of the best-known women in the small community of mathematicians, which probably numbered only three thousand or so.[12]

Before World War II, mathematics in the United States was still generally behind Europe. Until the end of the 1920s, promising American mathematicians often went to Europe to obtain doctorates. Many of them returned to teach and advance the field in America, though, and by the time Rees was at Chicago she thought the number going to Europe to study was about equal to those staying home. In the years following, more and more graduate students in mathematics chose American universities. The mathematics being developed in the United States, however, was different in emphasis from the European in its tendency to be highly abstract. Applied mathematicians were generally looked down on by their colleagues in pure mathematics due to the widespread belief that "you turned to applied mathematics if you found the going too hard in pure mathematics." Among the few proving otherwise was Richard Courant, who had come to the United States from Europe in 1934 and had pulled together a small group to study applied mathematics at NYU. William Prager at Brown University in Rhode Island—another immigrant—established a program of advanced instruction and research in applied mechanics in 1941.[13]

The situation in mathematical statistics, another applied field, was similar. Only a handful of universities were offering serious work in the field by 1940: Harold Hotelling taught at Columbia in New York City, Jerzy Neyman was at Berkeley in California, and S. S. "Sam" Wilkes gave his first course on mathematical statistics at Princeton University in the spring of 1937. In Europe, by contrast, there was much more interest in mathematics research conducted with a practical application in mind. With the coming of Hitler in Europe and the flight of many top scholars, the United States fell heir to some of the greatest applied mathematicians in the world, who formed the nucleus of an extraordinarily gifted community. It would become Rees's wartime task to tap the talents of that community.[14]

Before World War II, the U.S. government had done little to develop science beyond encouraging states to establish institutions of higher education. The national scientific organizations that emerged over the years had generally come about as a result of wars. In 1863 the Civil War gave birth to the National Academy of Sciences, intended to focus the nation's scientific talents. World War I led to the creation of the National Research Council to help the Academy of Sciences meet its governmental obligations, and the National Advisory Committee for Aeronautics (NACA, the predecessor of NASA). But heavy-handed efforts by the military to control science during the war, including controlling research priorities, had soured many scientists on the idea of cooperating with the government.[15]

In the 1930s, while the isolationist mood that gripped the country kept military appropriations at a modest level, significant advances in radar were nevertheless being made at the army's Signal Corps Laboratory and at the Naval Research Laboratory. Signal Corps and NRL radar sets would make enormous contributions to the war effort in the Pacific during the first year after the United States entered the war. Many scientists, moreover, were quicker than the general public to see the Nazi menace for what it was and were anxious for the United States to cooperate with the British and Canadians. The British Tizard Mission to the United States in the summer of 1940 paved the way for a crucial Allied exchange of scientific information.[16]

In a 1970 House of Representatives subcommittee hearing on science research and development, Harvey Brooks, a Harvard theoretical physicist who had headed the Harvard Underwater Sound Lab during the war, re-created the atmosphere of the time:

> In a certain sense World War II and the subsequent period of the Cold War might be characterized as a love affair between the intellectual community and the government, which affected not only the development of science but a much broader range of academic scholarship. The Nazi menace united the American intellectual community as nothing else has or could. Nazism was a specific attack on the values that the academic community held in highest priority, and the reality of its threat was brought home to American academics by a stream of

refugees from Europe whose names were bywords among American scientists. . . . Thus academic intellectuals were well prepared, emotionally and intellectually, to close ranks behind the American war effort.[17]

With the fall of France it seemed to some key scientists that U.S. participation in the war was inevitable. In part to avoid being preempted by the military again, and yet recognizing the need to organize the scientific war effort, a group of American scientists began to mobilize. They were led by Vannevar Bush, an electrical engineer, former vice president and dean of engineering at MIT, chairman of the National Advisory Committee for Aeronautics (NACA), president of the Carnegie Institution, and well known throughout the scientific community for creating the differential analyzer. With the support of Bush and a number of prominent colleagues, President Roosevelt established the National Defense Research Committee (NDRC) in June 1940. Among those involved from the beginning, in addition to Bush, were Karl T. Compton, a physicist and president of MIT; James B. Conant, a chemist and the president of Harvard; and Frank B. Jewett, an electrical engineer and president of the National Academy of Sciences and the Bell Telephone Laboratories. Their premise was that science had advanced so far since the last conflict that America's military leaders did not have a good grasp of what might be scientifically possible. Therefore, instead of reverting to the former pattern of having the military request from science the weapons it wanted, science should acquaint itself with the needs of the military so that it could advise on what was possible. Much of the initiative for scientific military research thus swung toward civilian scientists.[18]

NDRC's mandate was to "correlate governmental and civil research in fields of military importance outside of aeronautics." Most research on aeronautical problems already fell under the purview of NACA. NDRC was also to "supplement, and not replace, activities of the military services themselves, and it should exist primarily to aid these services." In these tasks it would "enlist the support of scientific and educational institutions and organizations, and of individual scientists and engineers, throughout the country."[19] There is hardly a better description of the nature of Rees's activities during World War II.

With Bush acting as chairman, the committee swung into action at once, impelled by a sense of urgency to develop new and more deadly weapons. In addition to the four initiators of the committee there was a physicist from Cal Tech; the commissioner of patents, who was an attorney; Rear Adm. Harold G. Bowen for the navy; and Brig. Gen. George V. Strong for the army. Five divisions were created to handle different categories of problems, and sections were established within the divisions as the need became apparent. Each division was supervised by a member of the committee who was given a great deal of autonomy in handling assignments within his own division and reported regularly to the committee. The committee decided to operate through contracts and followed this procedure through the end of the war. NDRC did not set up its own laboratories, nor did its own staff conduct research. Recommendations for contracts were usually initiated at the section level and were passed to the committee through the division chair, the committee reserving for itself the final decision on all contracts. The military members advised on the relation of the proposed project to research already under way in the services.[20]

At this early stage in its operation, while NDRC was still an unfamiliar organization, relationships with academic and research institutions had to be carefully negotiated. The eminent status and national reputation of its members were instrumental in the committee's success. When the committee approved a proposal, the chairman of the relevant division was then responsible for negotiating a contract. Usually, preliminary discussion had already been held between NDRC and scientists at the designated institution to ascertain that the proposed contractee had the facilities and manpower to perform the desired work within the financial terms of the agreement. NDRC had to be satisfied that the work would be done well there. The secretary of the committee then drew up a contract that, after being approved by the committee and checked for accuracy by the division involved, was sent to the institution for signature. Eventually, such contracts became routine and were quickly implemented.[21]

NDRC deliberately limited the scope of its activities to matters of primary concern to the national defense, although in a period of total war it was sometimes difficult to determine if there was any part of the national economy not related to national defense. Once the United States actually entered the war, there was a proliferation of agencies to handle the war effort, and NDRC sought to work cordially with all of them. The army technical branches and the navy matériel bureaus continued to manage their own research, working through military labs and industry contracts. There was no overriding authority guiding wartime scientific development, but rather a number of independent agencies pursuing their own agendas with liaison that was sometimes effective, sometimes not. Apart from a special committee to look into atomic fission—out of which grew the Manhattan Project—which President Roosevelt specifically assigned to NDRC, the committee reserved the right to initiate research without the support of the services. As it turned out, however, much of the work undertaken by the committee was at the request of the army, the navy, or both.[22]

NDRC's first job was to compile lists of institutions, academic and commercial, where suitable research might be undertaken, and of scientists who would be suitable to undertake such work. The committee needed to find out what research projects that might have a military application were already under way and who was working on them. The committee also needed to know the current status of army and navy research projects, as well as developments the services would recommend but could not undertake themselves.[23]

While the committee at first tried to disrupt educational programs as little as possible, this inhibition receded as war approached. The lack of facilities for studying antisubmarine warfare problems, for example, quickly led to contracts with Columbia University and the University of California at San Diego to establish such centers. Similarly a contract was negotiated with MIT to undertake a microwave radar research program —resulting in the enormous Radiation Laboratory—and Cal Tech and George Washington University were pressed into service to take on different phases of rocketry. Eventually, academic and research institutions all over the country were drawn into war work, including Mary Sears's Woods Hole and Florence van Straten's NYU. While Grace Hopper left Vassar to work in uniform at Harvard in a lab taken over by the navy, there were also civilian scientists at Harvard from many other places. The director of Harvard's Radio Research Laboratory, for example, was F. E. Terman from Stanford University, and of the six hundred people on his staff there were more from California institutions than from Harvard. MIT's Rad Lab was directed by Lee A. DuBridge from the University of Rochester, and the associate director was F. Wheeler Loomis from the University of Illinois.[24]

NDRC engineered this massive exchange of personnel and paid the full-time salaries of so many scientists not in the cause of advancing scientific research but to bring a speedy end to the war. As Harvey Brooks recalled, "Natural scientists left their home universities and flocked to the war laboratories" set up by NDRC, where many were pressed to work on problems well outside their fields and about which they had previously known little or nothing. It was not just the navy that made such demands on its scientists.[25]

Money was not generally a problem. After Pearl Harbor the emphasis of the work changed from research to development and costs rose rapidly, but so did the funds provided, which Harvey Brooks called "virtually unlimited." NDRC was fortunate, too, in its personnel. President Roosevelt set the pattern at the beginning by arranging for many top scientists to serve the government without compensation (or WOC, as it was known to personnel people). Much of the success of NDRC was the result of work performed under these terms. All members of the committee itself served without compensation: Bush continued to hold his position at the Carnegie Institution, Conant at Harvard, and Compton at MIT. The creative use of part-timers was also effective with the many scientists who willingly served one or two days a week.[26]

In an effort to improve cooperation with the army and navy, military liaison officers were appointed to division and section projects, or groups of projects, to keep the scientists informed of military requirements and to introduce the military to new areas of scientific research. While this system was far from perfect, and cooperation varied from bureau to bureau and also depended a great deal on the inclination and technical knowledge of the officers involved, it tended to improve as the military men developed respect for the competence of the scientists. The Tizard Mission had already made it clear that much could be learned from liaison with the British, who were facing Germany's newest military hardware and techniques. Consequently, Roosevelt sent Conant to London in February 1941 to organize an exchange of information with Britain and to establish an NDRC office in London. Much was accomplished in one year to create a civilian-led mechanism for harnessing the nation's scientists to the war effort without placing them under the direct control of the military. By June 1941 Bush had recruited six thousand physicists, chemists, mathematicians, and engineers, a number that grew to thirty thousand by the end of the war.[27]

Germany, on the other hand, had no organization devoted to weapons research. Confident of a quick victory, it intended to win with the weapons it had already developed. At first there was little disruption of normal research programs in the belief that whatever the scientists were working on would be useful to the postwar German state. Perhaps, too, there was a reluctance to use the services of scientists of whose loyalty the Nazi regime was not sufficiently confident. In the early years of the war, therefore, such war research as went on was conducted in military laboratories and in the war industries, and even there basic research was frequently dropped in favor of testing already existing weapons. Industrial scientists were placed under the control of the production system, and regimentation stifled creativity. There were few opportunities for liaison among the military, academics, and industry, and little cooperation was possible among the different groups. Many Jewish scientists and those belonging to other oppressed groups were eliminated, and many others were indiscriminately drafted. Germany quickly lost the scientific lead it had held going into the war, and although its war research was conducted more effectively from 1942 onward, when academic scientists were finally drawn in, it was by then too late to regain the initiative.[28]

Japan's top civilian scientists, many of whom had been educated overseas, were very able, but their talents were never properly harnessed during the war. They generally remained outside the war effort, distrusted by the military and hampered by small budgets and excessive security. Military scientific programs, moreover, tended to attract only second-class men, and the bitter rivalry between the army and the navy prevented coordination of their research projects. Neither Italy nor Germany was of much help to their Axis ally, sending little in the way of scientific information—except in the field of underwater sound—and most of it too late to affect the outcome of the war.[29]

By contrast, British scientists, once enlisted in the war effort, proved very effective in creating innovative weapons and technologies. Everyone knows about the gallant pilots who saved Britain from German bombers, but not so many realize the debt owed to the small group of physicists who developed the chain home radar warning system. Although Britain never established a central organization to coordinate war research, its scientific community proved extremely productive, and Anglo-American scientific cooperation was of immense value to the Allied war effort.[30]

In June 1941 the Office of Scientific Research and Development (OSRD) was created by executive order and was placed within the Office of Emergency Management of the Executive Office of the President. Its purpose was to build on the success of NDRC by adding a number of new functions to the old ones. NDRC's mandate was to organize weapons research, but it made no provision for their development. OSRD—as the word *development* in its name suggests—would also provide for the intermediate step of engineering development. In theory, OSRD was also charged to improve the coordination of research projects with the army, navy, and NACA. In fact, OSRD was little more successful in this effort than NDRC had been. Finally, NDRC had been aimed exclusively at research on weapons and instruments of war, and OSRD was given a parallel committee structure to handle the development of military medicine. President Roosevelt placed Vannevar Bush at the head of the new organization, which was divided into an Advisory Council; NDRC; the Committee on Medical Research; the Administrative Office, handling administrative affairs; the Liaison Office, which exchanged information with Allied governments; the Scientific Personnel Office; and the Office of Field Service.[31]

Initially there was little structural change in NDRC, even in the wake of Pearl Harbor. Conant took over the chairmanship from Bush, and the other committee members continued to serve on what was reconstituted as an advisory committee of OSRD. NDRC was no longer responsible for drawing up contracts; this job now fell to the Administrative Office of OSRD, whose main problem became fitting a rapidly expanding research and development network into the established framework of government funding. To do this the Administrative Office adapted the concept of the procurement contract, routinely used by the government for the purchase of goods and equipment, to cover the purchase from universities of research and development in support of military needs. Harvey Brooks called this kind of contract "an important new social invention . . . which permitted great flexibility in the deployment of new skills for new purposes." In addition, OSRD took over NDRC's former liaison activities with the Allies. Otherwise the organization into divisions and sections remained essentially the same, as did the work they accomplished.[32]

By December 1942, however, after almost a year of war, the work of NDRC had expanded to such a degree that it was no longer possible for the committee members to oversee divisions and also devote sufficient time to matters of general policy. For that reason a complete reorganization of NDRC was effected. Its work was now divided among eighteen new divisions and two panels. A nineteenth division was added later.

Division 1 was concerned with ballistics research, Division 2 with structural defense and offense, Division 3 with special projectiles, Division 4 with ordnance accessories, Division 5 with new missiles, Division 6 with subsurface warfare, Division 7 with fire control, Division 8 with explosives, Division 9 with chemistry, Division 10 with absorbents and aerosols, Division 11 with chemical engineering, Division 12 with transportation development, Division 13 with electrical communication, Division 14 with radar, Division 15 with radio coordination, Division 16 with optics, Division 17 with physics, Division 18 with war metallurgy, and Division 19 with miscellaneous weapons (mostly for the Office of Strategic Services). The two panels were the Applied Mathematics Panel and the Applied Psychology Panel. Each of the two panels had important functions that were somewhat different from those of the regular divisions. They had to provide expert consulting service to the divisions, and they were to carry out any authorized studies. Projects could come from the army, the navy, Allied governments, or from OSRD itself.[33]

Chiefs were appointed for each division, and once again the work within divisions was divided into sections. The new division chiefs, many of them carried over from the old organization, were men of high standing in their fields accustomed to independence in research. The decentralization of the organization and the wide latitude given the division chiefs were largely responsible for the speed with which NDRC was able to operate and accounted in large measure for its success. Vannevar Bush even believed that "the entire success of OSRD depended upon [the] extreme decentralization and great autonomy of individual units." One of the leaders accorded that autonomy was Warren Weaver, who had served as chair of the Controls Section of NDRC's old Division D.[34]

With NDRC's reorganization, Weaver was appointed chief of the Applied Mathematics Panel (AMP). There was an interesting reason for creating a separate agency just for mathematicians, and it had to do with the divergence between pure and applied mathematics. Again, it is characteristic of World War II (and perhaps all wars) that the lines between science and technology, between theory and practice, were blurred. Karl T. Compton, of the University of Chicago, made that very clear when he wrote to Weaver in October 1942 asking him on behalf of the NDRC Executive Committee to take over AMP. "There are several reasons back of this," he wrote, but the principal one is the fact that thus far the mathematicians as a group have not been brought into the war picture very effectively. For example; the committee headed by Marston Morse has not been effective; I think this is because it is too "pure." Apparently what is needed is to bring mathematics and the various instrument problems together through the intermediate ground of Applied Mathematics. You have had an outstanding interest in this field and have intimate contact with particular mathematicians on one side and with the working affairs of the instrument designers on the other.[35]

The position of panel chief was comparable to that of division head; Weaver was to be the administrative and executive head of AMP, responsible for its organization and functioning. All divisions requiring extensive mathematical investigations, computing, or statistical work had to have at least one member who also sat on AMP. James Baxter, the president of Williams College and author of the brief official history of OSRD published in 1946, referred to the creation of AMP as "one of the most important features of the reorganization." While its purpose was "to make the most appropriate and advanced mathematical techniques more available to all NDRC divisions," its relation to Division 7 (fire control) was "particularly close and significant. . . . The mathematicians broke new ground over the whole field of fire control."[36]

The work of each division varied considerably, as did the frequency of its meetings, the number of sections, the size and cost of its contracts, and the number of scientists it employed. One thing all divisions and panels had in common was the requirement to present semiannual budgets and progress reports. Annual budgets varied from a high of $51,265,300 for Division 14 (radar) for July 1944 to June 1945 to a low of $22,552 for Division 19 (miscellaneous weapons) for July 1945 to June 1946. AMP had a high budget of $1,477,350 for July 1944 to June 1945 and a low of $60,500 for July 1945 to June 1946. In their five most active years NDRC and OSRD together contracted for more than $500,000,000.[37]

In most cases, once a contract was approved a technical aide from the relevant division undertook the supervision of the work. Technical aides were full-time employees paid by the civil service; some of them were young scientists and some were scientists of a distinction equal to that of the division chiefs. Among other things they kept the division informed of progress being made by the contractee, usually supplementing the contractee's monthly reports with site visits of their own. After the war, Irvin

Stewart, the president of West Virginia University, who had been deputy director of OSRD, wrote an administrative history of the organization. He said of technical aides that "taken as a whole . . . [they] were an exceedingly capable group who deserve a large share of the credit for the successful execution of the broad policies laid down by the director [OSRD] and the NDRC."[38] Mina Rees became the chief technical aide to the Applied Mathematics Panel.

After the Japanese attack on Pearl Harbor, Rees felt a great sense of frustration. She believed she could be useful in the war but did not know how to go about making a contribution. "I thought of joining the WAVES," she later recalled, "but then I decided that wasn't apt to be a good way of getting into the right kind of job." "Actually," she continued, thinking back:

> . . . what's her name, who was at Vassar, she joined the WAVES. . . . Grace Hopper, who was an associate professor of mathematics at Vassar just as I was at Hunter. She was assigned to work at Harvard for Howard Aiken who had the first operating computer, and she retired from the navy and is now called back as a captain; called back from retirement because she's practically indispensable. She's a famous person in the whole software field. So there was a way, but I didn't assess it as probable, and it might not have been probable for me; that depends.[39]

Rees's opportunity arose when she was called by Warren Weaver and invited to meet him. By then Weaver was heading the Applied Mathematics Panel and had found that he could not operate with only his secretary, especially as he still maintained his position at the Rockefeller Foundation and was trying to juggle the two jobs. The panel agreed that he needed an assistant who would be a full-time employee of the panel to take care of its central operations. Rees was offered the dual job of technical aide to the panel and executive assistant to Weaver. "When I was invited to do this I was delighted," Rees explained, "because I really wanted, as most young people did, I think, at that time, to have some part in trying to save the world." She began work on 1 August 1943, as soon as she was approved for a civil service appointment. She knew that as a woman she would have found it "harder to get a job that would be really significant in the war effort," so she did not hesitate to accept Weaver's offer. Rees had been in high school during World War I and had been very aware of the conflict in which two of her brothers had served. Now she felt that it was her turn to play her part.[40]

Rees believed she was offered the job on AMP because of the extensive connections she had cultivated among mathematicians around the country. Although there were women mathematicians at all the eastern women's colleges, few were better known than she. Her contacts had already given her an overview of what was going on in the field, so she was comfortable with the proposed job. "I had the basis for understanding what was needed," she said. "I wouldn't have taken a job that I didn't feel I could do." Rees knew that OSRD was engaged in the most urgent problems of the operations of war, and it appealed to her to be working in that environment. She was also attracted by the high repute of the men who were in charge of OSRD. She knew of Vannevar Bush as a "world famous engineer, the inventor of the differential analyzer, an analog computer whose function was largely to solve the differential equations of engineering." Warren Weaver had been a professor and chairman of the Mathematics Department at the University of Wisconsin, but initially he had studied engineering and had experience in applied mathematics, something then still quite rare. According to Rees, "Wisconsin was a place where he could get that kind of background." It is surely no coincidence that Howard Aiken—the quintessentially practical mathematician —had studied undergraduate calculus under Weaver at Wisconsin. Even before the Mark I was completed, Aiken had been in touch with Weaver about putting it to use, and Weaver remembered and acted on the proposal when AMP was studying computing devices.[41]

After leaving Wisconsin in 1932, Weaver had become the director of the newly created Division of Natural Sciences of the Rockefeller Foundation in New York City. Whereas previously the foundation had concentrated its scientific efforts on a few major institutions and on funding new research institutions, such as Woods Hole (to the benefit of Mary Sears), Weaver inspired a shift of emphasis toward the biological sciences and the support of the work of individual scientists. Weaver's activities at the Rockefeller Foundation before the war were very important to his work on NDRC. He had developed strikingly effective procedures to identify the most promising young scientists in Europe and America before their quality was generally recognized. Under his guidance, the Rockefeller Foundation "pioneered in establishing the general institutional traditions and specific administrative techniques for the patronage of individual research on a large scale." These were exactly the skills he would need as head of AMP. Moreover, his work had also brought him in touch with the leaders in many scientific fields, giving him a familiarity he used well to recruit scientists and mathematicians to war work.[42]

Weaver had been working for NDRC for more than a year when he took over AMP. In July 1940 Vannevar Bush had invited Weaver to head the committee's fire control section (D-2). Weaver intended to resign from the Rockefeller Foundation but was persuaded to retain his appointment even though the majority of his time would go to NDRC. One of the most pressing problems at the beginning of the war was how to produce effective fire control for antiaircraft weapons so that they could shoot down fast, high-altitude planes. The navy already had fairly advanced fire control devices with gyroscopic stabilization, rapid computation, and automatic power control of the guns. The army's existing mechanical devices, on the other hand, based on gears and cams, had hardly changed from World War I and were not fast enough or accurate enough to do the job, and anyway required precision machine tooling, which made them expensive and difficult to produce in quantity. The solution came from Bell Telephone Laboratories, which proposed using an electrical gun director. The computation process such directors would rely on, however, depended on a number of electrical devices of unproven design. Although the army was skeptical about using anything electrical under battle conditions, Weaver persuaded them to approve the proposal, and D-2 took full responsibility for supervision of the work.[43]

By the fall of 1942, when Vannevar Bush determined to reorganize NDRC, it was clear that the demand for sophisticated mathematical studies had increased rapidly, as had the need for mathematical assistance throughout the organization. Warren Weaver noted in his autobiography that "as the war went on, the emphasis [at NDRC] on the design and production of hardware necessarily tapered off somewhat, for the practical reason that by then a brand-new device simply could not be conceived of, designed, built in pilot model, tested, improved, standardized, and put into service in time to affect the conduct of the war."[44] In tune with the calendar of events in the war, this meant an increasing emphasis on analyses of the effectiveness of existing weapons, devices, and procedures. The task assigned to AMP, or "the Panel," as it was called, was to help with the increasingly complex mathematical problems that were becoming more and more important and that required the creation of new theory.

The Panel also helped with those problems that were relatively simple mathematically and required no new mathematical results, but needed mathematicians to formulate them properly. Before he could accomplish anything, however, Weaver first had to find the mathematicians, and there was plenty of competition for this relatively scarce commodity.

Mathematicians had been involved in government programs before World War II, for example, in the work of the Coast and Geodetic Survey and of the Agricultural Extension Service. Now they were to be recruited in large numbers to sustain a total war fought across two oceans. Some of those who found themselves in uniform were sent to serve in an army or navy installation that needed mathematicians. Herman Goldstine, for example, was ordered to the Aberdeen Proving Ground in Maryland, where he became the army's liaison with the Eckert-Mauchly team working on ENIAC at the University of Pennsylvania. The ENIAC connection brought Goldstine in touch with John von Neumann, who consulted on the project, and this relationship had a profound effect on his subsequent career. Just as it happened to Hopper in the navy, army service introduced Goldstine to the world of computers.[45]

Other mathematicians found themselves working in operational research groups. Some were attached to various air commands or to navy units like the Anti-submarine Warfare Operational Research Group (ASWORG) directed by MIT physicist Philip M. Morse. Yet others were associated with British and Canadian research efforts. There were also posts in industry. Bell Telephone Laboratories was perhaps the largest wartime employer of mathematicians, but others worked at RCA, Westinghouse, Bell Aircraft, and other companies with war contracts. There were mathematicians working on the Manhattan Project and on cryptanalysis. Of all the groups dealing with mathematicians, however, OSRD had by far the greatest influence on wartime mathematics, and it had the greatest influence in shaping the development of postwar mathematics as well.[46]

In order to meet his need for personnel, Weaver invited the participation of a broad array of mathematicians without regard to their field of specialization. He recruited several hundred—practically all of them academic mathematicians—to provide assistance in military research even though many of them in peacetime were theoretical mathematicians. Everyone clearly understood that these arrangements were for the duration only and that at the end of the hostilities they would return to their former jobs.[47]

Weaver's mathematicians worked on AMP problems in groups set up at eleven universities across the country, including Princeton, Columbia, NYU, the University of California at Berkeley, Brown, Harvard, and Northwestern. Rees maintained that Brown and NYU were the only two universities of stature in the United States actually prepared for the kind of work required by the war because they were the only two with established applied mathematics activities. In addition, Princeton and Berkeley were already doing useful advanced work in statistics. Most of the other OSRD contracts were with universities that had to recruit the necessary personnel from other universities. Columbia, for example, got some of its people from the University of Chicago.[48]

Economists and experts in statistical techniques joined the Panel when such skills were needed. Two economists in particular, W. Allen Wallis of Stanford and Milton Friedman, who later won a Nobel Prize in economics, assisted the Panel as statisticians. Some of the nation's most able mathematicians were employed on these university contracts, among them John von Neumann, who had come to Princeton's Institute for Advanced Study from Hungary in 1933. The eminent NYU mathematician Richard Courant, himself deeply engaged in AMP work, told Weaver that "an attempt should be made to channel [von Neumann's] extraordinary energy and ingenuity so that various Panel activities can receive optimum benefit from it." Weaver took Courant's advice and AMP profited enormously.[49] In addition to aiding other divisions of OSRD when asked, the main responsibility of AMP was to provide mathematical assistance to the military services. In every case, before accepting a problem, the Panel considered whether or not they had a reasonable chance to accomplish something useful. By demonstrating versatility and effectiveness in meeting military requirements they won the confidence of the military officers with whom they worked. By the end of the war AMP had undertaken 194 studies, almost half of them the result of direct requests from the armed services. Navy liaison with the Panel was maintained by Lt. Cdr. R. D. Conrad and Lt. T. C. Wilson of the Office of the Coordinator of Research and Development. For most of the war Rear Adm. Julius A. Furer was the coordinator. Another frequent navy visitor to AMP was Lt. Cdr. W. E. Bleick, the liaison from the Bureau of Ordnance.[50]

Rees joined the Panel in August 1943. By January 1944 AMP needed more technical aides, and Weaver initiated a search for suitable candidates. At that time he defined the duties to include "reading a large amount of report material, both British and American, visiting contracts, consulting on studies, suggesting material and contacts, and establishing inter-relationships between Panel personnel and the services." With her considerable charm, her aptitude for solving, not creating, problems, and her skill at making people feel like valuable members of a team, Rees was very well qualified for the job.[51]

In addition to her duties as chief technical aide, Rees was also Weaver's executive assistant. Weaver had not worked directly in mathematics for some time, so he gathered around him some of the acknowledged leaders in American mathematics to act as an executive committee responsible for the general policy of the Panel. Rees served as secretary to this group —the Committee Advisory to the Scientific Officer—which at various times included Richard Courant, Griffith C. Evans, Thornton C. Fry (deputy chief), Lawrence M. Graves, Harold Marston Morse, Oswald Veblen, and Samuel Stanley Wilkes. Among the other technical aides were Ivan S. Sokolnikoff and Sam Wilkes. The executive committee got together once a week in Weaver's office at Rockefeller Center to consider applications for the Panel's help. Rees's office, the Panel's operating office, was on the sixty-fourth floor of the Empire State Building with a magnificent view of New York harbor that Rees very much appreciated. Each of the other technical aides had an office there as well, and in addition to office clerical staff they shared a secretary. Everyone on the Panel had an identification badge reading "Mathematical Studies Relating to Warfare."[52]

Rees's role at AMP is expressed well in a citation offered to her at the Hunter College commencement on 5 June 1973 which states that she had been deeply involved "in deploying and sustaining the efforts of this country's mathematicians in the war effort."[53] Rees herself described her role as "quite a general one." Her major responsibility as Weaver's assistant was to take care of the central operations of the Panel. Weaver also delegated to her many of his administrative functions, such as recommending AMP contracts to OSRD. As AMP projects progressed, Rees's duties also required a considerable amount of travel to visit the military originators of the problems the Panel's mathematicians were working to solve. On one such trip to Wright Field in Dayton, Ohio, she witnessed a buzz bomb run in which "the racket was prodigious in spite of stuffed

Mina Rees's AMP ID card, 1945
*Mina Rees Collection, City University of New York Graduate School and University
Center Archives*

ears." During these visits Rees had a lot of contact with the military as
well as a chance to become familiar with a large number of the country's
mathematicians and their work. She also had contact with many of the
country's important universities, and with the men (there were few women)
running them. According to Vannevar Bush, the result of such contacts
for OSRD was to create "an effective partnership of scientists, engineers,
industrialists and military men such as was never seen before."[54]

Rees worked from early morning until late at night, sometimes thinking that only the view of the harbor kept her sane. "I was always so tired
that I remember going to parties every now and then and not opening my
mouth. Everybody thought I was so full of top secrets that I didn't dare
talk, but it was just that I was too tired to talk." She generally worked
seven days a week and did not take a vacation the whole time—not until
1946. Of course, many people worked like that during the war, and as at
the Harvard Computation Lab, the Panel members sometimes relieved the
stress with light banter. One time Rees wrote to reprimand Thornton Fry

for "what looks like the beginning of a bad habit—too frequent absence from ExCo meetings. I hope you are not planning to continue these bad beginnings." George Stibitz, enclosing some information Rees needed, added a note explaining their significance: "The slide rules are all very special applications of old and well known principles (except mine, of course), and the applications are so special that they are of little interest. In other words, pfui." The note is signed "love and kisses, George R. Stibitz, Technical Jackass, Div. 7." This was the same George Stibitz who gave his name to the Stibitz method of measuring the amount by which a tracer bullet misses a towed target by means of two sets of motion pictures.[55]

Each of the Panel's technical aides had responsibility for the work that was going on in the contracts according to their own specialties. Sam Wilkes, one of the best statisticians in the country, according to Rees, was in charge of statistics. Ivan Sokolnikoff, a Russian by birth whom Weaver knew from Princeton, was in charge of much of the applied mathematics. Rees, whose specialty was abstract algebra—about as abstract as you can get, according to her own description—nevertheless was in charge of much of the computation work, including the development of electrical and electronic computers. Vannevar Bush distributed the following guidelines regarding the work of technical aides:

> There are two functions to be performed in the administration of a research project carried on by a contractor under one of our contracts. One of these is the appropriate conduct of a business relationship. The other is the supervision of the scientific program. Neither, of course, should interfere with proper internal management by the contractor. Both elements, however, should be adequately present in order that the contractor may perform to maximum advantage.[56]

In practice, supervising a contract for AMP meant keeping in touch with the progress of the work and with the techniques that were being used to attack the problem. It meant discussing the procedure chosen, not to act as final authority but merely to participate actively in the decision making. Each contract had a project director who made the ultimate decisions; the technical aides and other Panel members who were experts in the field were there for consultation. On the whole, Rees believed the scientists working on AMP contracts were glad to have visits from the technical aides because they were the people who knew if something similar was going on elsewhere. For the aides, it sometimes meant the strain of dealing with difficult people, "ones with strong personality, each one a big shot." Yet it was important for the technical aides to make their presence felt because they were "responsible for the performance of the contracts."[57]

In the early days of AMP, Rees sometimes had difficulty persuading scientists to accept Panel contracts. She knew very well that researchers were jealous of their freedom to pursue research independent of direction, and at the beginning of World War II there was a general reluctance among mathematicians to work with industry for that reason. Those who were asked to work for the military faced many of the same problems that they would have faced in industry. In most cases the mathematicians had to solve other people's problems. This was very trying for them because when a problem is defined by someone who does not know the techniques available for solving it, the definition is apt to be wrong. Researchers jealously guarded their right to choose the approach they would use, and they did not take well to instruction from people who knew the problem but not the methods of research. This issue forced technical aides to develop formidable skills as intermediaries; they were the government source of funding standing between the contractee (the scientists) and the contractor (often the military), interpreting the project back and forth between them and making its completion possible.[58]

Thirty-three years after it had closed up shop, Rees asked Warren Weaver what value he thought the military had put on the work of AMP. He pointed out that with a few exceptions, not many in the army had had the background to understand what might be done. On the whole, aviators had more scientific background and were generally more receptive, as were one or two individuals at Aberdeen Proving Ground. Navy people, on the other hand, were generally eager for help. They, and later the army air forces, were the first true believers. In fact, Rees sometimes thought some naval officers placed too much faith in science. They tended to think it could do everything, and she had to disabuse them of that notion.[59]

In 1944 Vannevar Bush described the procedure for initiating projects for NDRC. "When the Services make a request," he wrote, "the chairman's office, through the Executive Secretary, assigns the problem to an NDRC Division, Panel, or Committee. If the British request our aid through the Liaison Office, the matter can take the same channel. A Division itself or one of its Sections may of course also initiate."[60] In practice, however, the usual procedure for AMP was for a military officer to write to Weaver directly stating a problem he thought the Panel might be able to address. Rees transmitted these requests to the Panel along with some background information with which the Panel could make a decision. Generally her work involved reformulating the problem in mathematical terms and then seeing if there were people available who had the right kind of mathematical specialty and the time to reach the answer to it. She selected scientists by field, so she needed to know what field people were working in and how busy they were.[61]

Looking back forty years later, Rees acknowledged her surprise at people's unexpected talents. Hassler Whitney, for example, a member of the Applied Mathematics Group at Columbia and one of the most famous of the young American mathematicians, "turned out to have an absolute genius for airplane problems from guidance studies." Rees once accompanied Whitney to perform some tests on a training machine for pilots. Whitney was developing mathematical principles to discover the best techniques for aerial gunnery, and he was going to test his theories on a flight simulator. Rees and Whitney each got into a simulator, and "he shot down all his planes and I only shot down a couple. It was quite clear that he really knew all about this mechanism which I didn't think he knew anything about. So a lot of people you didn't really appreciate until you saw what they'd actually done." This sort of understanding made Rees highly effective at finding suitable scientists. It was also a skill that was to prove invaluable after the war when she worked for the Office of Naval Research.[62]

If, after Rees's presentation, the Panel thought the request seemed important, and if, in their judgment, they had the personnel to handle the study, a group would go down to Washington for a meeting with the military petitioners. Rees was the first point of contact, traveling to Washington with the mathematician who was going to carry out the project, making frequent visits to the Navy Department, various navy bureaus, the Pentagon, the Naval Research Laboratory, the David Taylor Model Basin, and many other facilities and agencies. Although Panel members had travel priority, they always went to Washington by train because it was so hard to get airplane seats. Rees used the time to learn all she could about each project because she wrote monthly reports on each to keep the project originators up-to-date on the standing of the study. In addition, Rees had to keep current with all the projects being undertaken that might in any way involve mathematics—in the navy especially, but also in the army or in other OSRD divisions—in order to avoid duplication of effort.[63]

According to Rees, one of the strengths of the system thus developed was that many of the most able mathematicians in the country either were working under OSRD contracts or were members of the Panel itself. "So if we were stuck," she recalled, "we always had somebody we could discuss it with who would know if we didn't know . . . would know who in the book was most apt to be able to do it." "I can't remember a case where we couldn't do something significant," she concluded. In spite of Rees's heavy travel schedule most of the Panel communication was by telephone. The deputy chief of AMP, Thornton Fry, was head of the Applied Mathematics Division of Bell Telephone Labs and a great exponent of using the telephone, so they all did. They had a direct line to Washington and also made frequent calls to California.[64]

Another strength of the system was based on the pragmatism of a group of dedicated professionals determined to get a job done. This was proved on a regular basis by the Panel's creative handling of the security clearance issue. Everyone on the Panel had to be cleared for Secret, and all AMP paperwork was classified Secret. But a fairly large number of the mathematicians whose services AMP wanted to use had no security clearance at all, usually because they had not been in the United States long enough. According to Rees, one of the most difficult problems in statistics was actually solved by a man (whom she did not name) who could not be cleared because he was a recent immigrant. The solution was to abstract the problem from its factual base so that it was not identifiable. Since Rees was responsible for finding the right person to fulfill each contract, and then persuading them to do so, it often fell to her to make such work possible by separating the word problem and its expression in mathematical terms. In some ways the situation is reminiscent of the mathematical problems solved by Hopper and her colleagues at the Harvard Computation Lab, sometimes without even knowing the problem's source.[65]

A further element of Rees's job as facilitator was to secure draft deferments or exemptions from military service. Quite a few of the men working under AMP contracts were of fighting age, and Rees had to demonstrate that the work they were doing for the Panel was more important to the war effort than anything they might do in the military. It was very often Rees who got them their original exemptions and kept them in that category. Even after the lessons of World War I this was not as easy as it should have been. Only some twenty-four hundred men made it onto the reserved list from among physically fit graduate students in the sciences, and even older, well-established scientists were frequently subjected to the scrutiny of the Selective Service Board. Scientific exemptions had to be carefully negotiated.[66]

Asked how her work on AMP differed from that of Warren Weaver, Rees pointed out that, first of all, she was a full-time employee while Weaver still had a very important job at the Rockefeller Foundation, although he put in the work of two men anyway. In general, however, Weaver dealt with proposals in which admirals and generals were involved, and Rees did the negotiating if navy captains or army colonels were involved. There, it seemed, Rees's gender was significant. "I mean, obviously the generals were not talking to me," she said. Rees was quick to point out, too, that Weaver was also qualified to deal with problems about which she knew nothing. In the beginning there were times when she had to ask for an explanation of what was being discussed at the executive committee meetings "because they were talking about a strictly engineering problem and I didn't even know what some of the words meant. Well, I learned, but that was early in the event."[67]

Rees was the member of AMP solely responsible for its contract with the Bureau of Standards. The contract concerned the Mathematical Tables Project funded originally as part of the Depression effort to find jobs for mathematicians. The Bureau of Standards had taken over the project, which in those precomputer days developed hand techniques for making tables of functions required for solving certain kinds of mathematical problems. People working in the applications of mathematics, especially in engineering tasks, needed to use those functions, so the task of computing tables had a clear, practical use. During World War II AMP took over responsibility from the Bureau of Standards for the continued production of tables of functions. It was through this work that Rees became aware of the extensive need for computing, especially for projects in applied mathematics. The just-emerging field of computers, which Rees also supervised, was soon to make hand calculations of all sorts seem absurdly inefficient, labor intensive, and time-consuming.[68]

Most of the AMP studies conducted between 1942 and 1946 concerned improving the accuracy of equipment by recommending appropriate design changes or ascertaining the best use of existing equipment in particular fields such as bombing and the barrage use of rockets. One of the first problems the navy brought to AMP was how to determine what kind of a torpedo barrage to lay down against Japanese vessels to maximize the chance of hitting them. The navy had no information on how fast Japanese vessels could accelerate in a straight line, how rapidly they could turn, etc. They did, however, have very good photographs of many Japanese vessels. The people at NYU knew that in 1887, British physicist Lord Kelvin—noted for his pioneering work in thermodynamics, electricity, and underwater telegraphy—had established that the speed of a ship moving in a straight line is indicated by the spacing of the cusps along the bow waves. Most of the navy photographs, though, showed Japanese ships in the process of turning, so Lord Kelvin's analysis had to be extended to ships in turns. This was rather simply done, and the speed of Japanese ships was figured from pictures of their bow waves or wakes. A test of the mathematical results in an experimental run with a new destroyer off the coast of Maine found an extremely good agreement of theory and observation, within a few percent margin of error for both speed and turning radius.[69]

The navy was so impressed with the result that its Photographic Interpretation Center (from which Mary Sears received data helpful for her reports) adopted the method developed by AMP and incorporated much of the material in an official handbook. As Rees pointed out, "This and similar experiences won over the armed services to the notion that mathematics could be of great help to them."[70]

Another of the early problems tackled by AMP had to do with aerial gunnery. Brig. Gen. Robert W. Harper, Training Division, assistant chief of staff, AAF, defined the issue in a letter to Vannevar Bush: "The problems connected with flexible gunnery are probably the most critical being faced by the Air Forces today. It would be difficult to overstate the importance of this work or the urgency of the need; the defense of our bomber formations against fighter interception is a matter which demands increasing coordinated expert attention." General Harper proposed that AMP should recruit and train mathematicians to be assigned to operations research sections in the field in different theaters to examine flexible gunnery problems. The Panel could handle this program because it had already been involved in studies of rules for flexible gunnery training and because it had access to the best mathematicians in the country. AMP fulfilled the assignment quickly as Study No. 103, initially training ten mathematicians for fieldwork and, when the demand continued, then training eight more. It was more difficult to recruit the second group because by then so many mathematicians were already engaged in war work. John W. Odle, who was recruited in the second group, reported:

> [The] training was extremely valuable to me and was directly applicable to my subsequent assignment in the flexible gunnery subsection of the Operations Research Group at the Eighth Air Force in England. Without the general orientation and the specialized instruction that I received . . . I would have been woefully lost in a field of endeavor that was completely new and unfamiliar to me. . . . The training certainly opened up immense new vistas to me. In fact, that introduction to Operational Research . . . and my later wartime experiences as a practitioner, completely changed the course of my career.[71]

Philip Morse of ASWORG had already been working closely with NDRC and now brought a good deal of business to AMP. He also served as AMP liaison to Division 6, subsurface warfare. Several of the projects he presented involved probability problems: for example, given a depth charge with a known lethal range, how should depth bombing be carried out for the most effective results? Another problem involved how an airplane could most effectively search for a submarine it had seen submerge, recognizing that the plane had a limited range of visibility and that the range of the submarine in a given length of time was also limited. Airplanes were needed to shield convoys, but they did not always know the exact location of the convoys. Another probability problem, therefore, was how a plane should search for a convoy, given a specified amount of gas. The AMP Executive Committee finally had to ask Morse to submit a statement of his priorities for computing jobs.[72]

In general, AMP enjoyed a good relationship with navy research organizations, better than did many NDRC divisions. This amicable situation included especially the Naval Research Laboratory, which frequently sought help for computations involving fire-control experiments. The navy's Mark VIII radar gun position set presented certain problems. When an attack was planned against a shore installation, the skipper plotted the curve along which the ship would go in—and the point at which it would open fire—on a Mercator projection. But when the operator looked in the radarscope he saw a different map. AMP was asked if it could devise a simple gadget so that the operator could draw points on the selected course the way the profile of the land would look on the scope presentation. The Panel was able to come up with an optical scheme that met the specifications. The numbers and varieties of problems presented to AMP for solution seem almost endless, reflecting the complications of a modern, worldwide, total, technical war. A large percentage of the problems were naval in origin; indeed, there were not many navy agencies that did not in some way or another call on AMP for help. The Hydrographic Office, for example, received assistance from the Mathematical Tables Project on a loran technical report.[73]

Among the issues that complicated naval problems was the movement of ships on water. Thus, while the navy used computers and directors for its guns, these were more complex than those developed for the army because the motion of the ships themselves had to be taken into account. Similarly, while the navy's 5-inch guns were used principally on long-range antiaircraft fire, in the event of a torpedo attack a battleship would shoot off everything, depressing the big guns to cause splash and use ricochet. Mathematical computations had to take these variables into account. AMP's Study No. 40 suggests the range of work the Panel accomplished for the navy. The problem for Study No. 40 came from the Jam Handy organization producing training films for the Bureau of Aeronautics. The challenge was to devise improved methods for calculating positions and orientations of airplane models in movie making to better simulate aspects of air warfare.[74]

Very often the tasks taken on by AMP required considerable work on the development of basic theory. Rees noted that some of the tasks involved what has been called "classical applied mathematics." At NYU, for example, work in gas kinetics concerned the theory of explosions in the air and underwater, which involved extensive study of the kinds of shock fronts that are created by explosions. Meanwhile, the Underwater Explosives Research Laboratory at Wood's Hole was making theoretical investigations in the pressure-time curve for explosives and in damage produced by explosive waves on underwater objects. A BuAer request for assistance in the design of nozzles for jet motors initiated Study No. 137, an extended analysis of gas flow in nozzles and supersonic gas jets involving the development of jet and rocket theory. By work of this sort AMP mathematicians gained expertise in new and important fields, ensuring that they would be frequently called on for consultation and advice. Rees remembered one trip in particular that she made to Pasadena in 1944, accompanying Richard Courant and Kurt Friedrichs to check on a problem Cal Tech was having launching rockets. Courant and Friedrichs were able to make some suggestions, and although it is not known how significant their influence was, the new experiments begun after their visit were successful.[75]

The mathematical aspects of the dynamics of compressible fluids also commanded considerable attention from the Panel. In response to many questions on this subject raised by wartime agencies, a shock wave manual was prepared at NYU, and AMP—under the auspices of OSRD —published its first version in 1944. Much of the Panel's work had a significance well beyond the immediate demands of the war, and the shock wave manual was one of the major documents produced by AMP that proved to be of continuing mathematical interest. Indeed, the 1944 manual became the basis for a 1948 book by Courant and Friedrichs: *Supersonic Flow and Shock Waves*. After the war, with support from all the military services, the NYU group continued to work on a number of the same problems, including studies of water waves and work related to computer applications.[76]

At Brown University work concentrated on problems in classical dynamics and the mechanics of deformable media, and the output in mathematical terms was considerable. William Prager, the head of the Brown group, also viewed the importance of the work from a long-term standpoint, as he made clear in a letter he wrote in 1978:

> While the Applied Mathematics Group at Brown University worked on numerous problems suggested by the military services, I believe that its essential service to American Mathematics was to help in making Applied Mathematics respectable. . . . The fact that the Program of Advanced Instruction and Research in Applied Mechanics, the forerunner of Brown's Division of Applied Mathematics, relied heavily on the financial support available under a war preparedness program illustrates the influence of the war on the development of the mathematical sciences in the United States.[77]

Ivan Sokolnikoff was the technical aide in charge of the Harvard contract concerning fluid mechanics, his specialty. The work of the Underwater Ballistics Committee under Garrett Birkhoff produced an important report and also created a group of experts who were much in demand for consultation, especially by the navy.[78]

The largest of the applied mathematics groups, AMG-C, was the one at Columbia. Initially its work was largely devoted to studies in aerial warfare, and particularly air-to-air gunnery. The group was concerned with aeroballistics, the motion of projectiles from airborne guns, and with the theory of deflection shooting. Aerodynamic pursuit curve theory (Study No. 153) was important because the standard fighter had guns that fired only in the direction of flight. The Columbia group was also involved in the design and characteristics of own-speed sights—devices designed for use in the case of pursuit curve attack on a defending bomber —and lead computing sights, which assumed that the target's track relative to the gun mount remained essentially straight over the bullet's flight time. These developments both improved the accuracy of gun sights and simplified their mechanization and operation. In addition, AMG-C investigated the basic theory of a central fire-control system, the analytical aspects of experimental programs for testing airborne fire-control equipment, and new developments such as stabilization and radar. The group's work on aerial gunnery and gyroscopic gun sights, in particular, was of such value to the navy that the group received the Naval Ordnance Development Award for its efforts.[79]

Hassler Whitney of the Columbia group undertook much of AMP's effort to study the use of rockets in air warfare. He integrated the work being done at Columbia with that of Northwestern in the general field of fire control for airborne rockets, and also maintained liaison between Division 7 (fire control) and the activities of many army and navy establishments. This was particularly relevant to the work of the Naval Ordnance Test Station at Inyokern (China Lake, where a number of Waves were employed), the Dover Army Air Base, the Wright Field Armament Laboratory, the Naval Bureau of Ordnance, and the British Air Commission.[80]

Probability considerations and statistical problems arose in such a large number of Panel studies that four contracts were created to deal with these issues. By the end of the war the major effort of three of the four groups was being spent on nineteen studies dealing with the probability and statistical aspects of bombing problems, which differed for each service. Whereas the AAF normally used formation bombing, the navy used the tactic of individually aimed releases in most of its attacks on shipping, warships, submarines, and shore installations. The Panel worked closely with the Navy Air Intelligence Group and with the Naval Air Training Station at Banana River, Florida, to provide statistical analyses of bombing tactics. Statistics were also used for the development of new fire effect tables and in studies related to such things as land mine problems and searches.[81]

The largest of the Statistical Research Groups, SRG-C, was at Columbia. Sam Wilkes was responsible for most of its work, as well as for statistical activities at Berkeley and other places. Mina Rees also worked closely with Columbia's highly effective statistical consulting group. "I can certainly attest," she wrote many years later, "that it was a tremendously productive group and an exciting one to be associated with."[82] The most striking concept developed at Columbia was that of sequential analysis, later a dominant theme in statistical research. In his summary of AMP's work Warren Weaver discussed the importance of sequential analysis:

> During the war, it was recognized by the Services that the statistical techniques which were developed by the Panel for army and navy use, on the basis of the new theory of sequential analysis, if made generally available in industry, would improve the quality of products produced for the Services. In March 1945, the Quartermaster General wrote to the War Department liaison officer for NDRC a letter containing the following statement: "By making this information available to Quartermaster contractors on an unclassified basis, the material can be widely used by these contractors in their own process control and the more process quality control contractors use, the higher quality the Quartermaster Corps can be assured of obtaining from its contractors. . . . With thousands of contractors producing approximately billions of dollars worth of equipment each year, even a 1% reduction in defective merchandise would result in a great saving to the Government. Based on our experience with sequential sampling in the past year, it is the considered opinion of this office that savings of this magnitude can be made through the dissemination of sequential sampling procedures."

"On the basis of this and similar requests," Weaver concluded, "the Panel's work on sequential analysis was declassified, the reports . . . were published," and the procedures were widely and successfully applied. In fact, as Rees pointed out, the money saved was more than the whole cost of running AMP several times over.[83]

While the work of Columbia's SRG had a positive effect on the war effort, as did the work of AMP in general, association with those groups was also good for many of the mathematicians involved. "One may say more generally, I think," recorded Rees, "that for a number of mathematicians, whether their work was in AMP or elsewhere, what they did during the war had a substantial impact on their subsequent careers." These benefits were not restricted to scientists alone. As Harvard professor Harvey Brooks observed, "An informal and extremely effective system of recruiting for the [scientific] war effort was established within the academic community. At the same time humanists and social scientists flocked to the Office of Strategic Services and to the various agencies set up to manage the war economy." The effect of the war on our improbable warriors was part of a pattern of new opportunities and new directions opened up to those able to see and take advantage of them.[84]

The Panel, naturally enough, found itself deeply involved in the efforts to expand computing power. In October 1943 the Bureau of Ordnance—which was in great need of help with its extensive ballistics computations at the navy's Dahlgren Proving Ground—asked AMP to suggest suitable computing equipment. According to Rees, it was partly at her urging that AMP decided to make a comprehensive survey of the various types of computing equipment available. The survey included differential analyzers of the Bush type, relay computers, electronic computers, and other related computing equipment developed by National Cash Register and IBM. The study—No. 92—eventually looked at both Aiken's Mark I and Eckert and Mauchly's work on ENIAC. Rees thus became very familiar with the most up-to-date work in computers, a knowledge that was to prove very useful in her position at the Office of Naval Research after the war. Among the sorts of computations eventually produced by AMP on a variety of machines were those for the Bureau of Navigation on shock waves, on surface waves, on the solution of heat conduction equations for explosives, and on Project Dolphin (Study No. 172) to determine the time of release of torpedoes fired in salvos from groups of PT boats.[85]

In her final appreciation of the accomplishments of the Applied Mathematics Panel, Rees went far beyond its obvious contributions to winning World War II. She pointed out ways in which the Panel created or introduced mathematical concepts that after the war became essential mechanisms for business and economics in the United States. Mathematicians did not work in blinders during the war, although they may have had to put off solving the many new problems they identified. Certainly "a big chunk of new math was developed at NYU and at Columbia, and probably elsewhere," she recalled, and "in the statistics at Berkeley a lot of new stuff was developed."[86] These new fields had permeated so many activities that wartime practices adopted by the Applied Mathematics Panel and other groups such as the navy's ASWORG can be said to have contributed materially to the "increasing mathematization of society."[87]

Among the examples of such mathematization cited by Rees were the attempts after the war to combine the use of numerical data with mathematical models. This expanding field, variously called management science, operations research, cost-benefit analysis, optimization theory, or mathematical programming, was introduced into the curricula of business schools. Mathematical models were also applied in the behavioral sciences taught in liberal arts colleges, and in some universities separate courses in mathematics were added in economics departments, schools of industrial management, engineering schools, and so on. "Thus," Rees concluded, "as the uses of mathematics have expanded in new directions, many institutions have adopted new organizational arrangements to accommodate the new content, much of which reflects developments in the mathematical sciences that grew out of military requirements in World War II."[88]

When she was asked how she felt about the influence and power she wielded—unusual for a woman in those days, especially as she was the only woman on AMP—Rees replied that she was always aware that she had to be a little cautious. For one thing, most of the people she was dealing with were more distinguished than she, and for another, because she was female she was "sort of an underdog by definition." Nevertheless, on the whole she believed she was treated with the greatest friendliness and cooperation. She was always kept well informed of developments, and people were responsive to her requests. She found dealing with the military even easier than dealing with civilians. Although she had never referred to herself as Dr. Rees before, that is how she was immediately addressed by the military. "They all had titles and you had to have a title. If you met an admiral you didn't ask him where he came from; he was an admiral. . . . In the same way they went on the assumption that if you were a doctor you were a doctor. I didn't have any problem because I was a woman."[89]

Rees noted that she dealt with very few other professional women during the war because "there just weren't any women in these positions."

She seems to have forgotten about Dr. Dorothy W. Weeks of the OSRD Liaison Office, with whom she corresponded regarding information from British scientific establishments and whom she met several times on visits to Washington. She also failed to mention Dr. Gladys Anslow, head of the Physics Department at Smith College who was appointed to the Office of Field Service in 1944 and whom she had also met. Perhaps, too, she did not know of Dr. Gladys Anderson Emerson, a biochemist working for OSRD on the effects of vitamin deficiencies. While it is true that there were not many women in the whole OSRD operation, there were a few other very able ones on the administrative side, like Margaret Moses and Dr. Louise Kelley in the office of the chairman of NDRC. Rather than a sense that women were discriminated against, Rees felt that there just were not many qualified women available. Of course, past discrimination in education and opportunities was at least partly responsible for that, but Rees did not make that inference.[90]

On the whole, however, Rees had a valid point. Quite a few women were doing very important work with the design of the computing that used desk computers, formulating problems so that desk computers could solve them. But they were not at the level of the research mathematicians. Rees did recall two women who worked with Jerzy Neyman at Berkeley who were very important mathematical statisticians, especially one of them, Elizabeth "Betty" Scott. After Neyman retired, Betty Scott took over from him as chair of the Department of Mathematical Statistics. And of course there was Grace Hopper, although she was just entering the field at the time and was not yet as outstanding as she later became. Rees also knew of a woman in England doing important work: Olga Taussky Todd. Her husband was head of the National Physical Laboratory's computing activity. During the war Olga Taussky worked in the aircraft establishment, and according to Rees, she was a first-class mathematician; but Rees did not know of her equivalent in the United States.[91]

Rees acknowledged lacking a strong sense of feminism in the war years. At the time it seemed—in her word—irrelevant. The main thrust of what they were doing was to win a war. Social norms were very different then, too, as seen in a request sent to AMP from Lt. Cdr. T. C. Wilson of the navy's Office of the Coordinator of Research and Development. Commander Wilson wanted help finding personnel for mathematical work, and in particular he needed "three unmarried women computers for Dahlgren." He did not explain why the women had to be unmarried. Today, of course, such a request would be unthinkable, but then it was perfectly normal. Unthinkable, too, would be the use of the expression "girl-months" to signify how long it took for one woman to do a certain calculation on a desk calculator. Rees herself used the expression freely. Furthermore, in what sounds very much like an echo of the other improbable warriors, Rees said that she did not have time to think about gender issues. Those who knew her well years later at the City University of New York noted that while she was very supportive of women, even then she could not be called a feminist. Rather she respected talent wherever it was.[92]

A common feminist concern of more recent times has been the issue of promotion. When her female interviewer asked Rees about this in the 1980s, her answer, as always, was pragmatic and straightforward. The rule was that no one should make more money working for AMP than they would have made in their regular job, she patiently explained. But it was not clear whether or not, in those years, Rees would have been promoted at Hunter College, so it was hard to get her promoted at AMP. But Warren Weaver saw that it happened. Rees admitted that women were not always greeted with enthusiasm when they first entered a profession. Her solution, like that of Hopper and Sears, was that women must "offer something extra." Rees also continued to believe that government service offered women the greatest opportunities because of its well-established tradition of treating women "as working equals of men."[93]

Certainly working for the government, and particularly for Warren Weaver, had a very positive effect on Rees's career. Like the other improbable warriors she was fortunate in her wartime boss, and like them she enjoyed a close working relationship that was at the same time highly professional and did not extend to social familiarity. In his autobiography, *Scene of Change,* Weaver acknowledged his debt to "the incomparably fine assistance of Dr. Mina Rees." After the war, when Rees was in Washington, Weaver would visit her office occasionally when he was in town, maintaining a cordial friendship until his death in 1978. It was Rees who wrote a biographical memoir of Weaver for the National Academy of Sciences, calling him an "extraordinary man," "witty, forthright, a superb raconteur [and] skilled in the use of words as few of us can hope to be." When she worked for him during the war it was his "rigid honesty" that particularly impressed Rees.[94]

Rees had had little administrative experience before going to AMP, and she watched Weaver closely, learning from his great skill in dealing with military officers, the Washington bureaucracy, and fellow scientists alike. His light touch made him a popular colleague and an effective leader. Writing to inform six mathematicians on the Panel that he wanted them to act as a temporary committee on notation in aerial gunnery, he approached the matter thus: "I suggest that it may be sensible for you to locate, as promptly as possible, the limits of the area over which you can agree without too painful concessions; and not to spend much time developing and substantiating differences that are almost surely irreconcilable. Mathematicians have strong and not necessarily very rational ideas about notation, and I would like to minimize duels and suicides."[95]

In her postwar career Rees followed a number of Weaver's administrative procedures. One was to keep subordinates well informed of anything that had to do with them or their operations. Weaver sent copies of his letters to everyone who might be affected by them, and when he did not write he telephoned. Rees was an apt pupil and she adopted these practices, giving Weaver much credit for her later formidable success as an administrator. In many ways their talents were very similar. Weaver wrote perceptively of himself that he "lacked that strange and wonderful creative spark that makes a good researcher." Rees knew that to be true of herself, too, and often said so. "Maybe I could be called eminent," she commented to an interviewer in 1984, "but I am certainly not an eminent *mathematician!*" (emphasis in original). "There are some women who are doing high-quality mathematical research, but I'm not," she stated with her usual certainty. Rees would probably have agreed that the description of her as a "leading science administrator" was accurate, and it was her service with AMP that set her on that path. For their war work both Weaver and Rees received the King's Medal for Service in the Cause of Freedom from the British government, and Weaver received the Medal for Merit of the United States, while Rees was awarded the U.S. President's Certificate of Merit.[96]

"Perhaps the highest tribute which could have been paid to the role of mathematicians in World War II," wrote Vannevar Bush, "was the complete lack of astonishment which greeted their contributions." The Applied Mathematical Panel began functioning with its first executive committee meeting on 27 January 1943. Forty months later it closed up shop with the last meeting on 25 April 1946. Rees joined the Panel on 1 August 1943 and remained until the end. On 15 February 1946 she terminated her activities as a full-time technical aide but continued on a part-time basis until the work of the Panel was complete. In January, when Rees told Weaver of her plan to return to teaching part time, he wrote a letter to President George N. Shuster of Hunter College that included the following comments:

> I wish that I could make you feel the appreciation and admiration that the members of the Applied Mathematics Panel have for Miss Rees. She has, as I think you know, been in administrative charge of our main office. She has worked, on the one hand, with a large number of mathematicians from all over the country; and, on the other hand, with officials of the Army, Navy and the Government. I know of no single case in which she has not commanded the respect and cooperation of the people she has worked with. Her administration of her own office, and her handling of the many complex organizational and scientific problems, have been simply superb. She has worked with a completely unselfish disregard for hours, for difficulties, and for her own strength. She made a large and distinguished contribution to the war effort. You have a right to feel very proud of her.[97]

It is not unknown for critics to write off military citations as standard hyperbole, but there is no denying the sincerity of the respect conveyed in this letter, nor the importance of Mina Rees's contribution to the war effort to which it attests.

After the war, Rees built on the broad contacts she had already made through AMP when she accepted an invitation to head the mathematics branch of the newly established Office of Naval Research (ONR). It would prove challenging to design and develop a mathematical program melding civilian and navy science in peacetime. While Warren Weaver often commented favorably on the technical competence of the navy men with whom he dealt, reflecting the generally good relations accomplished by AMP, the feeling among some civilian scientists was not so sanguine. In 1944 Bush wrote that "the navy does not yet fully grasp how to manage and collaborate with civilian scientific personnel." Nevertheless, he favored continued government funding for the sciences after the war and he wrote a report to President Roosevelt, published in 1945 as *Science: The Endless Frontier,* appealing for public support for research. This initiative eventually led to the creation of the National Science Foundation in 1950.[98]

In the meantime, there were a number of navy reserve officers—very

Dr. Mina Rees at the Office of Naval Research, March 1946
U.S. Navy photo, Mina Rees Collection, City University of New York Graduate School and University Center Archives

able scientists themselves—who convinced the officers responsible for the continuing readiness of the navy that it was in the national interest to maintain the mutually beneficial relationship established with the nation's civilian scientists. Rear Adm. Harold G. Bowen, coordinator of research and development and from May 1945 head of the new Office of Research and Inventions, also supported the project. They did not try to persuade any other service: "Anybody in uniform would have more sense than that," Rees thought.[99]

In February 1945 James V. Forrestal, the secretary of the navy and soon to be the first secretary of defense, sent a memorandum to President Roosevelt in which he said: "The problem . . . is how to establish channels through which scientists can [contribute to the nation's security by carrying on research] in peace as successfully as they have during the war." The first part of a solution was for Congress to establish the ONR in 1946, making it responsible for funding basic research at the country's universities in the fields of science of interest to the navy. That August, Rees went to Washington to set up the ONR's program in mathematical sciences. Building on the groundwork prepared by the naval reserve scientific officers and by Admiral Bowen, Rees supported the idea that it was important to maintain pure research in order to provide the foundation for applied research when it was needed. A portion of her budget was accordingly allocated for that purpose. Having learned something from its war experience, the navy was inclined to be broad and generous in its interpretation of what might be of interest to it. Rees was given an expansive charter that in addition to mathematics included statistics and computer development.[100]

Initially, Rees had had grave reservations about the job. She doubted that the mathematicians of the country would welcome support from the military, and she doubted that the whole concept would work. Certainly Harvard, once the war was over, was anxious to shed the military connection as soon as possible. Other universities had the same attitude. "I just didn't think people in the United States, who had unwillingly in a sense, but with all their hearts, participated in this huge military effort, would wish to extend having the military in their lives," recalled Rees. "They wanted to go back to being civilians and not have anything to do with the military."[101]

She soon found that the range of interests of mathematicians was so varied, and the understanding of the naval officers with whom she dealt was so professional, that her initial doubts as to the feasibility of the relationship disappeared. She had the freedom to support good mathematical research conducted by able and interested mathematicians. ONR had no power to make grants or award fellowships, and all the support actually came in the form of contracts between the navy and the university or research institution. ONR had developed the practice, however, of making the contracts undemanding and generous, increasing the popularity of the program with university academics and administrators alike. Her experience with AMP had given Rees plenty of practice in flexibility as well as advanced information about the sorts of people she would be dealing with and what she could expect in her relationships with them. With this head start she soon created a flourishing program. Due in large part to her own reputation and to her use of recommendations from a committee of eminent advisers, she was able to secure funding for a wide range of applied and pure research projects. Her office supported the work of senior researchers and also postdoctoral research by promising young mathematicians.[102]

The notion that the military would spend money on basic research without trying to direct, control, or restrict the research was still novel to many. Therefore, Rees had to persuade researchers that this was all being done under the aegis of a group of civilians who really were concerned about the welfare of mathematics. In fact, ONR reported directly to the secretary of the navy, a civilian, and not to the CNO. By 1951 Rees was able to tell a commencement crowd at her alma mater, Hunter College, that so far, the representatives of the government had "shown such understanding and judgment that university people feel they are dealing with partners in a great intellectual undertaking." For Rees herself, an important result was that she became even better acquainted with university campuses across the country and with senior faculty members at those institutions. Her broad understanding of graduate education in the United States made her eminently suited for her later academic administrative assignments.[103]

The original staff of ONR was largely influenced by OSRD scientists and the naval officers who had been involved in scientific work during the war. There was a naval sciences division of mostly military officers whose concern was to get answers to immediate naval problems, rather like during the war years. Then there was a research division dominated by civilian scientists like Rees. Roger Revelle, the oceanographer and friend of Mary Sears who had transformed himself into a population specialist, was at ONR; a physicist headed the mechanics branch; and the head of the electronics group was E. R. "Manny" Piore, who later became the chief scientist at IBM. Rees found the intellectual climate at ONR extremely stimulating, with everyone not only very able, but also very compatible.[104]

Working conditions, too, were very different in peacetime. In her new job Rees worked nine-hour, sometimes even eight-hour days. She played —better than average—tennis every day and even took weekends off. One of her young assistants in New York later noted that when Rees was working she really worked, but when she was relaxing she really knew how to relax. No one would dream of disturbing her vacation unless the sky fell in, and she had her staff so well trained that it never did. In Washington, and from then on, Rees also had time to paint again, one of her favorite pastimes, producing marine landscapes and abstracts. The intellectual environment in Washington was different, too, from what she had experienced in academia. The scientists and mathematicians at ONR were all very motivated and dynamic. It was a more interesting mathematical setting than in most universities, where people were apt to work only on the relatively few things they knew about. At ONR, by contrast, people would come in with new ideas just because they seemed interesting, and anybody could pick them up and work on them. A powerful incentive, of course, was the awareness that applied mathematics, especially, was being vigorously pursued abroad, in Russia, Germany, England, and the Netherlands.[105]

When OSRD closed up shop, ONR became the chief government office subsidizing scientific research. One of Rees's first accomplishments was to provide for the continuation of the Mathematical Tables Project. Working with the Bureau of Standards, Rees helped establish the National Applied Mathematics Laboratories. One section of the Applied Mathematics Lab was the Computation Laboratory created to carry on the work of the Mathematical Tables Project, but with more emphasis in the future on problem solving. Rees continued to work closely with the Bureau of Standards, particularly sponsoring developments in computing, and it was largely through her energy and initiative that ONR took a leading position in the field. Rees was quick to perceive the ramifications of digital computers and "eager to establish a program that would stimulate their development, keep the navy in touch with progress being made, and enable the navy to benefit from what we anticipated would be spectacular achievements of the new technology."[106]

Under Rees's guidance, therefore, the mathematics branch was able to establish what Rees described as "a very limited program in support of digital computers." It participated in activities at the Bureau of Standards and facilitated the transfer of funds to develop computers for the Census and Weather Bureaus and to provide support for the growth of a computer industry. By the time Eckert and Mauchly's UNIVAC I was delivered to the Census Bureau, large commercial companies were showing signs of interest in building computers. The branch also supported two other major academic computers: von Neumann's machine at the Institute for Advanced Study and the Whirlwind computer at MIT. At the same time, Rees's group at ONR organized computer conferences, published reports, and wrote the *Digital Computer Newsletter,* published quarterly, explaining what was happening with every computer under construction in the United States. In the summer of 1946 the group supported the first course in the theory and techniques of electronic digital computers, given at the Moore School, and supported Howard Aiken's graduate training course in computing machinery at Harvard during 1947–48. ONR also started a research program in logistics that was carried on at Princeton for many years from 1948 onward, and the Logistics Research Project at George Washington University.[107]

Until the Association for Computing Machinery was established in 1947—with the help of members of the mathematics branch—Rees's group played a unique role in providing information to everyone interested in computing. The mysteries of the new field were still strong, though. "For an adequate discourse on the military applications of automatically sequenced electronic computers," Rees wrote in a 1950 article, "I direct you to recent Steve Canyon comic strips in which an electronic brain that could see and shoot down planes at great distances was saved from the totalitarian forces of evil."[108]

Within two years of her arrival in Washington, Rees's mathematics branch, in addition to its computing activities, had become involved in sponsoring a large research project on numerical analysis. This included, among other things, support for the establishment of the Institute for Numerical Analysis at UCLA. By 1949 there was so much going on in mathematics that the branch was expanded to become the Mathematical Sciences Division with Rees as director. The division had a branch for mathematics, one for statistics, one for computers, and one for logistics. Later, a mechanics branch was added as the division was already sponsoring work in fluid mechanics.[109]

As chief of the Mathematical Sciences Division, Rees had accomplished the distinction of being the only woman division head in the navy's research program. She had also received a number of distinguished appointments that spread her influence on postwar mathematics developments even more broadly. Among these positions she was the U.S. government representative on the UNESCO Panel on Applied Mathematics, the navy member and chairman of the National Bureau of Standards Applied Mathematics Advisory Council, and a member of the National Research Council's Committee on High Speed Computing Machines. In her final year at ONR Rees became the deputy research director, responsible for the entire research activity. When she left Washington in 1953, the first generation of machines produced by the computer industry had arrived. Automatic programming, as it was then called, was just appearing, "shepherded by Grace Hopper," according to Rees, "whose work then and in the following years made major contributions to the emerging software revolution." Looking back on her ten years of government service, Rees wrote that she left Washington convinced that "computers would be exploited in the future by the large commercial companies and that the role of the government vis-à-vis the computer would be quite different from what it had been during the zesty days of my service at the Office of Naval Research."[110]

For her work at ONR Rees has been called "the architect of the first large-scale, comprehensively planned program of support for mathematical research." It has also been noted that her programs and policies had a strong influence on the structure of the National Science Foundation; she was both an exceptionally able administrator and an innovative thinker. With all the resources she could command she unstintingly encouraged the new areas of mathematical science that she had been instrumental in supporting at AMP: linear programming, operations research, computer development and application, and numerical analysis. Both the American Mathematical Society and the Institute of Mathematical Statistics adopted resolutions of appreciation for her work at ONR.[111]

In 1953 Rees was offered the position of dean of the faculty at Hunter College. By then she was ready to leave ONR. "I'm an academic," she stated. "I expected to have my life in academia." She also wanted to get married to the man she had been seeing for many years, and she wanted to return to New York. ONR had established the postwar pattern of federal support for universities, and Rees had built up her own model program for funding mathematical research. With the creation of the National

Science Foundation the concept was secure. Another possible motivation for the timing of the move was the change in administration. An interviewer asked Rees if she left Washington because Eisenhower came in. While not replying directly, she did admit, "When Mr. Eisenhower was elected president, the budget was cut . . . the Republicans cut budgets."[112]

6

AFTER THE WAR

In 1943 five young women joined the WAVES. Joan Deffes and Ida Rambo were from California; Rose Gonzales had grown up on a farm in Minnesota; Hazel Nilsen, born on a homestead in Wyoming, was living in Nebraska; and Terry Wiruth, from Illinois, was working at the Savannah Ordnance Depot near Dubuque, Iowa. None had ever been far from home before, and the train trip to Hunter College in New York City for boot training was a great adventure for them all. From New York the women were sent to California, where they volunteered for duty at the new Naval Ordnance Test Station, Inyokern (China Lake), in the desert north of Los Angeles. In spite of the primitive conditions of a station still under construction they fell in love with the desert and never left. When the war ended they married and settled down at China Lake, continuing to work for the navy as civilians. They are still there today, their lives changed, expanded, and enriched by the few years they spent in the navy more than fifty years ago.[1] Like the China Lake Waves, our four improbable warriors found themselves and their lives irrevocably changed by their war service.

In 1947, following a year of research in Copenhagen where she held a

Rask-Orsted Foundation Grant and received the Johannes Schmidt Bronze Medal, Mary Sears returned to work full time as a scientist at Woods Hole. She built a house and settled down to being primarily an editor of oceanographic journals. Prevented from actively pursuing hands-on research, Sears turned instead to the advancement of the marine sciences by editing books and journals. Through her wartime navy assignment she had worked with many oceanographers, and the contacts thus established proved invaluable after the war. She became a founding editor of the internationally renowned oceanographic journal *Deep-Sea Research,* editing it from 1953 to 1974, and she helped to establish and edit the journal *Progress in Oceanography.* Her control over the selection of papers gave her a powerful influence on the direction of the postwar field. Sears also edited WHOI's *Annual Report,* its annual volume of *Collected Reprints,* and a number of other books, notably *Oceanography* (1961), a compendium of marine sciences that set the standard for the evaluation of marine research. She authored or coauthored only eleven publications, a very slim record for a scientist, but a record more than made up for when her vast collection of index cards was amalgamated and published in a fifteen-volume *Oceanographic Index.* In addition to her editing activities, Sears organized international conferences on oceanography, beginning by serving as chairman of the Steering Committee for the first International Oceanographic Congress held at the United Nations in 1959.[2]

Both in her various editing roles and in a private capacity Sears kept up an extensive correspondence (Columbus Iselin called it "huge") with oceanographic friends and colleagues all over the world, including Denmark, Sweden, Russia, Japan, and England. Her home in Woods Hole and the various other houses she bought to rent out were always available to these international visitors. As she wrote to J. N. Carruthers of the National Institute of Oceanography in England, "Even in midsummer when my own house is full of guests, I might have a vacant apartment in another house I own—as I did this summer, which provided for my overflow!" Carruthers and his wife, friends of many years, responded that they would "always have a very warm corner in our hearts for your abundant and unforgettable kindness to us both." Undoubtedly Sears was a wonderful hostess, and according to Mary Swallow, her longtime coeditor of *Deep-Sea Research,* she was also "a splendid cook and housekeeper."[3]

These contacts and her indefatigable attendance at international conferences gave Sears an influence on the emerging science of oceanography and the careers of budding oceanographers well beyond what might be expected from her official role. Much of this influence was exercised informally. While she herself was never in a position to hire and fire directly, many who were sought her advice. Her blunt yet fair assessments were respected and usually followed. In 1980 Roger Revelle, a longtime friend, called Sears "an institution within an institution at Woods Hole." She was, moreover, "the conscience of oceanography who initiated and maintained an uncompromising standard of excellence in scientific publications about the oceans. . . . She played a major role in creating the present world community of oceanographers from numerous countries and almost as many specialties."[4]

In spite of these accomplishments, Sears's life was deflected from her preferred path of active research and writing by gender bias. Toward the end of her career Sears told Betty Bunce, a junior colleague at WHOI and the first woman to sail in the institute's research vessels, that she envied her enormously. "I've spent all my years here, wanting desperately to take my data to sea," she admitted, "and no one would let me."[5]

Sears belonged to numerous professional organizations, among them the American Association for the Advancement of Science, the American Academy of Arts and Sciences, the Society of Women Geographers, and the American Geophysical Union. She was also deeply committed to local politics. She was active on the town's Republican Committee and was a long-standing town meeting member for the town of Falmouth. Another passion of hers was education. For more than two decades Sears sat on the Falmouth School Committee, serving as chair from 1960 to 1969, and at the same time maintained an active membership in the Massachusetts Association of School Committees.[6]

During her lifetime Sears received many honors in addition to the navy's recognition of her accomplishments. She received honorary doctor of science degrees in 1962 from Mount Holyoke College and in 1974 from Southeastern Massachusetts University (now UMass–Dartmouth). In 1992 Radcliffe College honored Sears with its Alumnae Recognition Award; in 1994 she was honored by WHOI's Women's Committee at its first Women Pioneers in Oceanography seminar; and in 1996 the Falmouth Business and Professional Women's Organization gave her its Woman of the Year Award.[7]

Even with all her other activities and interests, Sears was not ready to hang up her uniform when she returned to WHOI, so she transferred to the

Dr. Mary Sears
© *Tom Kleindinst, Woods Hole Oceanographic Institution*

naval reserve and became the officer in charge of Naval Reserve Research Company 1-8, Woods Hole. To maintain her reserve status, she had to spend two weeks each year on active duty. This meant annual "refurbishing" (letting out) of her uniform to ensure that it would fit. Her summer service was at the Office of Naval Research's branch in downtown Boston. When Sears first checked in there and asked what her duties would be, she was invited to go to the ONR library and brush up on her specialty. Careful search of the library revealed that the only book remotely dealing with oceanography was *Tides and Currents*, by Harald Sverdrup. When she saw it Sears felt a sense of familiarity and realized that she had probably contributed to portions of the book.[8]

Right after the war Sears had been afraid that the navy would lose interest in oceanography, perhaps even canceling its contracts with WHOI and Scripps. But Operation Crossroads and the need to understand the effects on navy ships and on the environment of atomic testing at Bikini Atoll made oceanography even more essential to the navy than before. Indeed, preparations for research activities at Bikini prior to the summer 1946 atomic bomb tests led to the development of a whole new branch of physical oceanography—experimental oceanography. So Sears was kept busy on reserve weekends and at the mandatory annual two-week stints working on oceanographic research projects for the navy. Finally, after twenty years in the reserve, Sears retired as a commander in 1963, although she remained active in the Association of Retired Naval Officers. What was to have been just a short wartime interruption of her civilian scientific career had turned into two decades of military service. Her postwar work for the Office of Naval Research was as competent as her wartime work, and was recognized as such.[9]

When word of her retirement from the naval reserve got around, Sears received a number of interesting job offers. One, from Rear Adm. Charles W. Thomas, USCG (Ret.), the assistant director of the Hawaii Institute of Geophysics, would have taken Sears to Honolulu, where she had tried to go with the WAVES twenty years earlier. However, she turned down the opportunity to head biological oceanography at the institute with the comment that she would not feel comfortable in the Pacific and was perfectly happy at Woods Hole. Sears received many other letters from serving naval officers who had known her. Typical was one from Capt. J. W. Jockusch, who had just left Washington to take up a new position as commanding officer of the San Francisco branch of ONR. Jockusch wrote that not long after he first arrived in Washington after the war, "word came to me of you and your work, both as Reserve Officer and in the scientific community. Certainly you have been one of the adornments of our Naval Reserve, and I mean this literally."[10]

Undoubtedly, Mary Sears did adorn the navy with her accomplishments, yet by almost any definition she was an improbable warrior. Even her name was a military handicap. When she was signing her first official navy forms, Sears left blank the space for a middle name as she did not have one. That would not do for navy regulations, however, and Sears was informed that if she had no middle name she must write "none" in the space provided. Sears complied under protest, and with very bad grace, frequently complaining about this little bit of bureaucratic inanity. For the rest of her life she was known to many old friends as "Mary None Sears."[11]

Sears had been under no obligation to volunteer her services to the navy for the duration of the war. In doing so she gave up, albeit temporarily, the work she loved. Her sacrifice did not pass unnoticed by navy authorities. On the occasion of her transfer to the retired reserve in 1963, Vice Adm. W. R. Smedberg, after expressing "sincere regret" at her retirement, wrote for the CNO: "Our country owes a debt of gratitude to you and to others of your caliber who, during your most productive years, sacrificed so much by making your service available to your country."[12]

Sears's assessment of her own career was modest in the extreme. Her correspondence abounds with invitations for her to appear as a guest speaker or to receive certain honors, most of which she turned down. Typical was her reply to a request from the American Geophysical Union's Visiting Scientist Program: "Since I am a biological oceanographer I doubt that I belong in the program outlined." Yet Sears was uncompromising in her editorial judgment, even when it was informally sought. For example, she answered an inquiry from a Russian oceanographer about Rachel Carson's book *The Sea around Us* that it "was a popular book and a so-called 'best seller.' The layman found it 'fascinating,' but I myself could never 'wade' through it!"[13] When the Radcliffe Alumnae Association, in recognition of her accomplishments, wrote that Sears had been head of the U.S. Navy Hydrographic Office, she was deeply embarrassed. "Only admirals ever head that office," she hastened to correct them. She might have been even more embarrassed had she read Columbus Iselin's observation that she "practically ran the Hydrographic Office single-handed."[14]

In 1977 Sears turned down a request to be interviewed for the Oral History Archives at Texas A&M University on the grounds that she had always had a very poor memory. Furthermore, she continued, "I do not verbalize well, although I am sometimes quite opinionated." She completely rejected the notion that she had "helped shape the discipline of modern oceanography," although that was the reason for the interview. Overlooking her two honorary degrees, Sears maintained that she had neither "been very productive as a scientist" nor "held any policy-making position." She did not even mention her wartime service in the navy.[15]

Sears's lifelong devotion to the internationalization of science was also a posture unexpected in a warrior, although it was right in line with Henry Bigelow's original vision for WHOI. He always intended Woods Hole to be a home for interdisciplinary as well as international studies, maintaining what was sometimes referred to as an open-door policy for research. Sears followed this intellectual scientific tradition, collecting half of the papers for a 1955 volume commemorating the twenty-fifth anniversary of WHOI from foreign scholars.[16]

In 1962, at the height of the cold war, a Russian scholar from the Geographical Society of the USSR sent Sears a copy of his book because, as he noted in the accompanying letter, "you do so much for international cooperation in the science of the sea." Sears was no pushover professionally, though, and believed it was essential to keep up with the Russians in oceanography because they had "the biggest research vessels, the most oceanographers, and arrive on the scene early and stay late."[17] Furthermore she made a very sharp distinction between science and politics. Earlier that year Sears, a lifelong and very active Republican, had written an old friend that "Russian and American scientists get on well together," but added, "Mind you I am talking about the scientists themselves, not their governments. *That is an entirely different matter.* Ten days in Moscow gave me the jitters." Yet in 1968, Sears characteristically rejected a request to join the editorial board of *Oceans* magazine, explaining bluntly that she was "bothered by the acute sense of nationalism that seems to be developing in non-professional periodicals." And she continued, "I would not want my name associated with anything of this sort, for scientists the world over are and should be friends working together. This, I believe . . . is a force for good in a warring world."[18]

Nonetheless, Sears continued to serve with pride in the U.S. Naval Reserve during peacetime, just as she continued to believe in her principled participation in the navy's scientific effort during World War II. Invited to meet Emperor Hirohito of Japan (well known as a student of oceanography) on his visit to WHOI in 1975, Sears declined because of a previous inescapable commitment. But she could not resist adding a postscript to her letter of refusal noting that her absence was probably just as well since she was afraid the words "World War II" might creep into her conversation, "innocuously, of course."[19]

Mary Sears died at her home in Woods Hole on 2 September 1997 at the age of ninety-two. In a note written some time earlier, her longtime friend and colleague Columbus O'Donnell Iselin, who was surely well qualified to judge, stated that Mary Sears "has done as much for the advancement of oceanography as anyone I know."[20] For a woman in a profession dominated by men such praise is sweet indeed. Perhaps sweeter still is the new oceanographic survey ship, T-AGS 65, launched on 19 October 2000 at the Halter Marine Shipyard in Mississippi and christened USNS *Mary Sears.*

After the war our second improbable warrior, Florence van Straten, became a civilian atmospheric physicist, eventually serving as lead analyst

Dr. Florence van Straten, Navy Weather Service meteorologist, 1958
National Archives photo no. 428-N-710258

and policy adviser in the Office of the Naval Weather Service, Chief of Naval Operations. In those days she frequently attended meetings of the Joint Meteorological Committee with Captain Orville, the postwar director of the Naval Weather Service. Among the subjects under discussion was numerical weather analysis and forecasting, which, as van Straten had predicted, became a practical possibility in the late 1940s and 1950s with the availability of high-speed computers.[21]

One of van Straten's first postwar assignments concerned long-range missiles. The navy was convinced that atmospheric conditions such as wind, temperature, and density would affect the flight of the new long-range missiles designed to enter the upper atmosphere, yet little was known about conditions at those heights. Consequently the Naval Weather Service established a project to use balloons to retrieve data in the atmosphere to a height of 100,000 feet. Van Straten was named to direct a program to prepare and analyze the data obtained. Her office eventually produced four detailed technical reports with the results of the analysis of the thousands of observations made from numerous locations scattered from Greenland to Japan. The reports were issued as they were completed over the course of two years and were available for immediate use by scientists. Until these reports some scientists had thought the stratosphere—30,000 to 40,000 feet above the earth—an area of storm-free calm. Van Straten's reports shattered that complacent belief by demonstrating that there were winds in the stratosphere of such strength that they caused violent oscillation to balloons with seventy-pound weights attached. Her analytical work on the conditions of the upper atmosphere assisted materially in the development of long-range missile technology.[22]

Van Straten was also engaged in work to improve the technology of high-atmosphere weather balloons. She designed equipment and developed new techniques, some successful, others not. She took out a patent on a sonic device to prevent ice formation on airplane wings, but it was not pursued any further. On the other hand, she created a radar-facsimile system to plot scope information automatically that the navy did develop. She also engaged in research in metal-gas catalysis, the upper atmosphere, and atmospheric physics.

Working on her own, van Straten began a study to investigate the pattern of radioactive fallout that could be expected in case of an atomic bomb attack on the United States. She knew that radioactive particles followed definite patterns influenced by atmospheric conditions that led to different densities at different locations not necessarily related to proximity to the explosion site. Moreover, she knew radioactive particle densities varied over time. She therefore formulated a scientific procedure for computing radioactive fallout patterns under all possible atmospheric conditions. After some revision and recalculation van Straten was ready to present her study, which the navy soon adopted. As a result, navy aerologists were able to plot graphs identifying the pattern of radioactive fallout under daily atmospheric conditions, and could direct ships away from potential zones of heavy concentration. This innovative work, which she had accomplished on her own initiative, was recognized in 1956 when van Straten was presented with the navy's Meritorious Civilian Service Award.[23]

During her postwar service van Straten also pioneered new techniques for weather modification. Her idea was to drop a small quantity of powdered carbon, which absorbs heat, into a cloud. She reasoned that the difference in temperature between the water droplets in a cloud and the warmer carbon powder sticking to them would produce enough large globules of water to create rain. The navy let van Straten use a Hurricane Hunter plane for her experiment and assigned observer photographic planes to record the result. In a series of tests off the Florida coast between 23 and 31 July 1958, she established the feasibility of creating or destroying cloud formations and producing rain by injecting carbon black into the atmosphere. Although this was not the first time clouds had been turned into rain by artificial means, it was the first time it had been done in a tropical area. Using the same carbon black seeding technique, moreover, van Straten was the first person to cause new clouds to form in the sky. With only five dollars worth of carbon black she and the other navy scientists working with her broke up seven clouds into rain and created four new clouds measuring several thousand feet in diameter where there had been none before. The successful experiment was recorded on film, and the incredulous reaction of the observers was caught on audiotape. In the end, however, politics and career ambitions folded van Straten's scheme unrecognizably into other projects.[24]

In 1958 van Straten was named Woman of the Year by the Women's Wing of the Aero Medical Association for her contributions to the study of atmospheric physics. In 1959, when the Bureau of Ordnance was consolidated with the Bureau of Aeronautics to become the Bureau of Weapons, van Straten was assigned to work there. That same year she was also named Alumnus of the Year by Washington Square College of New York University for her meteorological work. She finally resigned from federal service in 1962 "because it wasn't as much fun anymore." After that she continued as a consultant for the navy on atmospheric physics, primarily concerned with defining atmospheric problems for computer solution.[25]

After retiring, van Straten returned to her first love, writing, and very successfully combined her two passions in *Weather or Not*, a popular treatment of meteorology published in 1966. She was also responsible for the publication "Radar as a Meteorological Tool," and she wrote articles on atmospheric radioactive fallout and radar, novels, short stories, and poems. Like Mary Sears and Grace Hopper, after the war van Straten continued to serve in the naval reserve, retiring with the rank of commander in March 1965. Little is known about her interests other than what is stated in her obituary: that she was a charter member, treasurer, and trustee of River Road Unitarian Church in Bethesda, Maryland; she was vice chairwoman of the Unitarian Universalist Housing Foundation; she tutored in public schools; and she volunteered at the Junior Village in Washington and at nursing homes, and made recordings for the blind. Florence van Straten died of cancer at her home in Bethesda on 25 March 1992 at the age of seventy-eight. She left no immediate survivors.[26]

After World War II our third improbable warrior, Grace Hopper, continued to work on UNIVAC for Eckert-Mauchly, Remington Rand, and Sperry (through all the company's various changes), at the same time also returning to teaching part time. For many years she taught a course or two at night, beginning at the University of Pennsylvania's Moore School with a seminar on "Computers and Their Future" and later teaching at George Washington University. She also remained an active navy reservist. When she turned sixty in 1966 the navy informed her that she had reached the mandatory retirement age, and on 31 December she was put on the naval reserve retired list with the rank of commander. "It was the saddest day of my life," she recalled.[27]

After only seven months without her, however, the navy recalled Hopper, and not just to the reserves but to temporary active duty in Washington. Initially her appointment was for six months only, but that six months stretched out to almost twenty years. At first she took a leave of absence from Sperry, but by 1971 it was clear that she would not be returning soon, so she converted her leave to retirement from the company. The navy was having trouble implementing the various versions of COBOL going around; not all were compatible with all computers. Hopper was the logical person to oversee a rigorous program of standardization and persuade the entire navy to use one standard COBOL. From 1967 to 1977, as director of the Navy Programming Languages Group in the Office of Information Systems Planning, Hopper undertook development of a COBOL certifier to check all COBOL compilers used by the navy for compatibility and standards.[28]

In 1973 Hopper was promoted to the rank of captain. Among her

Capt. Grace Hopper,
July 1974
*Courtesy Mary Murray
Westcote*

other assignments she helped to develop a tactical data system for nuclear submarines. In a 1979 interview when she was already seventy-three, Hopper was typically candid about her future options:

> When the Navy throws me out, which they are bound to do eventually, because I'm going to be over age, . . . since UNIVAC made me famous, they cannot afford to have me wandering around the country in a starving condition. Therefore, they will hire me back at an extremely high salary. So I may be back at UNIVAC before too long because the Navy is running out of money.[29]

Yet the navy would not throw her out for another seven years, in spite of her age, and perhaps in spite of her outspokenness. Never one to stand in awe of rank, she was forthright even when addressing the Joint Chiefs of Staff.

> And I went down and I told them, I said, "You're going to have to learn to listen to your juniors." They looked at me and I pointed out that they had piles of reports they had to read, major decisions to

make, and they had not had time to keep up with really rapidly changing technology. They were going to have to present their problems to
their juniors who would come up with solutions; they could put on
the political aspects and the strategic aspects, but they were going to
have to learn from their juniors because they were the ones that knew
today's technology.[30]

From 1977 to 1983 Hopper was at the Naval Data Automation Command Headquarters (NAVDAC) in Washington, D.C. Her mission, as
designed especially for her in the NAVDAC organizational manual, was
to "survey the state of the art in computer technology on a continuing
basis. Review and evaluate the new knowledge from all sources, government and civilian, to determine the applicability of such knowledge to
major design and development problems[, and to] . . . provide technical
assessments of the possibility of applying new concepts in existing systems."[31] "Amazing Grace," as her colleagues fondly called her, became
the navy's foremost propagandist for its computer program, serving as
NAVDAC's representative to learned societies, industry associations, and
technical symposia. In 1980 Hopper was awarded the Navy Meritorious
Service Medal, and three years later, although she was technically too
old, Secretary of the Navy John Lehman promoted her to the rank of
commodore, which was changed to rear admiral later that year by special
presidential appointment.[32]

Hopper enjoyed her second full-time navy stint. She had three apart-
ments in Washington, the largest of which had a magnificent view of the
capital. She needed all the space, as well as six or seven walk-in closets,
to house her many collections, including books, dolls, Wedgwood china,
clothes, and shoes. A lifelong knitter, Hopper relaxed by knitting beautiful
and complicated sweaters for her nieces and nephews. When she finally
retired, she would take her knitting with her to board meetings. According to her sister, Hopper also loved to shop, especially at Brooks Brothers,
and although her best-known photographs show her in uniform, she seldom wore one in summer, preferring her own extensive wardrobe instead.
Always aware of her worth when it came to negotiating a contract, one of
Hopper's happiest days was when she turned seventy and was earning a
full navy salary as well as receiving social security. When she finally retired
in 1986, Grace Hopper, then seventy-nine, was the oldest active officer in
the U.S. Navy.[33]

Never one to sit around, shortly after leaving the navy Hopper was hired as a senior consultant to the Digital Equipment Corporation, where she was still employed at the time of her death. After a lifetime of activity, slowing down was hard for Hopper. When President George Bush awarded her the National Medal of Technology in September 1991, she refused to attend the ceremony because she did not want to appear in the wheelchair to which she was by then confined.[34]

Hopper's long life was full of accomplishment and recognition. She published more than fifty papers and articles, most of them about programming languages, the design and applications of software, and the uses and misuses of computers. She received at least twenty-four honorary doctorates in science, letters, laws, and engineering. Her awards are too numerous to list, but among the most notable was the Legion of Merit in 1973. That same year Hopper became the first woman and the first person from the United States to be made a Distinguished Fellow of the British Computer Society. Of all the awards she received, however, Hopper was proudest of her first: the 1946 Naval Ordnance Development Award for her World War II work on the Mark I computer.[35]

In 1987 the navy named its impressive new computer center in San Diego for Grace Murray Hopper. Eleven years after that, Harvard tore down its computer center named for Howard Aiken, a caption in the university magazine reading "Aiken Adieu." Today, perhaps unfairly, Hopper's name is much better known than Aiken's, and it is she, not he, who symbolizes the navy's early computer scientists.[36]

Finally, our fourth improbable warrior, Mina Rees, returned to New York after her seven years at the Office of Naval Research and served as dean of the faculty at Hunter College from 1953 until 1961. In June 1955 she married Leopold Brahdy, a physician, and enjoyed with him a devoted relationship until his death in 1977. In 1961 Rees became the first dean of graduate studies in the newly created City University of New York, a position she held until 1968. Once again she had embarked on a significant experiment, this time to promote a large-scale program of graduate study in the arts and sciences by creating a graduate school based on a consortium of all the colleges in the university. At that time she was the only woman dean of a graduate school in a coeducational institution in the nation. According to her research assistant, Rees was absolutely the right person to take on this challenge. She "had an incredible mind and could zero in on things. She was knowledgeable in all fields" and determined to offer only programs that would meet her high standards for quality. She

Dr. Mina Rees with Prof. Richard Courant at his NYU retirement party,
June 1969
*Mina Rees Collection, City University of New York Graduate School and University
Center Archives*

recruited top people like Arthur Schlesinger Jr., Irving Howe, and Alfred
Kazan—well-known men of letters—and gradually built outward from
a core of only four programs. In 1968 Rees became the provost of the
Graduate Division, and finally, from 1969 to 1972 she served as the first
president of the Graduate School and University Center, CUNY.[37]

During those years she also accomplished other notable firsts. She was
the first recipient of the Mathematical Association of America's Award for
Distinguished Service to Mathematics (1962) and the first woman chairman of the Council of Graduate Schools in the United States (1970). In
December 1969 Rees became the first woman since its founding more than
a century earlier to be elected president of the 122,000-member American
Association for the Advancement of Science. Given that in mathematics,
physics, chemistry, geology, and astronomy the proportion of active senior researchers who were women was usually well below 10 percent, her
national recognition was a particularly notable accomplishment. In an

interview Rees once said that "being a mathematician is useful chiefly because it is highly correlated with a well-organized mind." According to those who worked closely with her, that was certainly true of her and, in part at least, helps to explain how she could achieve so much.[38]

Among her other accomplishments Rees was the recipient of eighteen doctorates in science, engineering, literature, and law. She was presented with the American Association of University Women's Achievement Award in 1965; the Chancellor's Medal, City University of New York, in 1972; the Public Welfare Medal, National Academy of Sciences, in 1983; and that same year was given the Distinguished Service Medal of Teacher's College, Columbia University. She edited and was part author of the three-volume *Summary Technical Report, Applied Mathematics Panel*, and published thirty-one articles and papers.[39]

All of this recognition, of course, came at a cost. Although she was an accomplished cook and hostess, a swimmer, and with her husband a world traveler, hiker, and avid birdwatcher, Rees lamented that "the only trouble with my life is that I don't have time to sew."[40] She had traveled far from her sewing days during the Depression, and yet, like Hopper's knitting, Sears's gardening, and van Straten's writing, she never gave up that link to the satisfying pastimes of youth. When she retired in 1972 Rees was able to enjoy all of these pursuits while also remaining very active on numerous boards of directors and educational organizations. Mina Rees died in Manhattan on 25 October 1997 at the age of ninety-five.

"It is often said that OSRD is the war agency most admired by other Washington agencies," wrote James P. Baxter in September 1944. "Perhaps it would be more accurate to say that it is the agency which other agencies would praise first, or second only to themselves. It deserves a history worthy of its extraordinary performance." Professor Baxter proceeded to follow up on his words and wrote a preliminary 473-page "short history" of OSRD. This work by no means exhausted the vast historical material generated by OSRD; nor could it do justice to every participant. Even Warren Weaver received only fleeting mention, and the Applied Mathematics Panel only a few references. Mina Rees does not appear in the book at all.

Baxter's intention was to follow this book with a multivolume, all-encompassing long history, but Baxter's duties at Williams College forced him to withdraw from the project. Letters went out from Vannevar Bush urging all OSRD divisions to undertake the work themselves for their own areas before the OSRD disbanded and everyone scattered. Numerous volumes were eventually produced and published under various titles. In any event, however, AMP decided against preparing the history, a project that Thornton Fry, by then the panel's acting chief, told Rees gave him "a pain in the neck that radiates for about six feet in all directions."[41]

In fact, nobody was willing to assume the task. There was no report on computing because John von Neumann, who had started one during the war, ultimately decided that he was not ready to write a final report on a subject that was still so much in a state of change. Like Hopper, he was moving into an unpredictable future. Some panel members suggested that Rees should write the AMP history, but apparently she declined. Her view, as expressed to Weaver in January 1946, was "that an adequate account of the Panel's history has been written in the preparation of the Summary Technical Report and of the Summary Report of Projects," which she would have ready shortly. "It is to be noted, however," she added, "that both of these are classified documents while it is intended that the OSRD history shall be published." Thornton Fry was left to explain to James Conant at OSRD that "the question of omitting an account of the Panel from the history of OSRD has been discussed with the members of the Panel, and the decision to omit such an account has been approved by them." In 1946 the three-volume *Summary Technical Report, Applied Mathematics Panel, NDRC* was printed under the auspices of OSRD with Rees as chairman of the board of editors and as editor and partial author of volume 2. But as Rees had pointed out, these volumes were not for general circulation. Every page was printed with the word "confidential," and there were limited numbered copies produced, with distribution restricted to those who had the proper clearance. The Department of Defense finally declassified the three volumes in 1960.[42]

THE FOUR WOMEN profiled in this book were among the few of their sex allowed to contribute their exceptional abilities and specialized training to the war effort. World War II rhetoric strongly deplored a national shortage of scientists and eagerly sought to find women with scientific training, but the truth seems to be that even highly qualified women were usually welcome only at the lowest positions, especially in industry. Women were recruited to teach science in universities, but when peace arrived the briefly suspended antinepotism rules that prevented spouses from working at the same institution were reinstated. It was generally the wives who left. Even during the war, in both industry and academia, men were promoted and women only filled the gaps. Although the number of women scientists doubled in those four years, most of the women held only bachelor's degrees and languished at the bottom of the career pyramid. In general, women scientists had done better working for the government. Although OSRD employed disappointingly few women in its extensive research efforts, the Manhattan Project hired at least eighty-five women scientists and engineers, many of whom made significant contributions. When the war ended, however, although some of these women went on to distinguished careers, others became so discouraged that they left science altogether. The employment of women scientists is estimated to have dropped 10 percent right after the war, and it was not just married women who left. Many single women were forced out for fear they might get married. The message was clear: women were expected to move over, make way for the returning men, and once again devote themselves to hearth and home.[43]

Many women, perhaps most, accepted this as a return to normalcy. There seems to be general scholarly agreement that after World War II "the majority of women continued to define themselves primarily as wives and mothers," and those who had to work were once again generally confined to traditional lower-paying feminized jobs. Many who had had positions of responsibility and perhaps even status during the war were forced to give these up to returning veterans. By the 1950s many of the women veterans who had returned to the civilian workforce held positions as secretaries. Many others, as before the war, were teachers, bank tellers, nurses, telephone operators, and social workers. Very few had jobs that related to their wartime occupations, and there were even fewer whose careers had been enhanced by their service to their country. World War II had been too brief to fundamentally change people's beliefs about the role of women in society. While the public image of acceptable occupations for women changed suddenly in response to the manpower shortages of the war, the change was generally accepted as a temporary expedient. Only after women had largely given back their wartime jobs to men did the influence of their accomplishments begin to be felt.[44]

Many women veterans who might have gone on for further education either did not know about the GI Bill or did not realize that it applied to them. This was hardly surprising because women had constituted less than

3 percent of the sixteen million service personnel, but it was also not accidental. Little was done to publicize the fact that the educational benefits were to apply equally to all, and in many cases women who did apply for college were told that all the places had been taken by men.[45]

The immediate postwar period that was so productive for Sears, van Straten, Hopper, and Rees was generally not good for women in science. Even highly trained women, or perhaps especially they, had a tough time in the job market. They continued to be underemployed, and women students gravitated to a few "soft" disciplines such as psychology, sociology, economics, and geography where it was possible for them to earn doctorates (and where there was less money), rather than to physics or engineering, where they were strongly discouraged by university faculties. The numbers gradually crept up, but it took persistence and time. In 1954–55 women were 10.50 percent of all mathematicians (there are no separate statistics for computer scientists), 10.74 percent of all biological scientists (with no category for oceanography), and 1.41 percent of all meteorologists in the country. By 1970 the numbers for women had improved to 11.15 percent of computer scientists, 11.43 percent of mathematicians, 1.54 percent of meteorologists, and 12.92 percent of those in the biological sciences.[46]

Signs of change began to be evident in the mid-1960s when, for example, the Danforth Foundation first opened its graduate fellowships to women. But the Ford Foundation continued to tie its grant money to the goal of completing the doctorate in four years, and there was strong resistance among the elite universities to part-time students and flexible schedules that would have made it possible for married women and mothers to attain graduate degrees.[47]

The great change in science after the war, when direct government funding for research became the norm in universities, had brought a steady increase in available money. This was true even though academic research represented less than 10 percent of federal expenditure on science and technology. On demobilization, army air forces meteorologist Charles Bates joined a meteorological consulting firm. In 1948 he wrote his wartime colleague Mary Sears to ask for some WHOI publications. "I wish we could argue over a beer whether scientists working for a firm are profit-making while those working for an institution are not," he wrote, evidently in response to a comment of hers. "Frankly," he continued, the biggest money-makers today are certain universities—for a struggling firm like us to land a contract of $100,000 is going to be tough going, yet Harvard, MIT, yes, even WHOI and SIO [Scripps] get them quite regularly and charge as much overhead as any private business concern. In fact, the U. of Washington is turning down a $50,000 contract because the overhead is only 40%! Jeepers—our overhead is about 5%—and you accuse us of making a profit![48]

The lack of basic research coming from devastated Europe and the buildup of the cold war further encouraged the trend in government funding. By 1968, Harvey Brooks, physicist and dean of the Division of Engineering and Applied Physics at Harvard University, could write: "In a remarkably short time the federal government has become the principle patron of science and of advanced education in the sciences and technology." At that time federal funds supported 70 percent of academic research. Acceptance of this situation came too late for Howard Aiken, however, as by then he had already retired from Harvard, in part over the issue of science funding. In general, too, it was many years before women were in a position to take advantage of the new structure of science.[49]

The number of women in the military was even lower than the number of women in the sciences. Nineteen-seventy was the watershed year when events forced Richard Nixon to go for all-volunteer armed forces. Nevertheless, it was 1973 before women were fully integrated into the army, navy, air force, Marine Corps, and Coast Guard, and in that year they formed only 2.5 percent of the armed forces, having been freed from the 2 percent ceiling imposed by the 1948 Women's Armed Services Integration Act. The number increased gradually to close to 10 percent a decade later, finally reaching an all-time high of 14.1 percent in June 1999. It was 1970 before any woman attained star rank, 1972 before the first woman—the chief of the Navy Nurse Corps—became an admiral, and 1976 before women were admitted to the service academies, ensuring a regular supply of well-trained women officers.[50]

While our improbable warriors were grand exceptions to the norm, the potential for change had indeed been unleashed during World War II, and though for a time afterward all the gains seemed to be lost, in fact they were not. In many cases it was the unmarried women like Sears, van Straten, Hopper, and Rees who prevented women in the professional world from losing their hard-won positions. They kept and built on the gains they had made, and while denying they were trailblazers they slowly moved the whole process forward, whether they meant to or not.

Much work has yet to be done before anyone can speak with authority about the contribution of women scientists to victory in World War II. Here, at least, is a beginning, a tale of four women, three in the U.S. Navy, whose motives and wartime accomplishments demonstrate what is possible when unusual opportunities are seized by an intelligent, hardheaded, and persistent few.

NOTES

Chapter 1. Women at War: An Overview

1. Parts of this chapter appeared previously in Kathleen Broome Williams, "Women Ashore: The Contribution of WAVES to U.S. Naval Technology in World War II," *The Northern Marine/Le Marin du Nord* 8, no. 2 (1998): 1–20. Statement by Adm. William H. P. Blandy, USN, U.S. Navy Press Release, 30 July 1947, Women in Regular Navy—Official Correspondence (1946–48), roll 13, series I, Records of the Assistant Chief of Naval Personnel for Women, 1942–72 [hereafter ACNP(W)], microfilm. The original collection is in the Operational Archives, Naval Historical Center, Washington, D.C.

2. Statement by Adm. Louis Denfeld, USN, U.S. Navy Press Release, 30 July 1947, Women in Regular Navy—Official Correspondence (1946–48), roll 13, series I, ACNP(W).

3. Zimmerman, *Top Secret Exchange,* 4.

4. Bates and Fuller, *America's Weather Warriors,* 52–53.

5. Rossiter, *Women Scientists in America, 1940–1972,* 14.

6. For quote, Gildersleeve, *The "Waves" of the Navy,* 267; Letters/Memorandum to District/Air Command Directors (1943–48), roll 4, series I, ACNP(W).

7. Mildred McAfee Horton, interview by John T. Mason Jr., typescript of tape recording, August 1969, 84, Oral History Office, U.S. Naval Institute, Annapolis. For a concurring view, see *History of the Women's Reserve,* 2 vols., 1:37, U.S. Naval Administrative Histories of World War II, no. 88 [hereafter *WAVES History,*], 1946 Navy Department Library, Naval Historical Center, Washington, D.C. [hereafter NDL/NHC]. This official history of the wartime WAVES notes that lack of professional indoctrination and guidance caused difficulties that lasted for fifteen months.

8. *WAVES History,* 1:2, 8, NDL/NHC; Lillian Budd, "Yesterday's News—World War I," *Register* [Newsletter of Women in Military Service for America Memorial Foundation] (winter 1996–97): 8.

9. *WAVES History,* 1:4–6, NDL/NHC.

10. *WAVES History,* 1:6–8, NDL/NHC.

11. Rear Admiral Jacob's and Senator Andrew's quotes are from Senate hearings on S.2527, 19 May 1942, Hearings on WAVES Legislation and Public Laws, 1942–48, roll 19, series III, ACNP(W). See also Hancock, *Lady in the Navy,* 55–56; *WAVES History,* 1:10–12, 15, 361, NDL/NHC.

12. Senate hearings on S.2527, 19 May 1942, Hearings on WAVES Legislation and Public Laws, 1942–48, roll 19, series III, ACNP(W).

13. Davidson, *The Unsinkable Fleet*, 128–31.

14. *WAVES History*, 1:235, NDL/NHC; Hancock, *Lady in the Navy*, 61. Limitations on rank and restrictions on promotion were eased somewhat on 25 November 1943 with the passage of Public Law 441; Hancock, *Lady in the Navy*, 69.

15. Holm, *Women in the Military*, 24–25, 30, 33; Larson, *'Til I Come Marching Home*, 29; Soderbergh, *Women Marines*, 159; Willenz, *Women Veterans*, 27.

16. *New York Times*, 9 May 1942, for coast watcher; Evans, *Born for Liberty*, 220–24; Telegram from Mrs. Robert Weeks Kelley to Rear Adm. Randall Jacobs, 24 June 1942, box 2329, Bureau of Personnel [hereafter BuPers], Record Group [hereafter RG] 24, National Archives, College Park, Md. [hereafter NA2]; Miss Hy Lee Small to Lt. Cdr. Charles Bittenger, Navy Department, 24 June 1942, box 1197, Bureau of Ships [hereafter BuShips], RG19, NA2.

17. Campbell, *Women at War*, 22–23; Kennedy, *Freedom from Fear*, 787; Nofi, *Marine Corps Book of Lists*, 18.

18. "Women Market for WAVES," 2 October 1942, roll 13, series II, ACNP(W); Rupp, *Mobilizing Women*, 168–69, maintains that the financial incentive was an important factor in explaining more successful mobilization of American than German women. However, this argument does not explain why many American women officers were prepared to accept a cut in pay to serve in the military. See Willenz, *Women Veterans*, for high-paying defense jobs.

19. Lt. Cdr. J. Harrison to Director of Public Relations, Subj. Recruitment of WAVES, 27 May 1944, Esso Recruiting Drive, 1944, ACNP(W) Papers, Shelf File box 1, Operational Archives [hereafter OA], Naval Historical Center, Washington, D.C. [hereafter NHC]; "Uniforms for Women," *Smithfield (N.C.) Herald*, 25 February 1944; "Navy Is Seeking Women, while Men Still Direct the Show," *Henderson (N.C.) Dispatch*, 21 February 1944; W. M. Sherrill, "Join the Service and Get a Girdle, Should Boost Women's Groups," *Concord (N.C.) Tribune*, 15 February 1944.

20. Jacobs to SecNav, 13 May 1943, roll 3, series I, ACNP(W); Holm, *Women in the Military*, 53; the historian quoted is Soderbergh, *Women Marines*, xvi; for Britain, see Braybon and Summerfield, *Out of the Cage*, 157–60.

21. "Rechecking Deferments," *Durham (N.C.) Herald*, 1 March 1944; quote is from "The 900,000," *Durham (N.C.) Sun*, 28 February 1944; for scientists, see Sapolsky, *Science and the Navy*, 20.

22. Stewart, *Organizing Scientific Research*, 262–63, 276–77.

23. Rossiter, *Women Scientists in America, 1940–1972*, 4–7; see chapter 1 for a thorough and detailed survey of the work of scientific women in World War II.

24. Ibid., 4–5, 7.

25. Ibid., 2–7; Ambrose et al., *Journeys of Women in Science and Engineering*, 20.

26. For the Mothers' Movement, see Jeansonne, *Women of the Far Right*.

27. This information is from Haruko Cook and Theodore Cook, *Japan at War,* and from correspondence with them. There is regrettably little in English about Japanese women during the war other than a number of accounts of comfort women. See, e.g., Hicks, *The Comfort Women.*

28. Stephenson, *Women in Nazi Society,* 177, 186–87; see Rupp, *Mobilizing Women,* 6–7, 10, for German versus U.S. mobilization of women.

29. *New York Times,* 13 December 1942.

30. Margaret Bassett, hired 9 July 1943, Monthly Payroll Book of Chapel St. Branch, Receiving Tube Division, Raytheon Corp., Raytheon Archives, Lexington, Mass.; and see, e.g., *Raytheon News* 1, no. 2 (16 July 1943): 14; and 1, no. 9 (5 November 1943): 11. For statistics, see Dunnigan and Nofi, *Dirty Little Secrets of World War II,* 122; Willentz, *Women Veterans,* 30; Dunnigan and Nofi, *Dirty Little Secrets of the Vietnam War,* 4–5.

31. U.S. Office of Education, Information Bulletin, February 1942, file 127, box 8, A-128, Elizabeth Reynard Papers [hereafter Reynard Papers], Schlesinger Library [hereafter SL], Radcliffe Institute for Advanced Study, Cambridge, Mass.

32. Progress Report, 13 March 1942, Faculty National Service Committee, box 8, A-128, Reynard Papers, SL.

33. U.S. Office of Education, Information Bulletin, February 1942; Faculty National Service Committee Report of Progress, 13 March 1942; and School of Engineering to Dean Gildersleeve, 28 January and 19 February 1942, box 8, A-128, Reynard Papers, SL.

34. Margaret S. Morriss, Chairman, Committee on College Women and the War, 19 February 1943, box 16, series I, RG 3.0.5; Chancellor Harry W. Chase to Dr. Francis T. Brown of the American Council on Education, 25 February 1943, box 16, series I, RG 3.0.5, Harry W. Chase Administrative Papers, NYU Archives [hereafter Chase Papers, NYU].

35. Leila Sears to author, 10 July 2000.

36. "ESMDT Courses," undated memo, file 127, box 8, A-128, Reynard Papers, SL; "Eight WAVES Hold Important Posts in Office of Naval Research," Navy Department Press Release, 27 July 1947, Women in Regular Navy—Official Correspondence (1946–48), roll 13, series I, ACNP(W).

37. Among the distinguished women were Deans Margaret Disert of Wilson College, Dorothy Stratton of Purdue, Elizabeth Crandall of Stanford, and Louise Wilde of Rockford College. See Ebbert and Hall, *Crossed Currents,* 40; and "History of the Naval Reserve Midshipmen's School (WR), Northampton, MA," 15, in *WAVES History,* 1:242, NDL/NHC; Smith graduate Jane Newhall Lyons to author, 28 September 1996.

38. Respondents to author's questionnaires, e.g., Hazel Nilsen. Born on a homestead in Wyoming, Nilsen had her first streetcar ride and saw her first elevator on the day she enlisted in the navy. See also Alice Kinman Eubanks to Marie Alsmeyer, 27 October 1982, box 3, series III, Marie Bennett Alsmeyer, Personal Papers [here-

after Alsmeyer Papers], OA/NHC; for the WRNS, see Braybon and Summerfield, *Out of the Cage,* 198; quote is from Holm (ed.), *In Defense of a Nation,* 47.

39. "Miss Saltonstall Waves Seaman," *Boston Herald,* 2 September 1942; "Article for Army Navy Journal by Captain Mildred H. McAfee," October 1944, Speeches, Statements and Articles of Captain M. M. [McAfee] Horton (1943–45), roll 12, series I, ACNP(W); Willenz, *Women Veterans,* 24.

40. Secretary of the Navy James Forrestal, Press and Radio Release, 30 July 1946, Women in Regular Navy—Official Correspondence (1946–48), roll 13, series I, ACNP(W); Director, Flight Div., to Admin. Re. "Enlisted WAVES with Communications Training for Navy Weather Central, Urgent Need for," 25 March 1943, box 1, Aer. Sec., RG38, NA2.

41. *Enlist in the WAVES, Serve in the Hospital Corps,* U.S. Government Printing Office pamphlet, 1943, folder "Memorabilia, Misc.," series II, box 3, Alsmeyer Papers, OA/NHC; "The Utilization of Womanpower in Navy Billets, Officer and Enlisted," 4 May 1951, Bureau of Naval Personnel, Various Status of Women Reports (1951–64), roll 13, series I, ACNP(W).

42. Papers in the personal collection of Elisabeth Gaskill Coombs, including copies of orders, certificates of training, her Officer Qualification Questionnaire, a biographical sketch, photographs, and a certificate of honorable discharge. See also Commander, Naval Air Training Station, to BuPers, 30 May 1944, box 33, Bureau of Medicine and Surgery [hereafter BuMed], RG52, NA2.

43. "Jam Handy" operators were film projectionists. The Jammison Handy Corporation made an enormous number of films for commercial and industrial operations from the 1930s into the 1950s, and apparently they had a special simplified projection system. BuMed to Capt. John B. Farrier, 18 September 1943, box 33, BuMed, RG52, NA2; BuMed to BuPers re. Establishment of requirements for clinical training, 19 July 1944, box 33, BuMed, RG52, NA2; Request from BuAer for development of aptitude tests, 15 February 1943, box 33, BuMed, RG52, NA2; BuPers memo to Vice Adm. McIntire re. WAVE corpsmen, 27 June 1944, box 28, BuMed, RG52, NA2.

44. BuPers memorandum: list of specialties open to WR, 20 March 1945, Policies for the Administration of Women's Reserve (1943–69), 15, roll 9, series I, ACNP(W); Holm (ed.), *In Defense of a Nation,* 73; and "Women Reservists Rapidly Relieving Men for Sea Duty," Navy Department Press Release, 23 December 1942, 2, box 2, A-128, Reynard Papers, SL. "I asked an ensign about the Mechanical Corps, and the blueprinting. She said enlisted WAVES don't make the blueprints, just build the airplane motors etc. from the blueprints available." Marie Bennett to her parents, 10 May 1943, folder May 1943, series I, box 1, Alsmeyer Papers, OA/NHC; 18 percent of WACs served in technical and professional fields according to Willenz, *Women Veterans,* 22.

45. *All Hands,* no. 339 (June 1945): 55.

46. "Charting the Road to Tokyo," *All Hands,* no. 331 (October 1944): 27; for

Adm. Bryan's quote, see McAfee speech: "Recruiting for North Carolina," 9 February 1944, Speeches, Statements and Articles of Captain M. M. Horton (1943–45), roll 12, series I, ACNP(W).

47. All the above information on Sears is from her biographical file in the Wellesley College Archives, Wellesley, Mass. Materials include Appendix to the President's Report, 1938; Letter from Department of Zoology and Physiology to College Recorder, 28 September 1939; *Wellesley Magazine,* December 1939, 98; Wellesley College Office of Publicity Press Release, 15 August 1941; and press clippings.

48. "List of Billets," 1 December 1942, 1–8, file 44, box 2, A–128, Reynard Papers, SL.

49. Author's interview with Terry Wiruth, 30 December 1996, Ridgecrest (China Lake), Calif.

50. House Armed Services Committee Subcommittee 3, hearings on S.1641, 18 February 1948, roll 19, series III, ACNP(W).

51. "General Statistics Concerning Women Reservists Assigned to the Third Naval District," 7 March 1943, box 8, A-128, Reynard Papers, SL.

52. See, e.g., "A Chronological Record of the Naval Training School (Pre-Radar) Harvard University, 23 June 1941–31 March 1945," Cambridge, Mass., 1 April 1945, HUE 61.3145, Harvard University Archives [hereafter HUA].

53. Ebbert and Hall, *Crossed Currents,* 53–55; for Jacksonville, response to author's questionnaire from Dorothy Wells Black; *BuPers: The Story of Navy Manpower,* 37.

54. *All Hands,* no. 319 (October 1943): 41.

55. "Script for New Year's Day Broadcast by Captain Mildred H. McAfee," 1 January 1944, Speeches, Statements and Articles of Captain M. M. Horton (1943–45), roll 12, series I, ACNP(W); responses to author's questionnaire from Charlotte A. Potter and Rose Nudo Clement, 1996.

56. *BuPers: The Story of Navy Manpower,* 37; *War History of the NRL,* 108, U.S. Naval Administrative Histories of World War II, no. 134, 1 November 1946, NDL/NHC; and response to author's questionnaire from Marie Klein Lemlein, 1996.

57. Miscellaneous newspaper clippings, box 6, Grace Murray Hopper Papers, [hereafter Hopper Papers], Smithsonian Institution [hereafter Smithsonian]; author's interview with Ruth Brendel Noller, 23 December 1996, Sarasota, Fla.

58. *WAVES History,* 1:281, NDL/NHC.

59. Ibid., 300.

60. Senate Naval Affairs Committee hearing on H.R.2859, 29 September 1943, roll 19, series III, ACNP(W).

61. House Naval Affairs Committee hearing on H.R.5915, 9 May 1946, roll 19, series III, ACNP(W); and Navy Department Press Release, 27 June 1947, Women in Regular Navy—Official Correspondence (1946–48), roll 13, series I, ACNP(W); Lewis, "WAVES Forecasters," 2199, 2201.

62. House Armed Services Subcommittee 3, hearings on S.1641, 18 February 1948, Hearings on WAVES Legislation and Public Laws, 1942–48, roll 19, series III, ACNP(W).

63. House Naval Affairs Committee, 22 June 1944, Hearings on WAVES Legislation and Public Laws, 1942–48, roll 19, series III, ACNP(W).

64. House Armed Services Subcommittee 3, hearings on S.1641, 18 February 1948, Hearings on WAVE Legislation and Public Laws, 1942–48, roll 19, series III, ACNP(W).

65. Ibid.

66. Once again it was Congresswoman Edith Nourse Rogers, with Congresswoman Margaret Chase Smith, who fought for the survival of women in the American military. Eventually, separate titles of the Integration Act created a permanent place for women in each of the military services, including the new U.S. Air Force. Holm, *Women in the Military*, 113–22.

67. For changes brought by the war to women's lives, see Chafe, *Paradox of Change;* and for a contrary argument that war work had little lasting effect on women's social, economic, and professional roles, see, among others, Anderson, *Wartime Women;* and Campbell, *Women at War.*

68. Taylor, "Women-at-Arms," 136.

Chapter 2. Mary Sears: Oceanographer

1. Alexander, *Utmost Savagery,* 3.

2. CNO to Lt. Cdr. Mary Sears, 20 May 1946, Sears Papers in possession of Denton Family, Woods Hole, Mass. [hereafter Sears Papers, Denton Family]. I am grateful to Mr. and Mrs. Paul Denton, the heirs of Mary Sears, for access to her papers, including official documents spanning her entire naval career.

3. Sears said she was between five foot three and five foot four inches in height, "depending on the particular [navy] corpsman who measured me!" Sears to Miss Elaine L. Weygand, 4 October 1962, folder "Misc. Personal 1962," box 1, Mary Sears Papers, MC9 [hereafter Sears Papers], Woods Hole Oceanographic Institution Data Library and Archives [hereafter WHOI], Woods Hole, Mass. For the inbred comment: Sears to Rear Adm. Charles W. Thomas, USCG, 23 January 1964, folder "Misc. Personal (1963) 1964," box 1, Sears Papers, WHOI.

4. "Radcliffe Centennial Survey" filled in by hand by Mary Sears, Radcliffe College Alumna File, Schlesinger Library, Radcliffe Institute for Advanced Study, Cambridge, Mass. [hereafter Mary Sears Radcliffe Alumna File].

5. Quoted in Urdang, "Women of Achievement," 25. The book's title was not changed to *American Men and Women of Science* until the twelfth edition, 1971.

6. Mary Sears interview by Victoria Kaharl, 29 September 1989, typed transcript [hereafter Sears interview 1989], 28, Sears Papers, WHOI; Leila Sears written comments to author, 21 June 1999.

7. Six-page typed manuscript entitled "Answers to Security Questionnaire Submitted through WHOI on 11 April 1956" [hereafter Security Questionnaire], Sears Papers, Denton Family; *American Men of Science, Physical and Biological Sciences,* 10th ed.; Winsor School, *Yearbook for the Class of 1923,* 32–33, Sears Papers, WHOI.

8. Sears had the choice of picking a lock on the cleaning women's distant closet in the public part of the museum or walking across the street to the facilities in the Geology Museum. Sears interview 1989, 27–29, Sears Papers, WHOI.

9. Leila Sears to author, 14 June 1999.

10. Ibid., 7 July 1999.

11. Sears quote from "International Cooperation and Communication in the Marine Sciences," p. 4 of typescript of speech given by Sears in 1962 at a seminar on marine sciences, box 4, Sears Papers, WHOI; Raitt and Moulton, *Scripps,* 104–27; Fye, "Woods Hole," 1–2.

12. Much of the information in this paragraph, including quotes, comes from a bundle of thirty-five handwritten pages of notes by Mary Sears. They are in no particular order and have no title and no dates, but were clearly written late in her life. Hereafter these notes will be referred to as Sears's History of WHOI, folder "Sears, Mary, MS of WHOI History," no box, Sears Papers, WHOI.

13. Bigelow's 1930 report was entitled "Report on the Scope, Problems and Economic Importance of Oceanography, on the Present Situation in America, and on the Handicaps to Development, with Suggested Remedies"; Burstyn, "Reviving American Oceanography," 59–61, 64. Also located in the small village of Woods Hole, and adding to the attraction of the place as a scientific center, was the Bureau of Fisheries Laboratory.

14. Haedrich and Emery, "Growth of an Oceanographic Institution," 81. In Europe, and particularly in Scandinavia, the term *oceanography* was applied only to the study of the physics and chemistry of the oceans. Raitt and Moulton, *Scripps,* 128.

15. Burstyn, "Reviving American Oceanography," 65.

16. The three oceanographers were T. Whelan Borne at Scripps, Dr. Bigelow at Harvard, and Tommy Thompson, a chemist at the University of Washington. Sears interview 1989, 5, 7, Sears Papers, WHOI; Sears's History of WHOI, Sears Papers, WHOI. "Harvard Yacht Club" remark is from Susan Schlee, "The R/V *Atlantis,*" 50.

17. A possible exception to the no Ph.D. rule noted by Sears was Lt. Edward H. Smith, "the Coast Guard guy, and he got a Ph.D. at Harvard [in 1925]," Sears interview 1989, 7, Sears Papers, WHOI. Also Gary E. Weir, "Finding a Niche: Columbus O'Donnell Iselin and Mobilizing Oceanography for War, 1940–41," unpublished paper presented at WHOI and later to the Physical Oceanography Seminar at the University of Rhode Island, 3, 6–7. Thirty-three years later, Sears recognized that, finally, "oceanography [was] a well recognized science." Sears to Capt. J. W. Jockusch, 28 August 1963, folder "Misc. Personal 1963," box 1, Mary Sears Papers,

WHOI; Burstyn, "Reviving American Oceanography," 65. For an assessment of Bjerknes's work, see Friedman, *Appropriating the Weather.*

18. Schlee, *Edge of an Unfamiliar World,* 65–67, 171, 249–52; Hughes, *A Century of Weather Service,* 19–28; Bates and Fuller, *America's Weather Warriors,* 6–8; Bush, *Modern Arms and Free Men,* 18–19.

19. Leila Sears written comments to author, 21 June 1999.

20. Sears's History of WHOI, Sears Papers, WHOI.

21. Ibid.

22. "In Memoriam," two-page printed obituary, Sears Papers, WHOI; Elizabeth T. Bunce transcript of interview by author, 10 July 1998, Woods Hole, Mass. [hereafter Bunce interview 1998], 16. Other early WHOI scientists came from Yale, MIT, and Rutgers; Sears interview 1989, 26, Sears Papers, WHOI.

23. "In Memoriam," Sears Papers, WHOI; *WHOI Report for the Year 1940,* 17, WHOI. The other woman on the staff in 1940 was Cornelia C. Carey, assistant professor of botany from Barnard College.

24. Sears interview 1989, 26, 32, Sears Papers, WHOI.

25. Sears's History of WHOI, Sears Papers, WHOI. *Head* is the term for toilet on a boat; Milliman, "Mary Sears—an Appreciation," 749; Meier, "Science Rewards Woman's High Aim," *Boston Evening Globe,* 21 May 1963; Schlee, "The R/V *Atlantis,*" 51.

26. For Revelle's remark, see his article "The Oceanographic and How It Grew," 13.

27. Sears, "Oceanography—Then and Now," five-page typescript, 11 June 1963, box 1, Sears Papers, WHOI.

28. Mary Sears, "Oceanography," *Winsor Graduate Bulletin* 14 (May 1947): 9, Sears Papers, WHOI [hereafter "Oceanography," Sears Papers, WHOI]; "Contract No. OEMsr-204, Monthly Reports for periods 8 December 1941 to 14 January 1942, through 15 July to 15 August 1942," folder: "Reports," box 15, UAV 885.95.5, WWII Government Contract Records, HUA; Sears, "Excerpt from Memoirs (Rough Draft)," two-page typed transcription in author's possession from Sears's own handwritten draft made sometime in the early 1990s [hereafter Sears Memoir], courtesy Charles Bates. According to the Denton Family, Sears began many drafts of her memoirs in her last years, though only a few fragments remain. In "Finding a Niche," Gary E. Weir, Naval Historical Center, gives an excellent account of WHOI activities 1940–41. Sears did not return to her Peruvian research until well after the war. In 1952 she wrote to a colleague that she had been a bit slow getting started again after the war, but that some short things were "now in the offing based on my trip to Peru in 1941." Sears to Prof. John E. G. Raymont, 20 March 1952, folder "R" 1949–59, box 1, Sears Papers, WHOI; Leila Sears to author, 14 June 1999.

29. "Contract No. OEMsr-204, Report for period 15 March to 15 April 1942," folder "Reports," box 15, UAV 885.95.5, WWII Government Contract Records, HUA.

30. *WHOI Report for the Years 1943, 1944, 1945,* 16, WHOI.

31. Iselin, "History of War Years," 3; G. S. Bryan to CNO, 9 October 1945, box 3, RG38, NA2.

32. Sears interview 1989, 5, 7, Sears Papers, WHOI; Iselin, "History of War Years," 4, 21, WHOI.

33. *WHOI Report for the Years 1943, 1944, 1945*, 15, WHOI; *WHOI Report for the Year 1946*, 19, WHOI; Raitt and Moulton, *Scripps*, 137–46.

34. *WHOI Report for the Years 1943, 1944, 1945*, 28–34, WHOI.

35. Quote is from Sears to Prof. John E. G. Raymont, 20 March 1952, folder "R" 1949–59, box 1, Sears Papers WHOI; *WHOI Report for the Years 1943, 1944, 1945*, 28–34, WHOI. See Weir, "Finding a Niche," for an explanation of the role of Columbus Iselin in getting war contracts for WHOI. Scripps, too, expanded during the war years: Raitt and Moulton, *Scripps*, 137–51.

36. For quote, see Sears interview 1989, 3, Sears Papers, WHOI; Director of Naval Procurement to Mary Sears, 17 November 1942, "Application for Women's Reserve, USNR," Sears Papers, Denton Family.

37. Sears, "Expansion of Oceanographic Work in the U.S. Navy Hydrographic Office during World War II," 1 [hereafter "Expansion of Oceanographic Work"], incomplete typewritten draft with handwritten corrections by Mary Sears, n.d., Sears Papers, WHOI; "Techniques for Forecasting Wind Waves and Swell" (U.S. Navy Hydro Publication No. 604, Washington, D.C., 1951), iv, box D-1860, Government Publications [hereafter Gov. Pub.], RG287, NA1; Seiwell, "Military Oceanography in Tactical Operations," 677. I am grateful to Charles Bates for information on Seiwell.

38. Sears, "Expansion of Oceanographic Work," 1, Sears Papers, WHOI; Raitt and Moulton, *Scripps*, 137; Sears Memoir; Sears interview 1989, 3, 13, Sears Papers, WHOI.

39. John Milliman, senior scientist at WHOI and in 1985 editor of *Deep-Sea Research*, wrote that Sears "was pressed into duty by Roger Revelle during WWII," Milliman, "Mary Sears," 749; Sears interview 1989, 3, 13, Sears Papers, WHOI; CNO to Mary Sears, 16 January 1943, "Waiver of physical defect for enlistment in the U.S. Naval Reserve," Sears Papers, Denton Family.

40. Milliman, "Mary Sears," 749; Mary Sears, "Oceanography," 9, Sears Papers, WHOI; *Hydrographic Office*, 195–96, 214, U.S. Naval Administrative Histories of World War II, no. 123 [hereafter *Hydro War History*], n.d., NDL/NHC; Annual Report of Hydro for FY ending 30 June 1944, p. 4, box 64, Hydro, RG37, NA1.

41. Chief of Naval Personnel to Lt. Mary Sears, 31 March 1943, "Appointment in the United States Naval Reserve," Sears Papers, Denton Family; Sears to Miss Pauline Wycoff, Scripps, 31 July 1958, folder "R" 1949–59, box 1, Sears Papers, WHOI; citation commending Cdr. Roger Revelle signed by James Forrestal, n.d., courtesy Charles Bates; Sears Memoir; Seiwell, "Military Oceanography," 677.

42. Hydrographer's Order No.10, 18 March 1942, box 2, A (Reports), Hydro Index 1924–45, RG37, NA1; CNO to Lt. Mary Sears, 31 March 1943, "Active duty with pay . . . ," Sears Papers, Denton Family.

43. Seiwell, "Military Oceanography in World War II," 202–3; Charles C. Bates, "Discussion of: 'Military Oceanography in Tactical Operations,' by H. R. Seiwell," 130–31.

44. Quoted in *Hydro War History*, xiv, NDL/NHC. The production of nautical charts for June 1943–June 1944 set new records, growing from a prewar average output of 1,000,000 to 41,946,494. Annual Report of Hydro for FY ending 30 June 1944, 9, box 64, Hydro, RG37, NA1; *Hydro War History*, 142, NDL/NHC; Roger Revelle, from "The Oceanographic and How It Grew," reprinted in part in *Woods Hole Notes* 17, no. 4 (December 1985): 2.

45. Asst. SecNav to Hydro, 21 August, 4 December 1942, box 2, A (Reports), Hydro Index 1924–45, RG37, NA1.

46. Hydrographer to Chief of BuNav, 5 March 1943, box 295, Hydro, RG37, NA1; and Hydrographer to Chief of BuNav, 6 March 1943, box 295, Hydro, RG37, NA1.

47. Hydrographer to CO, Potomac River Naval Command, 10 April 1944, box 295, Hydro, RG37, NA1.

48. Lt. Cdr. S. R. Jackson to Lt. K. K. Burke, 19 June 1945, and reply, 22 June 1945, box 295, Hydro, RG37, NA1.

49. For Adm. Bryan's quote, see Hydrographer to Asst. Ed., *Fairchild Aviation News*, 16 August 1943, box 295, Hydro, RG37, NA1; Annual Report of Hydro for FY ending 30 June 1944, 2, 10–11, box 64, Hydro, RG 37, NA1. Photogrammetry is the process of making measurements from photographs, used especially in the construction of maps from aerial photographs.

50. Hydrographer to Chief of Nav. Pers., 19 February 1943, box 295, Hydro, RG 37, NA1.

51. By November 1942 Hydro was already requesting "the assignment of three officers of the Women's Reserve . . . to the Air Navigation Division." Hydrographer to Director of the Women's Reserve, 19 November 1942, box 295, Hydro, RG37, NA1; Hydrographer to VCNO, 31 December 1942, box 2, A (Reports), Hydro Index 1924–45, RG37, NA1; Hydrographer to VCNO, "Relief of Officers and Enlisted Men by Waves," 28 January 1943, box 295, Hydro, RG37, NA1; Hydro to CO, Potomac River Naval Command, 23 June 1943, box 295, Hydro, RG37, NA1; *Hydro War History*, 141–44, 171, NDL/NHC.

52. Mildred H. McAfee to Admiral Bryan, 18 December 1943, box 295, Hydro, RG37, NA1; Bryan quoted by Capt. H. W. Underwood to CO, Potomac River Naval Command, 16 April 1945, box 295, Hydro, RG37, NA1.

53. Revelle, "The Oceanographic and How It Grew," 2.

54. Quote is from Mary Sears, "Oceanography," 9, Sears Papers, WHOI; Mary Grier was described by Sears in 1972 as "the one really well-trained oceanographic librarian in the United States . . . [who] worked for me during the war (as a civilian)." Sears to A. S. Lowe, 25 April 1972, folder "DSR Misc. 1971–75," box 3, Sears Papers WHOI. The University of Washington oceanography program, which flourished in the 1930s, was shut down during the war.

55. Sears also mentioned [W. E.] Bill Schevill working on Submarine Supplements for Sailing Corrections, Sears interview 1989, 15–18, Sears Papers, WHOI; Sears, "Oceanography—Then and Now," 4, box 1, Sears Papers, WHOI. Hydro became the Oceanographic Office in 1962. A limnologist is an expert on bodies of fresh water, including their plant and animal life.

56. Sears, "Expansion of Oceanographic Work," 21, Sears Papers, WHOI; Bates and Fuller, *America's Weather Warriors*, 56–57. For biological oceanography, see Mills, *Biological Oceanography*. I am grateful to Louis Brown of Carnegie Institution's Department of Terrestrial Magnetism for information that Sverdrup was a DTM associate in 1917–25 when he was measuring magnetic data on Amundsen's *Maud* expedition, in which the vessel was deliberately frozen into the ice of the polar sea and drifted for three years recording scientific data.

57. Sears Memoir. The British oceanographic reports were mostly prepared under the direction of J. N. Carruthers. He and his wife became lifelong friends of Sears: Sears's History of WHOI, Sears Papers, WHOI; Indian Ocean example is from "Trip to United States by Lts. Crowell and Bates," typed itinerary courtesy Charles Bates. For additional information on oceanographic cooperation with Britain, see Iselin, "History of War Years," 13–14, WHOI.

58. *Hydro War History*, 163, NDL/NHC; Sears interview 1989, 15, Sears Papers, WHOI. See also the same comment in Sears Memoir.

59. The survey vessels were *Sumner, Bowditch, Pathfinder, Oceanographer*, and *Hydrographer*, Annual Report of Hydro for FY ending 30 June 1944, 13–14, box 63, Hydro, RG37, NA1; Hydro to C-in-C, U.S. Pacific Fleet, 19 August 1944, box 64, Hydro, RG37, NA1.

60. "Techniques for Forecasting Wind Waves and Swell," iv, Hydro Publication No. 604, box D-1860, Gov. Pub. RG287, NA1; Iselin, "History of War Years," 16–17, WHOI; "Trip to United States by Lts. Crowell and Bates," typed itinerary courtesy Charles Bates.

61. Naval message from Hydro Washington, Maritime Security, to NOIC, New Guinea, 22 May 1944, box 63, Hydro, RG37, NA1.

62. CO, USS *Sumner*, to Island Commander, Tarawa, 29 January 1944, box 60, Hydro, RG37, NA1; Iselin, "History of War Years," 34, WHOI.

63. Port Director's Office, Naval Transportation Service, San Pedro, Calif., to Hydro, Washington, D.C., 13 July 1943, box 51, Hydro, RG 37, NA1.

64. Sears, "Expansion of Oceanographic Work," 15, Sears Papers, WHOI; Annual Report of Hydro for FY ending 30 June 1944, 11, box 64, Hydro, RG37, NA1. In a letter of August 1944, B. E. Dodson, Sears's boss and head of Pilot Charts, suggested that Japanese data might be overrated. He mentioned errors found in captured Japanese tide tables and urged caution in using them. "Similar careless errors have been observed throughout their records of oceanographic data," he continued, "although it seems evident that no deliberate falsification was attempted." Dodson to Joint Intelligence Center, Pacific Ocean Areas, 30 August 1944, box 64, Hydro, RG37, NA1. Perhaps the accuracy of Japanese record keeping fell off under

the stress of war; for lack of charts, see *Hydro War History,* 164, NDL/NHC; for inferior charts, see Sears, "Expansion of Oceanographic Work," 15, Sears Papers, WHOI; and for Hydrographer's complaint, see *Hydro War History,* 164, NDL/NHC.

65. See, e.g., Lt. Edward J. Bloom, U.S. Naval Station, Seattle, to O-in-C, Joint Intelligence Center, Pacific Ocean Areas, Pearl Harbor, 7 March 1945, and related correspondence in box 54, Hydro, RG37, NA1. See also O-in-C, Pacific Ocean Areas, to Distribution List, "Translation of Captured Japanese Documents," box 64, Hydro, RG37, NA1; letter from Intelligence Center, Pacific Ocean Areas, to CNO regarding captured Japanese tide tables, 10 February 1944, box 62, Hydro, RG37, NA1. Leila Sears believed the Japanese documents must have come from the Communications Intelligence Division, where she worked.

66. Bates, "Discussion of: 'Military Oceanography,' by H. R. Seiwell," 130; Iselin, "History of War Years," 32–33, WHOI. On a letter from the CO USS *Sumner* to Hydrographer, 1 January 1944, enclosing tidal information for Tarawa Atoll, Sears penciled a note: "Enclosure transmitted to Coast and Geodetic Survey for analysis," box 58, Hydro, RG 37, NA1.

67. "Dr. Mary Sears," untitled, unsigned, undated four-page typewritten draft [hereafter "Dr. Mary Sears, Draft"], 1–2, folder "Misc. personal (1963) 1964," box 1, Sears Papers, WHOI. The records of the Hydrographic Office (RG37) contain many "Boarding Reports" with up-to-date navigation information obtained from merchant captains and forwarded to Hydro by the Office of Naval Intelligence; Iselin, "History of War Years," 27, WHOI; Personnel Officer, Op43 to Personnel Officer, CNO-Op211E, 22 May 1946, "Lt. Cdr. Mary Sears, collateral duty orders for," Sears Papers, Denton Family.

68. Sears interview 1989, 16, Sears Papers, WHOI; Sears's History of WHOI, Sears Papers, WHOI. Charles Bates—lieutenant AAF weather service during the war—suggests that the army private from Scripps was probably Walter Munk.

69. Sears interview 1989, 16, Sears Papers, WHOI; Sears Memoir.

70. Seiwell, "Military Oceanography in World War II," 202–3.

71. Bates, "Discussion of: 'Military Oceanography,' by H. R. Seiwell," 130–31.

72. "Breakers and Surf: Principles in Forecasting," H.O. No. 234, November 1944, box N-324, Gov. Pub. RG287, NA1.

73. Sears interview 1989, 17–18, Sears Papers, WHOI.

74. Sears's History of WHOI, Sears Papers, WHOI. Mrs. Montgomery was MBL librarian from 1919 to 1947.

75. Status of Work Underway in Hydro, U.S. Navy Department, 1 March 1944, 1, box 60, Hydro, RG37, NA1. Specter, *Eagle against the Sun,* provides a detailed account of planning for the Pacific campaigns.

76. Sears, "Expansion of Oceanographic Work," 15, Sears Papers, WHOI.

77. "Yanks Land on Luzon as Navy Planes Sweep China Coast," *All Hands,* no. 335 (February 1945): 2; "Dr. Mary Sears, Draft," 2, folder "Misc. personal (1963) 1964," box 1, Sears Papers, WHOI.

78. Undated, untitled newspaper clipping (sometime in 1963), Mary Sears Radcliffe Alumna File; "Hydrographic Office WAVES Worked on Invasion Charts," *WAVES Newsletter,* November 1945, 6, roll 13, series II, ACNP(W), OA/NHC.

79. Sears to Dr. Erwin Schweigger, 13 December 1949, folder "S 1949–1956," box 1, Sears Papers, WHOI.

80. Mary Sears, "Oceanography," 9–10, Sears Papers, WHOI; Iselin, "History of War Years," 24, 28–29, WHOI; Raitt and Moulton, *Scripps,* 142; "Hydrographic Office WAVES Worked on Invasion Charts," *WAVES Newsletter,* November 1945, roll 13, series II, ACNP(W), OA/NHC.

81. Sears to Sec., JMC, 26 September 1944, box 3, Aer. Sec., RG38, NA2.

82. Hydrographer attn: Lt. (j.g.) Mary Sears, from NRL, 30 July 1943, Hydro, RG37, NA1; Adams, "Radio Acoustic Ranging," 232; Sears interview 1989, 15, Sears Papers, WHOI; Iselin, "History of War Years," 13–14, WHOI.

83. R. Revelle, BuShips, "Submarine Bathythermograph—Use of in Diving Operations," 30 March 1944, box 62, Hydro, RG 37, NA1; Iselin, "History of War Years," 12–14, 18, 28, WHOI.

84. Sears interview 1989, 16–17, Sears Papers, WHOI; Vine quoted in Weir, "Finding a Niche," 22. For other instructional efforts undertaken by WHOI personnel, e.g., teaching naval officers at the Sound School at Key West, Fla., see Iselin, "History of War Years," 11, 30, WHOI.

85. Sears, "Expansion of Oceanographic Work," 20–21, Sears Papers, WHOI; Adams, "Radio Acoustic Ranging," 233; American Meteorological Society Meteorological and Geastrophysical Abstracts, 33–34, folder "Misc. Personal 1966," box 2, Sears Papers, WHOI.

86. Mills to Hydro, 11 December 1945, box 3, CNO, RG38, NA2.

87. *Hydro War History,* 196, NDL/NHC for quote. The Oceanographic Unit was responsible for chapter 3 of the JANIS reports; Annual Report of Hydro for FY ending 30 June 1944, "Summary of charts and misc. printing in the Hydro during FY1944, sheet 2," box 64, Hydro, RG 37, NA1. Following is a representative sampling of Hydro publications resulting from the work of the oceanographic unit: *Atlas of Sea and Swell Charts, North Atlantic Ocean,* Hydro Misc. Pub. 10, no. 721A, 1943; *Monthly Surface Temperature Charts of the Indian Ocean,* Hydro Pub. 10, no. 619, 1943; *Atlas of Current Charts, Southwestern Pacific Ocean,* Hydro Pub. 568, 1944; *Atlas of Surface Currents, Northwestern Pacific Ocean,* Hydro Pub. 569, 1944; *Atlas of Monthly Pilot Charts of the Upper Air, North Atlantic and North Pacific Oceans,* Hydro Pub. 560, 1945.

88. Hydro to VCNO, 4 September 1943, box 295, Hydro, RG37, NA1. In April 1943 Sears had gone directly to Hydro at the Suitland Federal Reservation ten miles southeast of the Capitol, letter from CNO to Lt. Mary Sears, Sears Papers, Denton Family. By April 1945 the number of enlisted WAVES had increased to more than four hundred and there were two WAVES lieutenants (j.g.) in administrative positions; letter from U.S. Naval Barracks, West Potomac Park, to CO, Potomac River

Naval Command, 16 April 1945, box 295, Hydro, RG37, NA1; and Charles Bates for information about Suitland; *Hydro War History,* 172, 175–77, 215–16, NDL/NHC.

89. Sears interview 1989, 13, Sears Papers, WHOI. Hydro was more of an exception than Sears may have remembered. In an April 1945 report on the Waves of Hydro a large number of the enlisted women had technical jobs; and while most WAVES officers had administrative and supervisory duties, some had "entirely technical assignments"; Report from Capt. H. W. Underwood to CO, Potomac River Naval Command, 16 April 1945, box 295, Hydro, RG37, NA1; *Hydro War History,* 263, NDL/NHC. Roger Revelle retired as a commander, with Commendation Ribbon.

90. For Revelle quote, see "The Oceanographic and How It Grew," 22; Milliman, "Mary Sears," 749.

91. Bunce interview 1998, 1; Milliman, "Mary Sears," 749–51.

92. Sears Memoir. I am grateful to Charles Bates for the information about Suitland Manor; for quote, Leila Sears to Dr. Charles Bates, June 1997, courtesy Leila Sears; Leila Sears written comments to author, 21 June 1999. Mary Sears described her own security clearance as "Secret–Top Secret," Security Questionnaire, Sears Papers, Denton Family.

93. Sears interview 1989, 14, Sears Papers, WHOI. For letters, see, e.g., Sears to Richard J. Sullivan, 23 October 1962, on behalf of Mrs. Lois F. Pasley, whom she had known since 1944 when "she was assigned to me as an enlisted girl in the WAVES"; quotes are from undated newspaper interview (sometime in 1963), Sears, Radcliffe College Alumna File.

94. Leila Sears written comments to author, 21 June 1999.

95. Sears interview 1989, 4 (for quote), 7, Sears Papers, WHOI; telephone interview with Leila Sears, 8 April 1999.

96. Jacket Copy, Officer's Qualification Report, Lt. Mary Sears, 28 February 1945, and Jacket Copy, Officer's Report, Lt. Mary Sears, 31 August 1945, Sears Papers, Denton Family. Sears traveled extensively and as often as she could. In addition to many trips to Britain and Scandinavia, Sears visited Russia at the height of the cold war in 1960 and again in 1963. See "Oceanographers Found Cordial Reception in Moscow," *Falmouth Enterprise,* 28 October 1960, folder "Biographical File," no box, Sears Papers, WHOI; Mary Sears, "Oceanography," 9, Sears Papers, WHOI.

97. Sears, "Expansion of Oceanographic Work," 23, Sears Papers, WHOI.

98. Minutes of Meeting in Hydrographer's Office, 19 October 1945, box 3, CNO, RG38, NA2; Hydrographer's Order No. 27, 1 February 1946, Sears Papers, Denton Family.

99. *Hydro War History,* 268, NDL/NHC; undated, untitled newspaper clipping, Mary Sears Radcliffe Alumna File.

100. Citation commending Cdr. Roger Revelle signed by James Forrestal, n.d., courtesy Charles Bates.

101. Annual Report of Hydro for FY ending 30 June 1944, 11, box 64, Hydro, RG 37, NA1.

102. Charles Bates to Dr. Mary Sears, 18 August 1948, folder "B 1948–1955," box 1, Sears Papers, WHOI. Bates worked with Sears on a number of occasions.

103. Annual Report of Hydro for FY ending 30 June 1944, 11, box 64, Hydro, RG37, NA1; Charles Bates to Mary Sears, 18 August 1948, folder "B 1948–1955," box 1, Sears Papers, WHOI; CNO to Lt. Cdr. Mary Sears, 20 May 1946, Sears Papers, Denton Family.

104. U.S. Navy Hydrographic Office, "Procedures for Officers Being Detached," Sears Papers, Denton Family; letter from O-in-C, USN Personnel Separation Unit (WR), U.S. Naval Barracks, N.Y., to Lt. Cdr. Mary Sears, 4 June 1946, Sears Papers, Denton Family; Lt. Cdr. Mary Sears to Chief BuPers, 21 June 1946, "Departure from the U.S.; notification of," Sears Papers, Denton Family.

Chapter 3. Florence van Straten: Meteorologist

1. Quoted in *Aerology*, 80, U.S. Naval Administrative Histories of World War II, no. 62, [hereafter *Aerology War History*] 1957, NDL/NHC. The war history does not cite the source of the quotation, saying only that it was made—with one or two other similar statements—by "the commanders of TF 38, Fifth Fleet and Third Fleet."

2. *Aerology War History*, 1, 5, NDL/NHC.

3. Orville, "Weather as a Weapon," 5–9; Charles Bates to Joanne Simpson, n.d. box 4, Charles Bates Papers, Special Collections, Cushing Library Archives, Texas A&M University [hereafter Bates Papers, TA&M].

4. Yost, *Women of Modern Science*, 126–28; "Florence W. van Straten Dies; Navy Atmospheric Physicist," obituary, *New York Times*, 31 March 1992; Florence van Straten, Military Service Information Form, FOIA, Military Personnel Records, National Personnel Records Center, St. Louis, Mo. [hereafter van Straten MPR].

5. Yost, *Women of Modern Science*, 126.

6. Ibid., 129. Van Straten's best-known work is a general-interest book, *Weather or Not*, published in 1966.

7. Bailey, *American Women in Science*, 400; F. W. van Straten and W. F. Ehret, "The Reaction of Zinc with Copper Sulfate in Aqueous Solution," 1798–1804; van Straten's application for membership, American Meteorological Society, September 1944, courtesy Evelyn Mazur, AMS.

8. Van Straten MPR; Bates and Fuller, *America's Weather Warriors*, 55–56. I am grateful to Charles Bates for supplying the names of the other women: Rachel A. Beard, Evelyn H. Beaulieu, Mary Elizabeth Brown, Zelda Carof, Mary Estelle Ellinwood, Margaret M. Finnigan, Katherine M. Hale, Helena C. Hendrickson, Laura H. Henry, Kathryn L. Howe, Marguerite F. Hunold, Loretta Mersey, Margaret Newman Moshier, Evelyn Parrick, Martha E. C. Perrill, Rosana J. Robuck, Dorothy A. Schmitt, Rosalyn J. Smith, Audry M. Stier, Henrietta P. Terry, Esther M. Turnbull, and Margaret E. Worden. For women chemists, see Rossiter, *Women Scientists in America, 1940–1972*, 16.

9. Hughes, *A Century of Weather Service*, 19–28; Bates and Fuller, *America's Weather Warriors*, 6–14. After the Civil War, Maury, who had left federal service for the Confederacy, became a professor of meteorology at VMI.

10. Hughes, *A Century of Weather Service*, 31, 34, 37; Bates and Fuller, *America's Weather Warriors*, 15–16; van Straten, "Meteorology Grows Up," 413.

11. *Aerology War History*, 1, NDL/NHC.

12. Ibid.; Bates and Fuller, *America's Weather Warriors*, 16–21; Hughes, *A Century of Weather Service*, 48.

13. Bates and Fuller, *America's Weather Warriors*, 23–26; Hughes, *A Century of Weather Service*, 96; Sapolsky, *Science and the Navy*, 13.

14. Hughes, *A Century of Weather Service*, 61, 63; Bates and Fuller, *America's Weather Warriors*, 30–31, 34; van Straten, "Meteorology Grows Up," 413.

15. *Aerology War History*, 10, NDL/NHC; Memo, Orville to Rear Adm. D. C. Ramsey, re "Cdr. F. W. Reichelderfer," 24 October 1944, box 16, Aer. Sec. RG38, NA2; Bates and Fuller, *America's Weather Warriors*, 33–35, 38. Rossby, joined by Jacob Bjerknes, later did important work on vertical waves (Rossby waves) extending through the atmosphere, which made relatively long-range weather forecasts in the Northern Hemisphere theoretically possible.

16. King quoted in Bates and Fuller, *America's Weather Warriors*, 38.

17. Bates and Fuller, *America's Weather Warriors*, 35, 41, 50, 51; "Howard Thomas Orville," *Bulletin American Meteorological Society* 41, no. 11 (November 1960): 649–50, courtesy Evelyn Mazur, AMS. Another study puts the number of navy "weather forecasters" in 1940 at forty-six: see Lewis, "WAVES Forecasters," 2187, n. 1.

18. *Aerology War History*, 17, 22–23, NDL/NHC; "The Aerological Service," chapter 2, Instruction Course for Officers, 5 May 1943, 1–2, box 10, Aer. Sec., RG38, NA2; Capt. H. T. Orville to Prof. H. U. Sverdrup, 4 January 1945, box 1, Aer. Sec. RG38, NA2; Col. Wood to CNO, Attn: Aerology Section, 10 May 1944, box 1, Aer. Sec., RG38, NA2.

19. *Aerology War History*, 17, 22–23, NDL/NHC; H. M. Bixby, Pan American Airways System, to Capt. John Harris, BuAer, 4 November 1943, box 141, Aer. Sec., RG38, NA2.

20. *Aerology War History*, 17, 22–23, 44, NDL/NHC. The war history states that the Aerological Section initiated the proposed formalized cooperation. On 30 June 1940 the Weather Bureau was transferred from the Department of Agriculture to the Department of Commerce.

21. Memo for Capt. Orville, "JANIS Reports, Data for," 27 November 1944, box 18, Aer. Sec., RG38, NA2; Reichelderfer Memo for Secretary, JMC, 18 October 1944, box 13, Aer. Sec., RG38, NA2.

22. C. W. G. Daking, M.O. Air Ministry, to Orville, 15 January 1945, and Orville to Daking, 18 January 1945, box 16, Aer. Sec., RG38, NA2.

23. *Aerology War History*, 26–27, NDL/NHC; U.S. Naval Academy Postgradu-

ate School Catalogue, 1941–42, 3:60, Records of the USNA, RG405, National Archives—Affiliated Archives, records on deposit at the USNA, Annapolis, Md. I am grateful to Prof. W. R. Roberts of Annapolis for locating these records.

24. Iselin to Rossby, 16 November 1944, box 1, Aer. Sec., RG38, NA2; "Aerological Section Annual Report," 10 August 1943, box 19, Aer. Sec., RG38, NA2; *Aerology War History,* 26–28, NDL/NHC.

25. Bates and Fuller, *America's Weather Warriors,* 55–56.

26. Lewis, "WAVES Forecasters," 2188–89.

27. Ibid.

28. Ibid., 2188.

29. Ibid., 2188, 2196; Stephenson, *Women in Nazi Society,* 177.

30. Lewis, "WAVES Forecasters," 2200.

31. Memo for Personnel Complement (Aerology), 30 September 1943, box 1, Aer. Sec., RG38, NA2; Lewis, "WAVES Forecasters," 2200.

32. Lewis, "WAVES Forecasters," 2187.

33. Ibid., 2189–90; Bates and Fuller, *America's Weather Warriors,* 276, n. 4.

34. Lewis, "WAVES Forecasters," 2190–91; Hughes, *A Century of Weather Service,* 114, 178.

35. Bates and Fuller, *America's Weather Warriors,* 54–55; Lewis, "WAVES Forecasters," 2191.

36. Bates and Fuller, *America's Weather Warriors,* 57, 277, n. 23.

37. Orville as "likeable" is in ibid., 137; Lewis, "WAVES Forecasters," 2192.

38. Lewis, "WAVES Forecasters," 2193–95; Yost, *Women of Modern Science,* 125.

39. Lewis, "WAVES Forecasters," 2196–98.

40. "Schools and Rates for Navy Women," n.d., NavPers 16,707, Training, General 1942–51, roll 12, series I, ACNP(W), OA/NHC; van Straten, *Weather or Not,* 138.

41. "Schools and Rates for Navy Women," n.d., NavPers 16,707, Training, General 1942–51, roll 12, series I, ACNP(W), OA/NHC. An aerograph was essentially a combination barograph, thermograph, and hydrograph that could be attached to a plane.

42. *Aerology War History,* 7, 9, 28, NDL/NHC.

43. Ibid.

44. "Naval Aerological Service," Memo to Cdr. R. L. Farrelly from H. T. Orville, 30 December 1943, box 10, Aer. Sec., RG38, NA2; *Aerology War History,* 32, NDL/NHC.

45. *Aerology War History,* 3–4, 8, 26, 75, NDL/NHC; Bates and Fuller, *America's Weather Warriors,* 59–60. On p. 277, n. 29, Bates and Fuller seem to have confused the number of weather ships with the number of carriers. See *Aerology War History,* 75, for correct numbers.

46. *Aerology War History,* 84–85, NDL/NHC.

47. *Aerology War History,* 34, NDL/NHC; Willoughby, *U.S. Coast Guard,* 89, 124–30; Memo from Aerology to OP-32, 21 January 1944, box 1, Aer. Sec., RG38, NA2.

48. Van Straten MPR; Bates and Fuller, *America's Weather Warriors,* 55–56, 58; *Aerology War History,* 47, 56, 60, NDL/NHC.

49. Memo re. Personnel Assignment under Proposed Reorganization of Aerology, 16 August 1943, box 10, Aer. Sec., RG38, NA2.

50. *Aerology War History,* 67–68, NDL/NHC.

51. Hughes, *A Century of Weather Service,* 116; van Straten, "Meteorology Grows Up," 413.

52. McCartney, *ENIAC,* 36–37; R. Revelle to Dr. H. U. Sverdrup, 9 October 1944, box 3, Aer. Sec., RG38, NA2. For Sears and Orville, see, e.g., Orville to Sears, 14 October 1944, box 3, Aer. Sec., RG38, NA2. Louis Brown of Carnegie Institution's Department of Terrestrial Magnetism informed me that Mauchly's father, S. J. Mauchly, was a staff member of DTM in the 1920s and 1930s, reducing global data into contour maps. His son worked part time with him as a schoolboy.

53. Memo, "Naval Officer Training in Sea and Swell Forecasting," 23 April 1945, box 1, Aer. Sec. RG38, NA2; from CO, NATS, Pacific Wing, to CO, NATS, 4 April 1945, box 1, Aer. Sec., RG38, NA2; van Straten, "Meteorology Grows Up," 416.

54. Memo, "Material on Aerology for Inclusion in Flight Division Article for Appropriations Committee," 11 November 1944, box 10, Aer. Sec., RG38, NA2.

55. For Lt. Mary E. Brown, see, e.g., Orville to OP-28, 24 July 1944; for Miss Alber, see John Harris to Dr. F. W. Reichelderfer, 1 September 1944, box 1, Aer. Sec., RG38, NA2; Memo, Weather Central to Orville, "Personnel Requirements," 17 December 1943, box 1, Aer. Sec. RG38, NA2. One of the Arlington Hall Waves, Jane Newhall Lyons, a 1942 Smith College graduate, recalled that "there were a number of different groups each with responsibility for a different type of message." Her group eventually consisted of four officers and twenty-five NSCs. Letter to author, 28 September 1996.

56. Ens. F. W. van Straten to Inspector of Naval Aircraft, Goodyear Aircraft Corp., 18 October 1943; Ens. F. W. van Straten to Capt. C. V. S. Knox, 2 November 1943; Capt. C. V. S. Knox to CNO, 2 November 1943, and to BuAer, Attn: Cdr. Orville, 3 November 1943, "forward for Comment"; all in box 141, Aer. Sec., RG38, NA2.

57. Recollections of van Straten are from former colleagues Cdr. Daniel F. Rex, USNR, and Lt. Earl G. Droessler, USNR.

58. "Navy Aerological Service," memo to Cdr. R. L. Farrelly from H. T. Orville, 30 December 1943, Box 10, Aer. Sec., RG38, NA2.

59. Van Straten, *Weather or Not,* 10–11.

60. "The Battle of Midway," Aerology and Naval Warfare, Aerology Section, March 1944, foreword, J. S. McCain, DCNO (Air), 18 January 1944, box 4, Bates Papers, TA&M.

61. Van Straten to Charles Bates, 5 August 1982, box 4, Bates Papers, TA&M.

62. Van Straten, "Meteorology Grows Up," 415; van Straten, *Weather or Not,* 11–12. For early use of naval radar, see Brown, *A Radar History,* 238–43.

63. Van Straten, *Weather or Not,* 11; Orville, "Weather Is a Weapon," 5.

64. Van Straten, "Meteorology Grows Up," 415; van Straten, *Weather or Not,* 13–16.

65. Van Straten, *Weather or Not,* 13–16; quote is from "Navy Aerological Service, " memo to Cdr. R. L. Farrelly from H. T. Orville, 30 December 1943, Box 10, Aer. Sec., RG38, NA2.

66. Van Straten, *Weather or Not,* 12; "The Battle of the Coral Sea," Aerology and Naval Warfare, Aerology Section, April 1944, box 4, Bates Papers, TA&M.

67. "The Battle of the Coral Sea," NAVAER 50-IT-12 (April 1944), box 4, Bates Papers, TA&M.

68. Van Straten, *Weather or Not,* 12–13; Millett, *Semper Fidelis,* 366.

69. Orville, "Weather as a Weapon," 5–6; "The Occupation of Kiska," August 1943, NAVAER 50-30T-2, box 4, Bates Papers, TA&M.

70. Orville, "Weather as a Weapon," 6, 8; Bates and Fuller, *America's Weather Warriors,* 121.

71. "Midway," NAVAER 50-40T-1; "Seventh Amphibious Force," NAVAER 50-30T-3; "Marshall Islands," NAVAER 50-30T-5; "Leyte," NAVAER 50-30T-6; all box 4, Bates Papers, TA&M.

72. Van Straten, "Meteorology Grows Up," 416; quote is from CNO to President, UCLA, 27 November 1943, box 10, Aer. Sec., RG38, NA2.

73. Van Straten, "Meteorology Grows Up," 416.

74. *Aerology War History,* 137, NDL/NHC; article for BuAer Newsletter, 1 June 1943, box 10, Aer. Sec., RG38, NA2.

75. Adm. Turner to CNO (Aerology Section), 3 June 1945, box 1, Aer. Sec., RG38, NA2.

76. Van Straten, *Weather or Not,* 16–17; for "Flossie" quote, Charles Bates to author, 14 August 1998. Orville retired from the navy as a captain in June 1950.

77. See, e.g., van Straten to CO, Naval Air Bases, Western Sea Frontier, 18 April 1945, box 541, Aer. Sec., RG38, NA2; van Straten to Chief of Forecast Branch, Army Air Forces, 26 January 1945, and Chief, Weather Division, AAF, to CNO, 17 March 1945, box 541, Aer. Sec., RG38, NA2; van Straten to Capt. H. E. Hall, c/o TWA, 28 May 1945, box 2, Aer. Sec., RG38, NA2.

78. Van Straten, "Memo to Capt. Orville, re. Visit to Aerological Observatory, USSR Hydrometeorological Service," 23 January 1945, box 21, Hydro, RG37, NA1.

79. See, e.g., van Straten to BuAer, re. "Aerological Supplies for PACT," 4 May 1945, box 541, Aer. Sec., RG38, NA2; van Straten to BuAer, re. "Recorder, Anemograph," 18 May 1945, box 541, Aer. Sec., RG38, NA2; van Straten to BuAer, re. "Additional Weather Patrol Vessels, Request for Equipment," 26 May and 5 June 1945, box 3, Aer. Sec., RG38, NA2.

80. "Seminar at the Weather Bureau—28 April 1945," box 10, Aer. Sec. RG38, NA2.

81. Memo, "Meeting at Weather Bureau, 9 May 1945, Subject: Stream Flow Forecasting," box 10, Aer. Sec. RG38, NA2.

82. Van Straten, comments on Conference on "Far Eastern Weather," rough draft, 15 May 1945, box 15, Aer. Sec., RG38, NA2.

83. Memo: "Seminars on Research in Forecast Improvement," 10 September 1945, box 11, Aer. Sec., RG38, NA2; Memo: "Aerological History Project," 28 August 1945, box 11, Aer. Sec., RG38, NA2.

84. *Aerology War History,* 41–42, NDL/NHC; JMC "Preparation of Chapter V, Climate and Meteorology, for Joint Army-Navy Intelligence Studies," 24 August 1944, box 18, Aer. Sec., RG38, NA2.

85. *Aerology War History,* 39–41, 69, NDL/NHC.

86. Orville's Aerological Section Annual Report, 10 August 1943, box 10, Aer. Sec., RG38, NA2; Van Straten, "Meteorology Grows Up," 417; Lt. Cdr. H. R. Carson to CO BuAer, re "Aerological Units in Combat Areas," box 951, BuAer, RG72, NA2.

87. Van Straten, "Meteorology Grows Up," 417; *Aerology War History,* 64, 74, NDL/NHC. Hattan Yoder, later a colleague of Louis Brown at Carnegie, was a naval aerology officer sent to Siberia. See his account: *Planned Invasion of Japan* (1997).

88. Van Straten, "Meteorology Grows Up," 417; *Aerology War History,* 58, NDL/NHC; van Straten, *Weather or Not,* 73, 75.

89. *Aerology War History,* 5, NDL/NHC; van Straten, "Meteorology Grows Up," 418–19; van Straten, *Weather or Not,* 70. Special microseismic stations were established in the Caribbean and in the Pacific.

90. Van Straten, "Meteorology Grows Up," 419–20; Appendix "D," Minutes of Meeting of Subcommittee on Meteorological Problems, Committee on Operating Problems," 16 April 1945, box 16, Aer. Sec., RG38, NA2. This appendix is the aerological research and development report for the Aerological Section, 1 April 1944 to 31 March 1945, and gives an excellent description of all the latest developments. For radar and meteorology, see also Brown, *A Radar History,* 442–43.

91. Van Straten, *Weather or Not,* 26–27; van Straten, "Meteorology Grows Up," 420–21.

92. Van Straten, *Weather or Not,* 113; Brown, *A Radar History,* 376–77, for "Battle of the Pips."

93. Van Straten, "Meteorology Grows Up," 420–21; Van Straten, *Weather or Not,* 14–16.

94. Van Straten, *Weather or Not,* 143.

95. Ibid., 150–52.

96. Ibid., 153.

97. Ibid., 155.

98. *Aerology War History,* 76–78, NDL/NHC.

99. Lewis, "WAVES Forecasters," 2199.

100. Laura E. Wintersteen to Charles Bates, 28 August 1982, box 4, Bates Papers, TA&M.

101. Reichelderfer to Orville, 27 August 1945, box 11, Aer. Sec., RG38, NA2.

102. Van Straten obituary, *Washington Post,* 31 March 1992; Bailey, *American Women in Science,* 400–401; information sheet courtesy Evelyn Mazur, AMS.

103. Van Straten, "Meteorology Grows Up," 421–22.

104. *Aerology War History,* foreword, NDL/NHC; Van Straten quoted in Yost, *Women of Modern Science,* 133.

Chapter 4. Grace Murray Hopper: Computer Scientist

1. Portions of this chapter appeared previously in Kathleen Broome Williams, "Civilians in Uniform: The Harvard Computation Lab in World War II," *Naval War College Review* 52, no. 3 (summer 1999): 90–110. I am grateful to Hopper's sister, Mary Murray Westcote, for generously giving me access to a large collection of her sister's papers and for sharing information with me in the course of several interviews. Program of launching of *Hopper,* 6 January 1996, Bath Iron Works Corporation; *New York Times,* 3 January 1992.

2. Grace Hopper interview by Christopher Evans, 1976 [hereafter Hopper interview 1976], OH81, Charles Babbage Institute, University of Minnesota, Minneapolis [hereafter CBI], 1.

3. Mitchell, *Contribution of Grace Murray Hopper,* 1–11, 24–37, 50–51, 63–64; Billings, *Hopper,* 30, 36–38, 47–53, 111, 115. Versions of these stories of Hopper's youth appear in many interviews conducted later in her life. For surveying, e.g., see Capt. Grace Hopper interview by Linda Calvert, 3 September 1982–28 February 1983, Women in Federal Government Oral History Project, OH46, Schlesinger Library, Radcliffe College [hereafter Hopper interview 1982–83, WFGOH46, SL], 159; and for disassembling clocks, see Grace Hopper interview 1976, OH81, CBI, 11.

4. Billings, *Hopper,* 18–20; for quote, see Hopper interview 1982–83, WFGOH46, SL, 18.

5. Chafe, *American Woman,* 103–4; Hopper's sister, Mary, graduated in 1930 and her brother, Roger, graduated from Yale in 1932. Mary Murray Westcote interview by author, 11 December 1999, Glen Ridge, N.J.

6. Tropp, "Grace Hopper," 8; for quote, see Hopper interview 1982–83, WFGOH46, SL, 4, 18. Hopper's brother later also earned a doctorate.

7. Chafe, *American Woman,* 89–111; Rees, "Support of Higher Education," 374.

8. Stephenson, *Women in Nazi Society,* 166–67.

9. Hopper interview 1982–83, WFGOH46, SL, 5–8, 113; Chafe, *American Woman,* 108–11; Rupp, *Mobilizing Women,* 3.

10. Hopper interview 1982–83, WFGOH46, SL, 10. Her great-grandfather was Rear Adm. Alexander Wilson Russell.

11. Hopper interview 1982–83, WFGOH46, SL, 17; Mitchell, *Contribution of Grace Murray Hopper,* 21.

12. Hopper interview 1982–83, WFGOH46, SL, 8–9, 10 (for quote), 161.

13. Aiken, "Proposed Automatic Calculating Machine," 62–69; Cohen, "Babbage and Aiken," 175–77.

14. "Robot Brain at Harvard Hot News Copy," *Boston News Week,* n.d., IBM Archives, Somers, N.Y.

15. Howard H. Aiken and Grace M. Hopper, "The Automatic Sequence Controlled Calculator –I," reprint from *Electrical Engineering* (August–September 1946): 1, box 1, folder 2, Grace Murray Hopper Collection 1944–65 [hereafter Hopper Papers], Smithsonian Institution, Washington, D.C.

16. "Aiken, Howard," in *Encyclopedia of Computer Science and Engineering,* 40; quote is from Cohen, "Howard Aiken and the Beginnings," 303; Gregory Webb Welch, "Computer Scientist," 38. Welch, a student of Cohen, convincingly supports this view of Harvard's attitude toward pure and applied sciences.

17. Bashe et al., *IBM's Early Computers,* 30–31; Hopper interview 1976, OH81, CBI, 3.

18. *Harvard Alumni Bulletin* 47, no.1 (September 1944), folder 21, box 6, Hopper Papers, Smithsonian.

19. Stewart, *Organizing Scientific Research,* 152; Baxter, *Scientists against Time,* 24–25.

20. "Harvard Gets Huge Calculator," *Boston Daily Globe,* 7 August 1944, n.p., folder 9, box 6, Hopper Papers, Smithsonian; "Algebra Machine Spurs Research," *New York Times,* 7 August 1944.

21. Pugh, *Memories,* 6; Welch, "Computer Scientist," 7; "General Purpose Digital Computers" (n.d.), folder "Bell Telephone Labs," box A–C, UAV 289.2005, Records of the Computation Laboratory, 1944– [hereafter Aiken Correspondence], HUA.

22. Richard M. Bloch, "Programming the Mark I," 2, unpublished manuscript courtesy of Dr. Bloch.

23. H. H. Aiken to Dr. Arnold Lowan, 1 November 1944, folder "(dead) BuOrd," box A–C, UAV 289.2005, Aiken Correspondence, HUA.

24. "IBM Automatic Sequence Controlled Calculator" (IBM Corporation, 1945), 5, IBM Archives; Hartree, *Calculating Instruments,* 74–79; Bashe et al., *IBM's Early Computers,* 29.

25. George Stibitz, "History of 7.5," n.d., but forwarded with letter of 22 March 1946, box 10, Applied Mathematics Panel General Records [hereafter AMP Gen. Recs.], RG227, NA2.

26. Hopper interview 1976, OH81, CBI, 3.

27. Contract NObs-14966, folder "BuShips Computing Project," box 6, UAV 885.95.2, World War II Government Contract Records [hereafter WWIIGCR], HUA.

28. Hershberg, *Conant,* 128; Spencer, *Great Men and Women,* 55; Zimmerman, *Top Secret Exchange,* 130, 134 n. 6, 194; Stewart, *Organizing Scientific Research,* for administrative history of OSRD.

29. Quoted in Zimmerman, *Top Secret Exchange,* 136; Burke, *Information and Secrecy,* 224.

30. Vannevar Bush, foreword, in Stewart, *Organizing Scientific Research,* ix–x. The section on liaison with the armed services, 151–67, suggests that in this regard the navy did a better job than did the army; Burke, *Information and Secrecy,* 224, 276, 291, 297.

31. Goldstine, *The Computer,* 134.

32. E.g., Mina Rees to Cdr. H. H. Aiken, 2 January 1945, folder "(dead) BuOrd," box A–C, UAV 289.2005, Aiken Correspondence, HUA; Warren Weaver to Capt. T. A Solberg, BuShips, NDRC, June 1944, 26, box 72, series II, Sperry Univac Records Accession 1825 [hereafter Sperry Acc. 1825], Hagley Museum and Library, Greenville, Del. [hereafter Hagley].

33. Burke, *Information and Secrecy,* 290–303; Cortada, *Before the Computer,* 203; for navy "bombes" built by NCR in Ohio, see R. Elaine Barlett, "Sugar Camp Reunion," 1.

34. Stewart, *Organizing Scientific Research,* 57; Hodges, *Turing,* 299; Zimmerman, *Top Secret Exchange,* 195–96.

35. Cortada, *Before the Computer,* 190–91; Hopper interview 1976, OH81, CBI, 12.

36. Bashe et al., *IBM's Early Computers,* 24; Spencer, *Great Men and Women,* 51, 54.

37. Folder "Bell Telephone Labs," box A–C, 289.2005, Aiken Correspondence, HUA; Hartree, *Calculating Instruments,* 80; Goldstine, *The Computer,* 115, 156; Cohen, "Howard Aiken and the Beginnings," 303; Spencer, *Great Men and Women,* preface.

38. Memo to AMP ExCo from Warren Weaver, 27 October 1943, box 2, AMP Gen. Recs., RG227, NA2.

39. Warren Weaver to Dr. Harlow Shapley, 10 January 1944, and Warren Weaver to Prof. E. L. Chafee, 2 March 1944, box 20, AMP Gen. Recs., RG227, NA2.

40. Diary of Mina Rees, 26 February 1945, box 1, AMP Gen. Recs., RG227, NA2.

41. Hodges, *Turing,* 298–99; Cohen, "Howard Aiken and the Beginnings," 306; Burke, *Information and Secrecy,* 264–65, 281.

42. See folder "(dead) BuOrd," box A–C, and folder "Visitors 1944 and 1945," box C–I, UAV 289.2005, Aiken Correspondence, HUA, for numerous examples; folder 22, box 6, Hopper Papers, Smithsonian.

43. "Staff of the Computation Laboratory," *Manual of Operation for the Automatic Sequence Controlled Calculator* (n.p.); Burke, *Information and Secrecy,* 291.

44. Assoc. Dir. of the Harvard Radio Research Lab and Assoc. Dir. of the Harvard Underwater Sound Lab to Mr. H. A. Wood and Pres. and Fellows of Harvard College, 22 May 1943, folder "Policies," box 2, UAV 885.95.2, WWIIGCR, HUA.

45. R. W. Hickham to John C. Baker, 28 August 1942, folder "Personnel," box 2, UAV 885.95.2, WWIIGCR, HUA.

46. *An Administrative History of the Bureau of Ships during World War II*, 4 vols., 3:127, U.S. Naval Administrative Histories of World War II, no. 89 [hereafter *BuShips History*], 1952, NDL/NHC. Among the Sperry Univac and Technitrol papers at the Hagley Museum and Library's extensive collection of documents on the development of the computer industry there are many examples of draft deferrals for scientists; Rodgers, *Think*, 143; Cohen, "Howard Aiken and the Beginnings," 305.

47. Capt. W. G. Schindler, Officer-in-Charge, Naval Ordnance Laboratory, to Dr. John Mauchly, 20 June 1944, box 70, series II, Sperry Acc. 1825, Hagley.

48. Cortada, *Before the Computer*, 203; Goldstine, *The Computer*, 130–31; J. G. Brainerd to Dean Harold Pender, 6 April 1945, box 71, series II, Sperry Acc. 1825, Hagley.

49. "Anonymous Research Contracts and Approximate Number of Employees at 8/31/44," folder "Personnel," box 2, UAV 885.95.2, WWIIGCR, HUA; Rudolph Elie Jr., "Harvard's Wonderful Achievements in Late War Are Told," misc. newspaper clipping, 24 May 1946, folder "clippings," box C–I, UAV 289.2005, Aiken Correspondence, HUA.

50. For Viking quote, see "Harvard Gets Huge Calculator," *Boston Daily Globe*, 7 August 1944, folder 9, box 6, Hopper Papers, Smithsonian; "Biography of Howard Hathaway Aiken," IBM Archives; Welch, "Computer Scientist," 43–44; Cohen, new foreword to *A Manual of Operations*, xiii; Campbell interview 1984, OH67, CBI, 12.

51. Bloch interview by author, 12 September 1997; Bloch interview 1984, OH66, CBI, 5.

52. Cohen, new foreword to *A Manual of Operations*, xiii.

53. Welch, "Computer Scientist," 47; Contract NObs-14966, folder "BuShips Computing Project," box 6, UAV.885.95.2, WWIIGCR, HUA.

54. Bloch, "Programming the Mark I," 3; Bloch interview 1984, OH66, CBI, 29; Hopper interview 1976, OH81, CBI, 6.

55. Rausa, "In Profile," 58.

56. Noller interview, 23 December 1996; *BuShips History*, 2:140–42, NDL/NHC.

57. Noller interview, 23 December 1996.

58. Campbell interview by author, 12 September 1997; Campbell interview 1984, OH67, CBI, 61, for quote.

59. Delo A. Calvin, three-page typewritten memoir in author's possession, 10 March 1998 [hereafter Calvin Memoir], 2.

60. Rodgers, *Think*, 170.

61. Calvin Memoir, 1–2; letter from John M. Hourihan to author, 14 March 1998.

62. Hopper interview 1976, OH81, CBI, 20–23; Pugh, *Memories*, 10; Campbell

interview by author, 12 September 1997; and Bloch interview by author, 12 September 1997 for "tough hombre" remark.

63. Robert Hawkins interview, 20 February 1984, Barnstable, Mass., OH64, CBI, 15.

64. Campbell interview by author, 12 September 1997; Cohen, "Howard Aiken and the Beginnings," 306.

65. Campbell interview by author, 12 September 1997; Calvin Memoir, 2, for quote; Bloch, "Programming the Mark I," 59.

66. Bloch, "Programming the Mark I," 3; Campbell interview 1984, OH67, CBI, 62; Campbell interview by author, 12 September 1997, for Mozart of computers.

67. "IBM Automatic Sequence Controlled Calculator," 6, IBM Archives.

68. "Biography of Howard Hathaway Aiken," IBM Archives; Pugh, *Memories*, 6; Hawkins interview 1984, OH64, CBI, 1, 6, 10, for quote.

69. Aiken, preface to the *Manual of Operations* (n.p.); *BuShips History*, 4:185, NDL/NHC.

70. Report No. 7, July 1944, BuShips Computation Project Reports 1944–45, Naval Research Laboratory, Washington, D.C. [hereafter NRL]; *Annals of the Computation Laboratory* 26 (1951): 5; Hopper interview 1976, OH81, CBI, 2, for quote.

71. Hopper interview 1982–83, WFGOH46, SL, 29.

72. Hopper interview 1976, OH81, CBI, 11.

73. Hopper, "Education of a Computer," 139, from reprint in Grace Murray Hopper Biographical Files, CBI.

74. Hopper interview 1976, OH81, CBI, 6, 11.

75. Ibid., OH81, CBI, 7, 11–12.

76. Grace M. Hopper, 20 July 1979, typed transcript, Oral History Interviews, [hereafter Hopper interview 1979], Sperry Acc. 1825, Hagley, 8.

77. Hopper, "Automatic Programming: Present Status and Future Trends," 10, n.d., Marvin L. Stein Papers (CBI 10), CBI; Hopper interview 1976, OH81, CBI, 10, for quote. Later the three programmers were joined by two lieutenant commanders and a lieutenant.

78. Hopper, "Automatic Programming," 10, Stein Papers, CBI; Hopper interview 1976, OH81, CBI, 13.

79. Hopper interview 1979, Sperry Acc. 1825, Hagley, 2; Hopper, "Automatic Programming," 2, Stein Papers, CBI.

80. Campbell, Bloch interview by author, 12 September 1997; Hopper interview 1982–83, WFGOH46, SL, 29.

81. L. S. Dederick to W. Weaver, 20 March 1945, box 5, AMP Gen. Recs., RG227, NA2; Stern, *ENIAC to UNIVAC*, 7.

82. Campbell interview 1984, OH67, CBI, 22; Reports No. 10, October 1944, No. 8, August 1944, No. 5, June 1944, BuShips Computation Project, NRL; Cohen and Welch, *Makin' Numbers*, 3, 57; Interim Progress Reports to AMP, 21 August 1944, 23 October 1944, 24 January 1945, box 13, AMP Gen. Recs., RG227, NA2.

83. Interim Report to AMP, 24 June 1944, box 13, AMP Gen. Recs., RG227, NA2.

84. Campbell interview 1984, OH67, CBI, 23; Cohen, "Howard Aiken and the Beginnings," 318.

85. Chief BuShips from NRL, 3 January 1945, folder "(dead) BuOrd," box A–C, UAV 289.2005, Aiken Correspondence, HUA.

86. Memo, Warren Weaver to Mina Rees, 9 March 1945, box 4, AMP Gen. Recs., RG227, NA2.

87. Mina Rees to Oswald Veblen, 9 June 1945, box 19, AMP Gen. Recs., RG227, NA2.

88. Memo to AMP ExCo from Warren Weaver, 27 October 1943, box 2, AMP Gen. Recs., RG227, NA2.

89. Diary of Mina Rees, 6 March 1944, box 1, AMP Gen. Recs., RG227, NA2.

90. Bloch interview by author, 12 September 1997, where he also notes his high regard for von Neumann's mathematical abilities; Hopper interview 1982–83, WFGOH46, SL, 12.

91. Progress Report to AMP from von Neumann, 23 October 1944, box 13, AMP Gen. Recs., RG227, NA2.

92. Bloch, "Programming the Mark I," 36.

93. Report No. 11, December 1944, BuShips Computation Project, NRL; Dr. Arnold Lowan from H. H. Aiken, 1 November 1944, folder "(dead) BuOrd," box A–C, UAV 289.2005, Aiken Correspondence, HUA; Bob Campbell to author, 16 August 1998. Von Neumann also worked on calculations for the hydrogen bomb, Hodges, *Turing,* 302. Cohen believes that no one at the lab knew the purpose of von Neumann's calculations until Hiroshima, *Howard Aiken,* 164–65.

94. H. H. Aiken to Dr. Arnold Lowan, 1 November 1944, folder "(dead) BuOrd, 13–11," box A–C, UAV.289.2005, Aiken Correspondence, HUA.

95. Hopper interview 1976, OH81, CBI, 20; Mitchell, *Contribution of Grace Murray Hopper,* 30, 32; Bloch interview 1984, OH66, 17, CBI.

96. Hopper interview 1976, OH81, CBI, 3. Even Cortada, *Before the Computer,* 203–4, gives an inaccurate date of 1945.

97. Herman Goldstine to Lt. J. J. Power, 6 July 1945, box 74, series II, Sperry Acc. 1825, Hagley.

98. Petzinger, "History of Software Begins"; and Petzinger, "Female Pioneers."

99. Hopper interview 1982–83, OH81, CBI, 4.

100. Hopper interview 1979, Sperry Acc. 1825, Hagley, 1.

101. A 1973 legal decision in a patent dispute found John Atanasoff's ABC machine and not the ENIAC the first electronic computer. Documents in the case are in the Sperry Univac Records, Hagley. Brian Levy, in "The Computer," *Newsweek,* special millennium edition (winter 1997–98): 28–30, makes no mention of the Mark I.

102. Bashe et al., *IBM's Early Computers,* 32.

103. Hopper interview 1982–83, WFGOH46, SL, 16, 130; Hodges, *Turing,* 301–2.

104. Rodgers, *Think*, 174.

105. Hartree, *Calculating Instruments*, v.

106. "Progress Report No. 12, Harvard Computation Laboratory, September 1950–October 1950," 1, box 1, series I, Technitrol Suit Records, Accession 1901, Hagley.

107. Welch, "Computer Scientist," 3, 94–95; Hopper interview 1976, OH81, CBI, 4; Cohen, "Howard Aiken and the Beginnings," 320–22; "Aiken, Howard," in *Encyclopedia of Computer Science and Engineering*, 41. See also *Annals of the Computation Laboratory*, vols. 16, 26.

108. Welch, "Computer Scientist," 4, 76, 101–2, 109, 115; Campbell interview by author, 12 September 1997; Cohen, "Babbage and Aiken," 183.

109. Hopper interview 1982–83, WFGOH46, SL, 13, 43–46.

110. "The Automatic Sequence Controlled Calculator," *Electrical Engineering* 65 (1946): 384–91, 449–54, 522–28; Cohen, *Howard Aiken*, 220; Cohen and Welch, *Makin' Numbers*, x. For a list of Hopper's publications, see Grace M. Hopper Officer Biography, box 313, OA/NHC.

111. McCartney, *ENIAC*, 154–55; Hopper interview 1982–83, WFGOH46, SL, 30.

112. Kennedy, *Freedom from Fear*, 787; Hopper interview 1982–83, WFGOH46, SL, 28, 41. For women dominating the early programming field, see Stern, *ENIAC to UNIVAC*, 63.

113. Hopper interview 1979, Sperry Acc. 1825, Hagley, 1; McCartney, *ENIAC*, 152; Burke, *Information and Secrecy*, 224, 276, 345; Hopper interview 1982–83, WFGOH46, SL, 32. ERA also succumbed to financial failure. Sperry later became UNISYS.

114. Billings, *Hopper*, 65; Hopper interview 1982–83, WFGOH46, SL, 16, 31, 36–37. Quote is from Hopper, "Education," 139, Grace Murray Hopper Biographical Files, CBI.

115. McCartney, *ENIAC*, 95–97, 151–52; Hopper interview 1982–83, WFGOH46, SL, 168. Holberton was later at the National Bureau of Standards where Hopper continued to keep in touch with her.

116. Hopper interview 1976, OH81, CBI, 22. See Stern, *ENIAC to UNIVAC*, for the place of Eckert and Mauchly in the development of computing. While Stern's is in many ways a careful, detailed study, it omits Hopper and Holberton.

117. Hopper interview 1979, Sperry Acc. 1825, Hagley, 1–2.

118. Ibid. Holberton went with the UNIVAC machine to work for the navy at the David Taylor Model Basin. She has only recently received some long overdue recognition of her accomplishments. See McCartney, *ENIAC*, 95–97, 151–52; Petzinger's two 1996 *Wall Street Journal* articles; and Light, "When Computers Were Women." In her several long interviews Hopper invariably gives credit to the pioneering computer work of other women, including Jean Smith, a Sperry engineer, and Peg Harper at the UNIVAC Division of Sperry.

119. Hopper, "Education," 139, 142, Grace Murray Hopper Biographical Files,

CBI; see Stern, *ENIAC to UNIVAC,* for exploration of the theme of industry's late entry into the computing field.

120. Hopper interview 1976, OH81, CBI, 14–15; McCartney, *ENIAC,* 152.

121. Hopper, "Education," 144, Grace Murray Hopper Biographical Files, CBI.

122. Billings, *Hopper,* 74; McCartney, *ENIAC,* 168–71; Hopper interview 1982–83, WFGOH46, SL, 39.

123. Hopper interview 1982–83, WFGOH46, SL, 13.

124. Hopper, "Education," 139, Grace Murray Hopper Biographical Files, CBI.

125. Hopper interview 1976, OH81, CBI, 12–13.

126. Hopper interview 1979, Sperry Acc. 1825, Hagley, 6.

127. Quote is from Billings, *Hopper,* 97; Hopper interview 1982–83, WFGOH46, SL, 47; Spencer, *Great Men and Women,* 144.

128. Hopper interview 1979, Sperry Acc. 1825, Hagley, 10–11. See McCartney, *ENIAC,* for the role of marketing in the early computer industry.

129. Hopper interview 1979, Sperry Acc. 1825, Hagley, 9. See Hopper interview 1982–83, WFGOH46, SL, 36, for another version of this story in which Hopper said the crisis occurred at Newport.

130. Hopper interview 1979, Sperry Acc. 1825, Hagley, 12.

131. Spencer, *Great Men and Women,* 144–45; Hopper interview 1979, Sperry Acc. 1825, Hagley, 18–23.

132. Hopper interview 1979, Sperry Acc. 1825, Hagley, 10–11. Among the others Hopper admired Nora Moser for her work at the Army Map Service and Kathleen McNulty and Jean Bartik at ENIAC.

133. Hopper interview 1982–83, WFGOH46, SL, 113–20.

134. Ibid.; Grace M. Hopper Officer Biography, box 313, OA/NHC.

135. Hopper interview 1976.

136. *New York Times,* 3 January 1992. See also *New York Times,* 22 April 2000.

137. Hopper interview 1979, Sperry Acc. 1825, Hagley, 13.

Chapter 5. Mina Spiegel Rees: Science Administrator

1. Baxter to Weaver, 26 September 1944, box 26, Applied Mathematics Panel General Records (AMP Gen. Recs.), RG227, NA2.

2. Bailey, *American Women in Science,* 322; Grinstein and Campbell, *Women of Mathematics,* 175; Mina Rees interview by Nina Cobb, 16 November 1983–20 January 1984, Women in Federal Government Oral History Project, OH40, Schlesinger Library, Radcliffe Institute [hereafter Rees interview 1983–84, WFGOH40, SL], 1–15.

3. Rees interview 1983–84, WFGOH40, SL, 19–24.

4. Grinstein and Campbell, *Women of Mathematics,* 176; Rees interview 1983–84, WFGOH40, SL, 27–40, for quotes.

5. Albers and Alexanderson, *Mathematical People,* 258.

6. Rees interview 1983–84, WFGOH40, SL, 37–46.

7. Ibid., 47–48, 76; Bailey, *American Women in Science*, 322; Rossiter, *Women Scientists in America, 1940–1972*, 31.

8. Rees is quoted in Albers and Alexanderson, *Mathematical People*, 258.

9. For a description of Rees, see "She Breaks a Hundred," *New York Herald Tribune*, 26 November 1963; "beguiling companion" comment is from "Presentation of Mina S. Rees for the Degree of Doctor of Sciences, 94th Wilson College Commencement, 31 May 1964," box 1, Mina Rees Collection, CUNY Graduate School and University Center Archives [hereafter Rees Collection, CUNY]. I am grateful to Joan Byers for access to this collection and for her generous assistance and information about Mina Rees.

10. Albers and Alexanderson, *Mathematical People*, 259, 261.

11. Rees interview 1983–84, WFGOH40, SL, 52–59.

12. Ibid., 78–81.

13. Brooks, *Government of Science*, 21–23; Rees, "The Mathematical Sciences and World War II," 607, the quote is from William Prager; Penick et al., *Politics of American Science*, 5; Brown, *A Radar History of World War II*, 79, 315: Courant's brother-in-law was the famous German radar engineer Wilhelm Runge.

14. Rees, "The Mathematical Sciences and World War II," 607.

15. Sapolsky, *Science and the Navy*, 3–4, 13.

16. Brown, *Radar History of World War II*, 42–44, 64–73, 159–63, 215–19. For the best account of the Tizard Mission, see Zimmerman, *Top Secret Exchange*. For a disparaging view of military scientific developments between the wars, see Stewart, *Organizing Scientific Research*, 3–4; and Bush, *Modern Arms*, 19.

17. H. Brooks, in U.S. House of Representatives, Subcommittee on Science, Research and Development, Hearings, 91st Cong., 2d sess., October 1970, quoted in Mina Rees, "Mathematics and the Government: The Postwar Years as Augury of the Future," 4, typescript, "Publications," box 1, Rees Collection, CUNY.

18. Stewart, *Organizing Scientific Research*, 6; Baxter, *Scientists against Time*, 14.

19. Baxter, *Scientists against Time*, 14–15.

20. Penick et al., *Politics of American Science*, 10–13; Stewart, *Organizing Scientific Research*, 9–12.

21. Stewart, *Organizing Scientific Research*, 12–14; Bush, *Pieces of the Action*, 38–39.

22. Sapolsky, *Science and the Navy*, 19–20; Stewart, *Organizing Scientific Research*, 17–18.

23. Stewart, *Organizing Scientific Research*, 23; Baxter, *Scientists against Time*, 16–17.

24. Baxter, *Scientists against Time*, 21–22.

25. Brooks quoted in Rees, "Mathematics and the Government," 8, "Publications," box 1, Rees Collection, CUNY; Stern, *ENIAC to UNIVAC*, 71.

26. Brooks quote in *Government of Science*, 23; Baxter, *Scientists against Time*, 19; Stewart, *Organizing Scientific Research*, 25–26, 278. Von Neumann's

annual salary at the IAS at Princeton was $12,500; the AMP covered about half of that from July 1943: Weaver to Dr. Frank Aydelette, 22 July 1943, box 13, AMP Gen. Recs., RG227, NA2.

27. Stewart, *Organizing Scientific Research*, 34; Baxter, *Scientists against Time*, 24; for a less sanguine view of the cooperation, see Sapolsky, *Science and the Navy*, 18–19, 29–30.

28. Baxter, *Scientists against Time*, 8–9, 24; Bush, *Modern Arms*, 18.

29. Baxter, *Scientists against Time*, 9–12.

30. For Anglo-American scientific cooperation, see Zimmerman, *Top Secret Exchange*.

31. Stewart, *Organizing Scientific Research*, 35–37.

32. Rees, "Mathematics and the Government," 4, "Publications," box 1, Rees Collection, CUNY; Brooks, *Government of Science*, 22–23.

33. Stewart, *Organizing Scientific Research*, 85–97.

34. Ibid., 60–63; Bush quoted in Baxter, *Scientists against Time*, ix.

35. Compton to Weaver, 27 October 1942, box 26, AMP Gen. Recs., RG227, NA2; see also Stern, *ENIAC to UNIVAC*, 71.

36. Stewart, *Organizing Scientific Research*, 80; Baxter, *Scientists against Time*, 216.

37. Stewart, *Organizing Scientific Research*, 25, 85–97.

38. Ibid., 81.

39. Rees interview 1983–84, WFGOH40, SL, 107.

40. Ibid., 107, 111.

41. Quotes are from ibid., 81, 99, 100–101. For Aiken, see Cohen, *Howard Aiken*, 11; and for Weaver and Aiken, see Weaver to Dr. Harlow Shapley, 10 January 1944, Weaver to Prof. E. L. Chaffee, 18 January 1944, Weaver to Chaffee 2 March 1944, all in box 20, AMP Gen. Recs, RG227, NA2.

42. Rees, "Warren Weaver, 1894–1978," 489–505; quote is by Robert E. Kohler.

43. Weaver, *Scene of Change*, 78–83.

44. *Ibid.*, 87.

45. Rees, "Mathematics and the Government," 1–4, "Publications," box 1, Rees Collection, CUNY; Stern, *ENIAC to UNIVAC*, 71–72.

46. Rees, "The Mathematical Sciences and World War II" 608–9; Rees, "Mathematics and the Government," 4, "Publications," box 1, Rees Collection, CUNY.

47. Weaver, *Scene of Change*, 88.

48. U.S. OSRD, *Summary Technical Report of AMP*, 2:vii. In an undated typescript entitled "Establishment of the City University of New York," 5, Rees put the number of university groups at thirteen, "Publications," box 1, Rees Collection, CUNY; Chicago is from Rees interview 1983–84, WFGOH40, SL, 106.

49. Weaver to Dean Edward L. Moreland, 22 July 1943, box 13, AMP Gen. Recs., RG227, NA2; Courant to Weaver, 27 March 1944, box 13, AMP Gen. Recs., RG227, NA2.

50. Weaver, *Scene of Change*, 88–89; U.S. OSRD, *Summary Technical Report*

of AMP, 2:vii; "Meeting of the ExCo of AMP," 3 May 1943, box 1, AMP Gen. Recs., RG227, NA2.

51. Rees Diary, ExCo, 31 January 1944, box 1, AMP Gen. Recs., RG227, NA2; author's interview with Norma Kenigsberg for insights into Rees's management style, 15 June 2000.

52. Rees, "The Mathematical Sciences and World War II," 609; for the ID badge, Rees Diary, AMP ExCo, 11 September 1944, box 1, AMP Gen. Recs., RG227, NA2. The Executive Committee had its first meeting on 27 January 1943, before Rees was brought onboard.

53. "Citation for Mina Rees," Hunter College Commencement, June 5, 1973, typescript, "Awards and Honors," box 1, Rees Collection, CUNY.

54. Rees Diary, "Visit to Wright Field," 1 December 1944, box 1, AMP Gen. Recs., RG227, NA2; Vannevar Bush quoted in Baxter, *Scientists against Time,* viii.

55. Rees interview 1983–84, WFGOH40, SL, 118–20; Rees to Fry, 25 September 1943, box 1, AMP Gen. Recs., RG227, NA2; Stibitz to Rees, 13 November 1945, AMP Gen. Recs., RG227, NA2; U.S. OSRD, *Summary Technical Report of AMP,* 2:166.

56. Rees interview 1983–84, WFGOH40, SL, 118–20; Bush quoted by Weaver in memo, 11 September 1944, box 2, AMP Gen. Recs., RG227, NA2.

57. Rees interview 1983–84, WFGOH40, SL, quotes on 122 and 124.

58. Weaver to Dr. Irvin Stewart, 9 September 1943, box 8, AMP Gen. Recs., RG227, NA2; Rees interview 1983–84, WFGOH40, SL, 131.

59. Rees, "The Mathematical Sciences and World War II," 617.

60. V. Bush to Members, Division and Panel Chiefs of NDRC, "Memorandum in Regard to Organization and Functions within OSRD insofar as NDRC Is Concerned," 24 May 1944, box 2, AMP Gen. Recs., RG227, NA2.

61. Rees interview 1983–84, WFGOH40, SL, 108, 112–14.

62. Ibid., 114; U.S. OSRD, *Summary Technical Report of AMP,* 2:x.

63. Rees interview 1983–84, WFGOH40, SL, 108, 112–13.

64. Ibid., 110, 113, 118.

65. Ibid., 110, 136.

66. Rees to Dr. Irvin Stewart, 31 December 1943, box 9, AMP Gen. Recs., RG227, NA2; Bush, *Science, the Endless Frontier,* 151–55.

67. Rees interview 1983–84, WFGOH40, SL, 116.

68. Rees, "The Computing Program of the ONR," 104.

69. Rees, "The Mathematical Sciences and World War II," 617; Rees Diary, AMP ExCo, 1 May 1944, box 1, AMP Gen. Recs., RG227, NA2.

70. Rees, "The Mathematical Sciences and World War II," 617.

71. Rees Diary, AMP ExCo, 6 March 1944, box 1, AMP Gen. Recs., RG227, NA2; Harper quoted in U.S. OSRD, *Summary Technical Report of AMP,* 2:3; Odle quoted in Rees, "The Mathematical Sciences and World War II," 617.

72. "Diary of ExCo Meeting," 8 March 1943, box 1, AMP Gen. Recs., RG227, NA2.

73. Rees Diary, AMP ExCo, 1 May 1944, box 1, RG227, NA2; Cdr. G. A. Patterson to Dr. A. N. Lowan, 12 April 1945, box 11, AMP Gen. Recs., RG227, NA2, for Hydro. Louis Brown suggests the radar operator was looking at a transverse Mercator map.

74. "Meeting of the ExCo of AMP," 3 May 1943, box 1, AMP Gen. Recs., RG227, NA2; "Notes on ExCo Meeting, 7 June 1943," box 1, AMP Gen. Recs., RG227, NA2; Rees Diary, AMP ExCo, 27 September 1943, box 1, AMP Gen. Recs., RG227, NA2.

75. Rees, "The Mathematical Sciences and World War II," 611, for quote; "Meeting of the ExCo of the AMP," 12 April 1943, box 1, AMP Gen. Recs., RG227, NA2, for Woods Hole; Rees Diary, AMP ExCo, 21 August 1944, box 1, AMP Gen. Recs., RG227, NA2, for Study No. 137; for Courant in Pasadena, Rees Diary, ExCo, box 1, AMP Gen. Recs., RG227, NA2.

76. U.S. OSRD, *Summary Technical Report of AMP,* 2:2; Rees, "The Mathematical Sciences and World War II," 611–12.

77. Prager quoted in Rees, "The Mathematical Sciences and World War II," 612.

78. Rees interview 1983–84, WFGOH40, SL, 121.

79. U.S. OSRD, *Summary Technical Report of AMP,* 2:10, 25, 45–56, 197–215; Rees Diary, AMP ExCo, 25 September 1944, box 1, AMP Gen. Recs., RG227, NA2; Arthur Sard, "Aerial Gunnery and Gyroscopic Gun Sights," 5 February 1946, 8, box 26, AMP Gen. Recs., RG227, NA2.

80. U.S. OSRD, *Summary Technical Report of AMP,* 2:x, 125–42. For AMP's role in the establishment of Inyokern, see Rees Diary, AMP ExCo, 5 June 1944, box 1, AMP Gen. Recs., RG227, NA2.

81. "Work of the Applied Mathematics Panel on Bombing Accuracy Analysis and Its Applications," 14 January 1946, 2, unsigned typescript, box 26, AMP Gen. Recs., RG227, NA2; U.S., OSRD, *Summary Technical Report of AMP,* 2:193–94.

82. Rees, "The Mathematical Sciences and World War II," 614.

83. Quoted in ibid., 614; see also Weaver, *Scene of Change,* 88–89.

84. Rees, "The Mathematical Sciences and World War II," 616; for Brooks quote, Rees, "Mathematics and the Government," 8.

85. Weaver to BuOrd, BTL, MIT, 23 December 1943, box 25, AMP Gen. Recs., RG227, NA2; Rees, "The Computing Program of the ONR," 104; "Final Report of Committee on Computing Aids for Naval Ballistics Laboratory," 28 April 1944, box 25, AMP Gen. Recs., RG227, NA2; Rees to Dr. A. N. Lowan, 4 December 1945, box 26, AMP Gen. Recs., RG227, NA2; Rees Diary, AMP ExCo, 1 November 1943, AMP Gen. Recs., RG227, NA2.

86. Rees interview 1983–84, WFGOH40, SL, 112.

87. Rees, "The Mathematical Sciences and World War II," 620; U.S. OSRD, *Summary Technical Report of AMP,* 2:215–22, for discussion of mathematical analysis in warfare.

88. Rees, "The Mathematical Sciences and World War II," 620.

89. Rees interview 1983–84, WFGOH40, SL, 128.

90. Margaret Moses to Rees, 26 January 1944, and Rees to Moses, 28 January 1944, box 23, AMP Gen. Recs., RG227, NA2; Minutes of Conference on Summary Technical Report, 30 August 1945, box 3, AMP Gen. Recs., RG227, NA2; for Gladys Emerson, see Yost, *Women of Modern Science,* 140–55.

91. Rees interview 1983–84, WFGOH40, SL, 139, 150–52; Rees to Dr. Dorothy W. Weeks, 8 March 1944, box 23, AMP Gen. Recs., RG227, NA2; MR to WW, 29 July 1944, AMP Gen. Recs., RG227, NA2, for Weeks and Anslow.

92. Rees interview 1983–84, WFGOH40, SL, 153; Weaver to Lt. Cdr. T. C. Wilson, 23 November 1943, box 7, AMP Gen. Recs., RG227, NA2. Weaver's suggestion to Wilson that he check with the Math Department at Hunter College has all the marks of Rees's input. For girl-months, see, e.g., Rees to Lt. James H. Wakelin, 17 September 1945, box 265, AMP Gen. Recs., RG227, NA2. See also Soderbergh, *Women Marines,* xx, for widespread and benevolent use of the term *girls.* The expressions *man-days* and *man-hours* were also widely used. The point about feminism is from author's June 2000 interviews with Nan Shaw and Norma Kenigsberg, and Joan Byers correspondence. Each worked for Rees for many years at CUNY.

93. Rees interview 1983–84, WFGOH40, SL, 154; quotes from "Hunter Group Told of Women's Gains," *New York Times,* 22 June 1951. See also Rossiter, *Women Scientists in America, 1940–1972,* 17, for advice that "self-discipline" was the best answer to discriminatory practices.

94. Weaver, *Scene of Change,* 87–88; Rees, "Warren Weaver," 522.

95. Weaver to CE, HCW, SM, EWP, GWT, RB, 7 August 1944, box 21, AMP Gen. Recs., RG227, NA2.

96. Weaver quoted in Rees, "Warren Weaver," 501; Rees quoted in Albers and Alexanderson, *Mathematical People,* 258; Mina Rees c.v., box 1, Rees Collection, CUNY Archives.

97. U.S. OSRD, *Summary Technical Report of AMP,* 2:v; Weaver to President George N. Shuster, 29 January 1946, box 8, AMP Gen. Recs., RG227, NA2.

98. Reagan, *Science and the Federal Patron,* 5–6, 264–66.

99. On navy officer technical competence, see, e.g., Rees Diary, AMP ExCo, 7 August 1944, AMP Gen. Recs., RG227, NA2; Bush is quoted in Sapolsky, *Science and the Navy,* 30; Rees quote is from Rees interview 1983–84, WFGOH40, SL, 155.

100. Rees, "Mathematics Program of the Office of Naval Research" [hereafter "Mathematics Program of ONR"], 1–2; Sapolsky, *Science and the Navy,* 5. Louis Brown notes that the ONR's support of science is seen as the golden age, and for the method of administration, not just the money.

101. Rees interview 1983–84, WFGOH40, SL, 165, 171. Confirming Rees's view, see Sapolsky, *Science and the Navy,* 5, 30, 40–41; and Penick et al., *Politics of American Science,* 22–23.

102. Rees, "Establishment of CUNY," 6–7, box 1, Rees Collection, CUNY Archives; Rees, "Mathematics Program of ONR," 2–3; Sapolsky, *Science and the Navy,* 8.

103. "Hunter Group Told of Women's Gains," *New York Times,* 22 June 1951;

Sapolsky, *Science and the Navy*, 41; Penick et al., *Politics of American Science*, 22–23.

104. Rees interview 1983–84, WFGOH40, SL, 157.

105. "Who's Who in Naval Research," *ONR Research Reviews* (February 1952): 14, box 1, Rees Collection, CUNY Archives; author's interview with Norma Kenigsberg, 15 June 2000; Rees interview 1983–84, WFGOH40, SL, 160; Rees, "Mathematics Program of ONR," 4.

106. Rees, "Mathematics Program of ONR," 1–2; quote is from Rees, "Computing Program of ONR," 104; Grinstein and Campbell, *Women of Mathematics*, 179.

107. Quote is from Rees, "Federal Computing Machine Programs," 733; Rees, "Computing Program of ONR," 104–6, 111–12; Stern, *UNIVAC to ENIAC*, 104, confirms Rees's interest in stimulating applied mathematics.

108. Rees, "Computing Program of ONR," 105–6; Sapolsky, *Science and the Navy*, 84–84; quote is from Rees, "The Federal Computing Machine Program," 731.

109. Rees, "Computing Program of ONR," 111–13; Albers and Alexanderson, *Mathematical People*, 267.

110. "Who's Who in Naval Research," *ONR Research Reviews* (February 1952): 13–14, box 1, Rees Collection, CUNY Archives; Rees, "Computing Program of ONR," 119, for quote; Rees, "Computing Program of ONR," 119.

111. F. J. Weyl, who served with Rees in ONR, is quoted in Grinstein and Campbell, *Women of Mathematics*, 176; Albers and Alexanderson, *Mathematical People*, 263.

112. Rees interview 1983.

Chapter 6. After the War

1. Author's interview with Deffes, Gonzales, Nilsen, Rambo, and Wiruth, 2 January 1997, China Lake, Calif.

2. Milliman, "Mary Sears," 750. During the years of Sears's editorship *Deep-Sea Research* increased from four to twelve issues annually, exceeding eighteen hundred pages a year by 1973; Roger Revelle describes oceanography as a science still considered young in 1961. Mary Sears, ed., *Oceanography* (Washington, D.C.: American Association for the Advancement of Science, Publication 67, 1961), v. In 1961 Dael Wolfle of the American Association for the Advancement of Science wrote to congratulate Sears on the publication of *Oceanography*, noting the "continuing evidence that the whole venture was a real help to oceanography." Dael Wolfle to Mary Sears, 17 May 1961, folder "AAAS 1959–64," box 4, Sears Papers, WHOI.

3. Sears to Dr. J. N. Carruthers, 22 September 1964, folder "Misc. Personal (1963) 1964," box 1, Sears Papers, WHOI. See Sears Papers, WHOI, for her extensive international correspondence. "Huge" reference is from Columbus Iselin, hand-

written page of notes headed "Mary Sears," n.d., folder "Biographical File," no box, Sears Papers, WHOI; J. N. Carruthers to Mary Sears, 26 May 1965, folder "Misc. Personal 1965," box 2, Sears Papers, WHOI; Mary Swallow, "Tribute to Mary Sears," 746.

4. Revelle, "The Oceanographic and How It Grew," 22. Roger Revelle had a profound influence on the development of oceanography during and after World War II and was a leading instigator of navy oceanographic programs. See Raitt and Moulton, *Scripps,* 146.

5. Sears interview 1989, 9, Sears Papers, WHOI. Quote is from Bunce interview 1998, 2. Bunce earned an A.B. from Smith College in 1937 and worked at WHOI during the war. She returned to Smith for an M.A. in physics in 1949 and spent the rest of her career at WHOI as a marine geophysicist.

6. Mary Sears c.v., folder "Biographical File," no box, Sears Papers, WHOI.

7. Ibid.

8. Mary Sears, "Oceanography," 9–10, Sears Papers, WHOI; Sears interview 1989, 31, Sears Papers, WHOI.

9. Sears interview 1989, 31, Sears Papers, WHOI. For the importance of Operation Crossroads to postwar oceanographic research, see Revelle, "The Oceanographic and How It Grew," 21; and Iselin, "History of War Years," 38, WHOI.

10. Thomas to Sears, 20 January 1964, and Sears to Thomas, 23 January 1964, folder "Misc. Personal (1963) 1964," box 1, Sears Papers, WHOI; Jackusch to Sears, 19 August 1963, folder "Misc. Personal 1963," box 1, Sears Papers, WHOI.

11. Fenner A. Chace Jr., Smithsonian Institution, to Sears, 13 September 1968, folder "Misc. Personal 1968," box 2, Sears Papers, WHOI. See, e.g., Sears's application for Veterans Administration National Service Life Insurance, 1 April 1943, Sears Papers, Denton Family.

12. CNO to Cdr. Mary Sears, 16 September 1963, Sears Papers, Denton Family.

13. Sears to American Geophysical Union, 3 August 1964, and Sears to Prof. L. Zenkevitch, 28 July 1964, folder "Misc. Personal (1963) 1964," box 1, Sears Papers, WHOI.

14. Sears to the *Radcliffe Quarterly,* 16 June 1992, Mary Sears Radcliffe Alumna File; Iselin, notes on Mary Sears, folder "Biographical File," no box, Sears Papers, WHOI.

15. Sears to Prof.. Robert A. Calvert, Texas A&M, College Station, 2 May 1977, folder "Misc. Personal 1975–1980," box 2, Sears Papers, WHOI.

16. George E. R. Deacon, "The Woods Hole Oceanographic Institution: An Expanding Influence," 25.

17. N. Gazsky to Sears, 26 May 1962, folder "Misc. Personal 1963," box 1, Sears Papers, WHOI; Sears, "Oceanography—then and now," 5, folder "Oceanography Then and Now—June 1963," box 1, Sears Papers, WHOI.

18. Sears to Mrs. William C. Ripley, 5 February 1963, folder "Misc. Personal 1963," box 1, Sears Papers, WHOI. Underlining is in the original; Sears to

Managing Editor, *Oceans,* 15 October 1968, folder "Misc. Personal 1968," box 2, Sears Papers, WHOI. There are many letters in a similar vein among the Sears Papers at WHOI.

19. Sears to Dr. Paul M. Fye, 3 September 1975, folder "Misc. Personal 1975–1980," box 2, Sears Papers, WHOI.

20. Iselin, notes on Mary Sears, folder "Biographical File," no box, Sears Papers, WHOI.

21. I am grateful to former colleagues Cdr. Daniel F. Rex, USNR, and Lt. Earl G. Droessler, USNR, for this information on van Straten.

22. Yost, *Women of Modern Science,* 134–35; van Straten obituary, *Washington Post,* 31 March 1992.

23. Yost, *Women of Modern Science,* 135–38; Bailey, *American Women in Science,* 400–401.

24. "What's Being Done about Weather?" *Junior Review* 31, no. 6 (October 13, 1958): 1; van Straten, *Weather or Not,* 204–12.

25. Emme, *Aeronautics and Astronautics,* 94–105; van Straten MPR; Bailey, *American Women in Science,* 400–401; quote is from van Straten to Bates, 5 August 1982, box 4, Bates Papers, TA&M.

26. Van Straten obituary, *Washington Post,* 31 March 1992; Van Straten MPR; Bates and Fuller, *America's Weather Warriors,* 277 n. 16.

27. Hopper interview 1982–83, WFGOH46, SL, 41; Hopper quoted in Billings, *Hopper,* 87.

28. Hopper interview 1979, Sperry Acc. 1825, Hagley, 21.

29. Ibid., 15.

30. Ibid., 16.

31. Hopper interview 1982–83, WFGOH46, SL, 49.

32. Billings, *Hopper,* 108–9; Mitchell, *Contribution of Grace Murray Hopper,* 63.

33. Mary Westcote interview by author, 11 December 1999.

34. "Rear Adm. Grace M. Hopper," *New York Times,* 3 January 1992; Mary Westcote telephone interview by author, 3 October 1999.

35. For a full list of Hopper's degrees, awards, and publications, see Grace M. Hopper Officer Biography, box 313, OA/NHC.

36. Mitchell, *Contribution of Grace Murray Hopper,* 1–11, 24–37, 50–51, 63–64; Billings, *Hopper,* 30, 36–38, 47–53, 110–15. For "Aiken Adieu," see "John Harvard's Journal," *Harvard Magazine* (September–October 1997): 68. Howard Aiken died on 14 March 1973 at the age of seventy-three.

37. Mina Rees c.v., box 1, Rees collection, CUNY Archives; "Women in Science," *New York Times,* 31 December 1969; quote is from Nan Shaw interview, 15 June 2000.

38. Mina Rees c.v., box 1, Rees collection, CUNY Archives; "Women in Science," *New York Times,* 31 December 1969; "Citation" AAUW Achievement Award, 1965, box 1, Rees Collection, CUNY Archives; quote is from Albers and Alexanderson,

Mathematical People, 260; author's interviews with Nan Shaw and Norma Kenigsberg, 15 June 2000.

39. Mina Rees c.v., box 1, Rees Collection, CUNY Archives.

40. "Citation of Mina Rees," Carnegie-Mellon University, 15 May 1972, box 1, Rees Collection, CUNY Archives.

41. Baxter to Warren Weaver, 26 September 1944, box 26, AMP Gen. Recs., RG227, NA2; Fry to Rees, 7 December 1945, box 26, AMP Gen. Recs., RG227, NA2.

42. Rees Diary, AMP ExCo, 25 April 1946, AMP Gen. Recs., RG227, NA2; Rees to Weaver, 5 January 1946, box 26, AMP Gen. Recs., RG227, NA2; Thornton Fry, Acting Chief, AMP to Dr. James B. Conant, 17 December 1945, box 26, AMP Gen. Recs., RG227, NA2. *Summary Technical Report,* vol. 2, copy no. 163, originally at the Naval Research Laboratory, is presently in the Duke University Library.

43. Ambrose et al., *Journeys of Women in Science and Engineering,* 20–21; Rossiter, *Women Scientist in America, 1940–72,* xv–xvi, 13–14, 24–25, 28–29, 35; Evans, *Born for Liberty,* 223.

44. Quote is from Gluck, *Rosie the Riveter Revisited,* 269; Soderbergh, *Women Marines,* 158–59; Rupp, *Mobilizing Women,* 4–5, 10, 174–75; Evans, *Born for Liberty,* 221–23, 230–31, 240.

45. Willenz, *Women Veterans,* xii; Rossiter, *Women Scientists in America, 1940–1972,* 38, for status of women scientists in the immediate postwar years, which Rossiter refers to as characterized by "overwhelming antifeminism."

46. Rossiter, *Women Scientists in America, 1940–1972,* 92–101.

47. Ibid., 92–96; Reagan, *Science and the Federal Patron,* 263–65; Penick et al., *Politics of American Science,* 21.

48. Brooks, *Government of Science,* vi; Bates to Sears, box 1, folder "B" 1948–1955, Sears Papers, WHOI.

49. Brooks, *Government of Science,* vi, 21–23.

50. Holm, *Women in the Military,* 202–3. The 2 percent limit was lifted in 1967.

BIBLIOGRAPHY

Author's Interviews and Correspondence

Bates, Charles C., World War II AAF meteorologist
Black, Dorothy Wells, World War II Wave
Bloch, Richard, Harvard Computation Laboratory
Bunce, Elizabeth T., WHOI marine geophysicist
Campbell, Richard V. D., Harvard Computation Laboratory
Clement, Rose Nudo, China Lake Wave
Coombs, Elisabeth Gaskill, World War II Wave
Deffes, Joan, China Lake Wave
Gonzales, Rose, China Lake Wave
Hourihan, John M., Harvard Computation Laboratory
Kenigsberg, Norma, Graduate School and University Center, CUNY
Lemlein, Marie Klein, World War II Wave
Lyons, Jane Newhall, World War II Wave
Nilsen, Hazel, China Lake Wave
Noller, Ruth Brendel, World War II Wave, Harvard Computation Laboratory
Potter, Charlotte A., World War II Wave
Rambo, Ida, China Lake Wave
Sears, Leila, World War II Wave, sister of Mary Sears
Shaw, Nanette, Graduate School and University Center, CUNY
Westcote, Mary Murray, sister of Grace Murray Hopper
Wiruth, Terry, China Lake Wave

Archival Sources

Archives Center, National Museum of American History, Smithsonian Institution
Grace Murray Hopper Collection 1944–65.

Charles Babbage Institute, University of Minnesota, Minneapolis
Grace Murray Hopper Biographical Files.

Marvin L. Stein Papers (CBI 10).

Oral Histories: Nos. 64 (Robert Hawkins), 66 (Richard Bloch), 67 (Robert Campbell), 81 (Grace Hopper).

City University of New York,
Graduate School and University Center Archives
Mina Rees Papers.

Cushing Library Archives, Texas A&M University, Special Collections
Charles Bates Papers.

Hagley Museum and Library Archives
Grace M. Hopper, 20 July 1979, Oral History Interviews.
Sperry Univac Records, Accession 1825.
Technitrol Suit Records, Accession 1901.

Harvard University Archives
Records of the Computation Laboratory, 1944– (Aiken Correspondence).
Records of the Naval Training School (Pre-Radar) Harvard.
World War II Government Contract Records.

IBM Archives
"Biography of Howard Hathaway Aiken." n.d.
"IBM Automatic Sequence Controlled Calculator" (IBM Corporation, 1945).

National Archives 1, Washington, D.C.
Record Group 37, Hydrographic Office.
Record Group 287, Publications of the U.S. Government.

National Archives 2, College Park, Maryland
Record Group 19, Bureau of Ships.
Record Group 24, Bureau of Personnel.
Record Group 38, Chief of Naval Operations.
Record Group 52, Bureau of Medicine and Surgery.
Record Group 72, Bureau of Aeronautics.
Record Group 227, Office of Scientific Research and Development.

National Archives—Affiliated Archives,
U.S. Naval Academy, Annapolis, Maryland
Record Group 405, Catalogues of U.S. Naval Academy Postgraduate School, academic years 1941–42, 1942–43, 1943–44, 1944–45, 1945–46.

National Archives—Regional Archives, Northeast Region (Boston)
Record Group 181, First Naval District.

Naval Historical Center, Navy Department Library
U.S. Naval Administrative Histories of World War II:
Aerology, Bureau of Aeronautics, no. 62, 1957.
History of the Women's Reserve, 2 vols., no. 88, 1946.
An Administrative History of the Bureau of Ships during World War II, 4 vols.,
    no. 89, 1952.
Hydrographic Office, no. 123, n.d.
War History of the Naval Research Laboratory, no. 134, 1 November 1946.

Naval Historical Center, Operational Archives
Marie Bennett Alsmeyer Personal Papers.
Records of the Assistant Chief of Naval Personnel (Women)—Shelf File boxes.

Naval Research Laboratory
Bureau of Ships Computation Project Reports 1944–1945: No. 5, June 1944; No. 7,
    July 1944; No. 8, August 1944; No. 10, October 1944; No. 11, December 1944.

New York University Archives
Henry Chase Administrative Papers.

Raytheon Archives
Monthly Payroll Books.
Raytheon News, 1943–.

Schlesinger Library, Radcliffe Institute for Advanced Study
Elizabeth Reynard Papers.
Mary Sears, Radcliffe College Alumna File.
Women in Federal Government Oral History Project: OH46 (Grace Hopper),
    OH40 (Mina Rees).

Sears Papers, Denton Family Collection
U.S. Navy service records, personal papers, and correspondence.

Wellesley College Archives
Mary Sears Biographical File.

Woods Hole Oceanographic Institution Data Library and Archives
Mary Sears Papers, MC9.
WHOI Reports for the years 1943, 1944, 1945.

Published Sources

Adams, K. T. "Radio Acoustic Ranging (R.A.R)." *Annual Report Smithsonian Institution* (1944): 232.

Aiken, H. H. "Proposed Automatic Calculating Machine." Ed. and preface by A. C. Oettinger and T. C. Bartee. *IEEE Spectrum* (August 1964): 62–69.

Aiken, H. H., and Grace M. Hopper. "The Automatic Sequence Controlled Calculator, I–III." *Electrical Engineering* 65 (August–September 1946): 384–91, 449–54, 522–28.

"Aiken, Howard." In *Encyclopedia of Computer Science and Engineering,* ed. Anthony Ralston. New York: Van Nostrand Reinhold, 1983.

Albers, Donald J., and G. L. Alexanderson, eds. *Mathematical People: Profiles and Interviews.* Boston, Basel, Stuttgart: Birkhäuser, 1985.

Alexander, Joseph H. *Utmost Savagery: The Three Days of Tarawa.* Annapolis: Naval Institute Press, 1995.

"Algebra Machine Spurs Research." *New York Times,* 7 August 1944.

Ambrose, Susan A., Kristin L. Dunkle, Barbara B. Lazarus, Indira Nait, and Deborah A. Harkus, eds. *Journeys of Women in Science and Engineering: No Universal Constants.* Philadelphia: Temple University Press, 1997.

Anderson, Karen. *Wartime Women: Sex Roles, Family Relations, and the Status of Women during World War II.* Westport, Conn.: Greenwood Press, 1981.

Annals of the Computation Laboratory of Harvard University. 35 vols. Cambridge: Harvard University Press, 1945–62.

Bailey, Martha J. *American Women in Science: A Biographical Dictionary.* Denver: ABC-CLIO, 1994.

Barlett, R. Elaine. "Sugar Camp Reunion." *Cryptolog* 17, no. 2 (spring 1996): 1.

Bashe, Charles J., Lyle R. Johnson, John H. Palmer, and Emerson W. Pugh. *IBM's Early Computers.* Cambridge: MIT Press, 1986.

Bates, Charles C. "Discussion of: 'Military Oceanography in Tactical Operations of World War II,' by H. R. Seiwell." *Transactions of the American Geophysical Union* 29, no. 1 (1948): 130–31.

Bates, Charles C., and John J. Fuller. *America's Weather Warriors, 1814–1985.* College Station: Texas A&M University Press, 1986.

Baxter, James Phinney. *Scientists against Time.* Boston: Little, Brown, 1946.

Belden, William, and Marva R. Belden. *The Lengthening Shadow: The Life of Thomas J. Watson.* Boston: Little, Brown, 1962.

Bellafaire, Judith. *The Army Nurse Corps.* CMH Publication 72-14. Washington, D.C.: U.S. Army Center for Military History, n.d.

———. *The Women's Army Corps.* CMH Publication 72-15. Washington, D.C.: U.S. Army Center for Military History, n.d.

Billings, Charlene W. *Grace Hopper: Navy Admiral and Computer Pioneer.* Hillside, N.J.: Enslow, 1989.

Binkin, Martin, and Shirley J. Bach. *Women and the Military*. Washington, D.C.: Brookings Institution, 1977.

Braybon, Gail, and Penny Summerfield. *Out of the Cage: Women's Experiences in Two World Wars*. London: Pandora Press, 1987.

Brooks, Harvey. *The Government of Science*. Cambridge: MIT Press, 1968.

Brown, Louis. *A Radar History of World War II: Technical and Military Imperatives*. Bristol and Philadelphia: Institute of Physics Publishing, 1999.

Budd, Lillian. "Yesterday's News—World War I." *Register* [Newsletter of Women in Military Service for America Memorial Foundation, Inc.] (winter 1996–97): 8.

BuPers: The Story of Navy Manpower, U.S. Bureau of Naval Personnel. Washington, D.C.: U.S. Government Printing Office, 1949.

Burke, Colin. *Information and Secrecy: Vannevar Bush, Ultra, and the Other Memex*. Metuchen, N.J., and London: Scarecrow Press, 1994.

Burstyn, H. L. "Reviving American Oceanography." In *Oceanography: The Past,* ed. M. Sears and D. Merriman. New York: Springer-Verlag, 1980.

Bush, Vannevar. *Modern Arms and Free Men: A Discussion of the Role of Science in Preserving Democracy*. New York: Simon and Schuster, 1949.

———. *Pieces of the Action*. New York: William Morrow, 1970.

———. *Science, the Endless Frontier: A Report to the President*. Washington, D.C.: U.S. Government Printing Office, 1945.

Campbell, D'Ann. *Women at War with America: Private Lives in a Patriotic Era*. Cambridge: Harvard University Press, 1984.

Chafe, William Henry. *The American Woman: Her Changing Social, Economic, and Political Roles, 1920–1970*. New York: Oxford University Press, 1972.

———. *The Paradox of Change*. Rev. ed. of *The American Woman* (1972). New York: Oxford University Press, 1991.

"Charting the Road to Tokyo." *All Hands,* no. 331 (October 1944): 24–27.

Cohen, I. Bernard. "Babbage and Aiken: With Notes on Henry Babbage's Gift to Harvard, and to Other Institutions, of a Portion of His Father's Difference Engine." *Annals of the History of Computing* 10, no. 3 (1988): 175–77.

———. "Howard Aiken and the Beginnings of Computer Science." *CWI Quarterly* 3, no. 4 (1990): 303–4.

———. *Howard Aiken: Portrait of a Computer Pioneer*. Cambridge: MIT Press, 1999.

———. New foreword to *A Manual of Operation for the Automatic Sequence Controlled Calculator*. Cambridge: MIT Press, 1985.

Cohen, I. Bernard, and Gregory W. Welch, eds. *Makin' Numbers: Howard Aiken and the Computer*. Cambridge: MIT Press, 1999.

Collins, Winifred Quick. *More Than a Uniform: A Navy Woman in a Navy Man's World*. Denton: University of North Texas Press, 1997.

Cook, Haruko Taya, and Theodore F. Cook. *Japan at War: An Oral History*. New York: New Press, 1992.

Cortada, James W. *Before the Computer: IBM, NCR, Burroughs, and Remington Rand and the Industry They Created, 1865–1956.* Princeton: Princeton University Press, 1993.

Davidson, Joel R. *The Unsinkable Fleet: The Politics of U.S. Naval Expansion in World War II.* Annapolis: Naval Institute Press, 1996.

Deacon, George E. R. "The Woods Hole Oceanographic Institution: An Expanding Influence." In *Oceanography: The Past,* ed. M. Sears and D. Merriman. New York: Springer-Verlag, 1980.

Douglas, Deborah G. *United States Women in Aviation, 1940–1985.* Washington, D.C.: Smithsonian Institution Press, 1991.

Dunnigan, James F., and Albert A. Nofi. *Dirty Little Secrets of the Vietnam War.* New York: St. Martin's Press, 1998.

———. *Dirty Little Secrets of World War II.* New York: William Morrow, 1994.

Ebbert, Jean, and Marie-Beth Hall. *Crossed Currents.* Washington, D.C.: Brassey's, 1993.

Emme, Eugene M. *Aeronautics and Astronautics: An American Chronology of Science and Technology in the Exploration of Space, 1915–1960.* Washington, D.C.: National Aeronautics and Space Administration, 1961.

Evans, Sara M. *Born for Liberty: A History of Women in America.* New York: Free Press, 1989.

Fletcher, M. H. *The WRNS: A History of the Women's Royal Naval Service.* Annapolis: Naval Institute Press, 1989.

Friedman, Robert M. *Appropriating the Weather: Vilhelm Bjerknes and the Construction of Modern Meteorology.* Ithaca, N.Y.: Cornell University Press, 1993.

Fye, Paul M. "The Woods Hole Oceanographic Institution: A Commentary." In *Oceanography: The Past,* ed. M. Sears and D. Merriman. New York: Springer-Verlag, 1980.

Gildersleeve, Virginia C. *The "Waves" of the Navy: How They Began.* New York: Macmillan, 1956.

Gluck, Sherna Berger. *Rosie the Riveter Revisited: Women, War and Social Change.* New York: Meridian, 1987.

Godson, Susan, H. "The Waves in World War II." *U.S. Naval Institute Proceedings* 107 (December 1981): 46–51.

Goldstine, Herman H. *The Computer: From Pascal to von Neumann.* Ormond Beach, Fla.: Camelot, 1996.

Grinstein, Louise S., and Paul J. Campbell, eds. *Women of Mathematics: A Bibliographic Sourcebook.* New York: Greenwood Press, 1987.

Grinstein, Louise S., Rose K. Rose, and Miriam H. Rafailovich, eds. *Women in Chemistry and Physics: A Bibliographic Sourcebook.* Westport, Conn.: Greenwood Press, 1993.

Gunter, Helen Clifford. *Navy Wave: Memories of World War II.* Fort Bragg, Calif.: Cypress House Press, 1992.

Haedrich, R. L., and K. O. Emery. "Growth of an Oceanographic Institution." In *Oceanography: The Past*, ed. M. Sears and D. Merriman. New York: Springer-Verlag, 1980.

Hancock, Joy Bright. *Lady in the Navy*. Annapolis: Naval Institute Press, 1972.

Hartree, Douglas R. *Calculating Instruments and Machines*. Urbana: University of Illinois Press, 1949.

"Harvard Receives $15 Million to Benefit Computer Science, Electrical Engineering." *Harvard University Gazette*, 31 October 1996, 1, 6.

Hershberg, James G. *James B. Conant: Harvard to Hiroshima and the Making of the Nuclear Age*. New York: Alfred A. Knopf, 1993.

Herzenberg, Caroline L. *Women Scientists from Antiquity to the Present: An Index*. West Cornwall, Conn.: Locust Hill Press, 1986.

Hicks, George. *The Comfort Women: Japan's Brutal Regime of Enforced Prostitution in the Second World War*. New York: W. W. Norton, 1994.

Hodges, Andrew. *Alan Turing: The Enigma*. New York: Simon and Schuster, 1983.

Holm, Jeanne, ed. *In Defense of a Nation: Service Women in World War II*. Washington, D.C.: Military Women's Press, 1998.

———. *Women in the Military: An Unfinished Revolution*. Rev. ed. Novato, Calif.: Presidio Press, 1992.

Hopper, Grace Murray. "The Education of a Computer." In *Proceedings, Symposium on Industrial Applications of Automatic Computing Equipment*, 139–44. Midwest Research Institute, Kansas City, Mo., 8–9 January 1953.

Hughes, Patrick. *A Century of Weather Service: A History of the Birth and Growth of the National Weather Service, 1870–1970*. New York: Gordon and Breach, 1970.

Jeansonne, Glen. *Women of the Far Right: The Mothers' Movement and World War II*. Chicago: University of Chicago Press, 1997.

"John Harvard's Journal." *Harvard Magazine* (September–October 1997): 68.

Kennedy, David M. *Freedom from Fear: The American People in Depression and War, 1929–1945*. New York: Oxford University Press, 1999.

Larson, C. Kay. *'Til I Come Marching Home: A Brief History of American Women in World War II*. Pasadena, Md.: Minerva Center, 1995.

Lewis, J. M. "WAVES Forecasters in World War II (with a Brief Survey of Other Women Meteorologists in World War II)." *Bulletin of the American Meteorological Society* 76, no. 11 (November 1995): 2187–202.

Light, Jennifer S. "When Computers Were Women." *Technology and Culture* 40, no. 3 (July 1999): 455–83.

Litoff, Judith Barret, and David C. Smith, eds. *We're in This War Too: World War II Letters from American Women in Uniform*. New York, Oxford: Oxford University Press, 1994.

Lyne, Mary C., and Kay Arthur. *Three Years behind the Mast: The Story of the United States Coast Guard SPARS*. Washington, D.C.: n.p., 1946.

Markoff, John. "Rear Adm. Grace M. Hopper Dies; Innovator in Computers Was 85." *New York Times*, 3 January 1992.

Mattfeld, Jacquelyn A., and Carol G. Van Aken, eds. *Women and the Scientific Professions: The MIT Symposium on American Women in Science and Engineering*. Cambridge: MIT Press, 1965.

McCartney, Scott. *ENIAC: The Triumphs and Tragedies of the World's First Computer*. New York: Walker and Company, 1999.

Meid, Pat. *The Marine Corps Reserve Women's Reserve in World War II*. Washington, D.C.: Historical Branch, U.S. Marine Corps, 1968.

Meier, Mary. "Science Rewards Woman's High Aim." *Boston Evening Globe*, 21 May 1963.

Meigs, Montgomery C. *Slide Rules and Submarines*. Washington, D.C.: National Defense University Press, 1990.

Millett, Alan R. *Semper Fidelis: The History of the United States Marine Corps*. New York: Free Press, 1991.

Milliman, John D. "Mary Sears—An Appreciation." *Deep-Sea Research* 32, no. 7 (1985): 749.

Mills, Eric L. *Biological Oceanography: An Early History, 1870–1969*. Ithaca, N.Y.: Cornell University Press, 1989.

Mitchell, Carmen Lois. *The Contribution of Grace Murray Hopper to Computer Science and Computer Education*. Ann Arbor: University Microfilms, 1994.

Nofi, Albert A. *Marine Corps Book of Lists: A Definitive Compendium of Marine Corps Facts, Feats and Traditions*. Conshohocken, Pa.: Combined Publishing, 1997.

Orville, Howard T. "Weather Is a Weapon." *All Hands*, no. 336 (March 1945): 5–9.

Penick, James L. Jr., Carroll W. Pursell Jr., Morgan B. Sherwood, and Donald C. Swain, eds. *The Politics of American Science 1939 to the Present*. Rev. ed. Cambridge: MIT Press, 1972.

Petzinger, Thomas Jr. "Female Pioneers Fostered Practicality in Computer Industry." *Wall Street Journal*, 22 November 1996.

———. "History of Software Begins with Work of Some Brainy Women." *Wall Street Journal*, 15 November 1996.

Poolman, Kenneth. *The Winning Edge: Naval Technology in Action, 1939–1945*. Annapolis: Naval Institute Press, 1997.

Pugh, Emerson W. *Memories That Shaped an Industry: Decisions Leading to IBM System 1360*. Cambridge: MIT Press, 1984.

Raitt, Helen, and Beatrice Moulton. *Scripps Institution of Oceanography*. [Los Angeles]: Ward Ritchie Press, 1967.

Randal, Brian. *The Origin of Digital Computers: Selected Papers*. New York: Springer-Verlag, 1973.

Rausa, Rosario. "In Profile, Grace Murray Hopper." *Naval History* (fall 1992): 58–61.

Reagan, Michael D. *Science and the Federal Patron.* New York: Oxford University Press, 1969.

Rees, Mina. "The Computing Program of the Office of Naval Research, 1949–1953." *Annals of the History of Computing* 4, no. 2 (April 1982): 102–19.

———. "The Federal Computing Machine Program." *Science* 112 (22 December 1950): 731–36.

———. "The Mathematical Sciences and World War II." *American Mathematical Monthly* 87, no. 8 (October 1980): 607–21.

———. "The Mathematics Program of the Office of Naval Research." *Bulletin of the American Mathematical Society* 54, no. 1 (January 1948): 1–5.

———. "Support of Higher Education by the Federal Government." *American Mathematical Monthly* 68, no. 4 (April 1961): 371–77.

———. "Warren Weaver, 1894–1978." *Biographical Memoirs* 57: 489–505. Washington, D.C.: National Academy Press, 1987.

Revelle, Roger. "The Oceanographic and How It Grew." In *Oceanography: The Past,* ed. M. Sears and D. Merriman. New York: Springer-Verlag, 1980.

Reynolds, Moira Davison. *American Women Scientists: 23 Inspiring Biographies, 1900–2000.* Jefferson, N.C.: McFadland and Company, 1999.

Rodgers, William. *Think: A Biography of the Watsons and IBM.* New York: Stein and Day, 1969.

Rossiter, Margaret W. *Women Scientists in America: Before Affirmative Action, 1940–1972.* Baltimore: Johns Hopkins University Press, 1995.

———. *Women Scientists in America: Struggles and Strategies to 1940.* Baltimore: Johns Hopkins University Press, 1982.

Rupp, Leila J. *Mobilizing Women for War: German and American Propaganda, 1939–1945.* Princeton: Princeton University Press, 1978.

Sapolsky, Harvey M. *Science and the Navy: The History of the Office of Naval Research.* Princeton: Princeton University Press, 1990.

Schlee, Susan. *The Edge of an Unfamiliar World: A History of Oceanography.* New York: E. P. Dutton, 1973.

———. "The R/V *Atlantis* and Her First Oceanographic Institution." In *Oceanography: The Past,* ed. M. Sears and D. Merriman. New York: Springer-Verlag, 1980.

Seiwell, H. R. "Military Oceanography in Tactical Operations of World War II." *Transactions of the American Geophysical Union* 27, no. 5 (October 1946): 677.

———. "Military Oceanography in World War II." *Military Engineer* (May 1947): 202–3.

Soderbergh, Peter A. *Women Marines: The World War II Era.* Westport, Conn.: Praeger, 1992.

Specter, Ronald H. *Eagle against the Sun: The American War with Japan.* New York: Vintage Books, 1985.

Spencer, Donald P. *Great Men and Women of Computing.* Ormond Beach, Fla.: Camelot, 1996.

Stephenson, Jill. *Women in Nazi Society*. New York: Harper and Row, 1975.

Stern, Nancy. *From ENIAC to UNIVAC: An Appraisal of the Eckert-Mauchly Computers*. Bedford, Mass.: Digital Press, 1981.

Stewart, Irvin. *Organizing Scientific Research for War: The Administrative History of the Office of Scientific Research and Development*. Boston: Little, Brown, 1948.

Stremlow, Mary V. *Free a Marine to Fight: Women Marines in World War II*. Washington D.C., Marine Corps Headquarters, History and Museums Division, 1994.

Swallow, Mary. "Tribute to Mary Sears." *Deep-Sea Research* 32, no. 7 (1985): 746.

Taylor, Hazel. "Women-at-Arms." *American Heritage* 51, no. 2 (2000): 136.

Treadwell, Mattie E. *The Women's Army Corps: The U.S. Army in World War II*. Washington, D.C.: Department of the Army, 1954.

Tropp, Henry S. "Grace Hopper: The Youthful Teacher of Us All." *Abacus* (fall 1984): 8

Urdang, Joan. "Women of Achievement: Government, Law, and Science." *Radcliffe Quarterly* (September 1992): 25.

U.S. Office of Scientific Research and Development, National Defense Research Committee. *Summary Technical Report of the Applied Mathematics Panel*. 3 vols. (Confidential) Washington, D.C., 1946.

Valian, Virginia. *Why So Slow? The Advancement of Women*. Cambridge: MIT Press, 1999.

Van Straten, F. W. "Meteorology Grows Up." *Scientific Monthly* (December 1946): 413–22.

Van Straten, Florence W. *Weather or Not*. New York: Dodd, Mead, 1966.

Weatherford, Doris. *American Women and World War II*. New York: Facts on File, 1990.

Weaver, Warren. *Scene of Change: A Lifetime in American Science*. New York: Charles Scribner's Sons, 1970.

Welch, Gregory Webb. "Computer Scientist Howard Hathaway Aiken: Reactionary or Visionary?" A.B. thesis, Harvard University, 1986.

———. "Howard Hathaway Aiken: The Life of a Computer Pioneer." *Computer Museum Report* 12 (spring 1985): 7.

Willenz, June A. *Women Veterans: America's Forgotten Heroines*. New York: Continuum, 1983.

Willoughby, Malcolm F. *U.S. Coast Guard in World War II*. Annapolis: U.S. Naval Institute, 1957.

Wingo, Josette Dermody. *Mother Was a Gunner's Mate: World War II in the Waves*. Annapolis: Naval Institute Press, 1994.

Wise, Nancy Baker, and Christy Wise. *A Mouthful of Rivets: Women at Work in World War II*. San Francisco: Jossey-Bass, 1994.

"Yanks Land on Luzon as Navy Planes Sweep China Coast." *All Hands*, no. 335 (February 1945): 2.

Yoder, H. S. *Planned Invasion of Japan, 1945: The Siberian Weather Advantage.* Philadelphia: American Philosophical Society, 1997.

Yost, Edna. *Women of Modern Science.* New York: Dodd, Mead, 1959.

Zimmerman, David. *Top Secret Exchange: The Tizard Mission and the Scientific War.* Montreal and Kingston: McGill–Queen's University Press, 1996.

INDEX

Aberdeen Proving Ground, 137; ENIAC
at, 127; Herman Goldstine at, 172;
Warren Weaver on, 177; weather
station at, 72; women calculators
at, 134
aerographers/aerographers' mates, 75,
99; definition of, 68; overseas, 104;
at sea, 86–87; Waves as, 18, 77,
85–86, 91–92
aerologists: definition of, 68; demobilization of, 109; and Luzon landings, 56; number of, 74, 86–87; and
Okinawa invasion, 99; overseas,
104; successes of, 95–99; training
of, 77–78; Waves as, 25
aerology: between world wars, 73–74;
definition of, 67; and oceanography, 51; role of women in, 78; successes of, 91; use of radar for,
106–7; wartime expansion of, 77,
105; war work of, 100, 103; in
World War I, 72. *See also* meteorology; weather forecasting
Aerology Section, 75, 110, 112; functions of, 53, 89–90, 101, 103;
Howard Orville as head of, 74, 89,
92; sources of information for,
99–100, 106; transfer of, 77, 87–89;
Waves at, 91–92
Aetna, 149
Agassiz, Alexander, 31
Agassiz, Louis, 31
Aiken, Howard H., 141, 187; character
of, 131, 133, 140; designs Mark I,
118; Grace Murray Hopper on,
122, 130–31; heads Harvard Computation Lab, 119–20, 123–24, 126;
legacy of, 137; on Mark I, 122;
Mina Spiegel Rees on, 169; in naval

reserve, 128; postwar career of,
142–44, 197, 219; and program-
ming, 133, 142–43; publications by,
143–44; and Warren Weaver, 125,
170
Alber, H., 91
American Academy of Arts and Sciences,
202
American Association for the Advancement of Science, 202, 214
American Mathematical Society, 159, 198
Anderson, Ella, 10
Annapolis, Md. *See* U.S. Naval Academy
Anslow, Gladys, 189
antisubmarine warfare, 48, 52, 65, 139,
163
Anti-submarine Warfare Operational
Research Group (ASWORG), 53,
138, 172, 182, 188
Applied Mathematics Group (AMG),
178, 185
Applied Mathematics Panel (AMP), 190,
192, 195, 198; computer survey by,
125, 170, 187; and computing at
Columbia, 138; and draft deferments, 179–80; and Harvard Computation Lab, 123, 134; and
Mathematical Tables Project, 180;
mathematicians at, 171–72, 174,
179, 183; and NDRC, 167; procedures of, 177–78; relationship with
navy, 173, 182–83, 185–86, 192;
task of, 171–72; technical aides at,
168–69, 176–77; trains mathematicians, 181–82; von Neumann
reports to, 139, 173; and war effort,
187–88; war work of, 181–82, 184,
186–88, 216. *See also* Office of Scientific Research and Development

Fye, Paul, 40

G. I. Bill (1944), 144, 217–18
Gaskill, Elizabeth, 17–18
GE. *See* General Electric
General Electric (GE), 12, 118, 152
George Washington University, 163, 197, 210
Germany: and computing, 125; and meteorology, 71, 78–80; and mobilization of science, 164–65; and mobilization of women, 12; and oceanography, 34; postwar mathematics in, 196
Gildersleeve, Virginia C., 2–3, 13, 15
Gleim, Karen, 78
Goldstine, Herman, 141, 172
Graves, Elizabeth Riddle, 10
Graves, Lawrence M., 174
Great Britain, 124; and computing, 118, 121, 135, 148; and Mary Sears, 201; and mobilization of science, 165, 172; postwar mathematics in, 196; scientific exchanges with, 49, 160, 164, 177; and women in meteorology, 80; and women in military, 2, 7, 16
Grieff, Lotti, 10
Grier, Mary, 48, 55–56
Groves, Leslie R., 126
Guggenheim Foundation, 78

Halsey, William F., 96, 98
Harper, Robert W., 181
Hartree, Douglas R., 142
Harvard Computation Laboratory, 123; contribution to war effort, 126; established, 119; Grace Murray Hopper at, 24, 118, 146, 147, 179; navy contract for, 125, 129; as navy facility, 124, 130; postwar funding for, 142–43; staff of, 127, 175; von Neumann at, 139–40. *See also* Mark I
Harvard University, 72, 144, 156; and AMP, 173, 184; and applied sciences, 120; attitude toward government funding, 142–43, 194, 219; Columbus O'Donnell Iselin at, 34; computer courses at, 143, 197; and computer science degrees, 150;

Howard Aiken at, 118–19, 131, 169; James Conant heads, 9, 161, 164; Mary Sears at, 34, 53; meteorology at, 71; Radio Research Lab at, 123, 127, 163; Richard Bloch at, 121, 128; Robert Campbell at, 128; Underwater Sound Lab at, 127, 160; and Vassar, 115; war programs at, 23, 163; Waves trained at, 24
Hawkins, Bob, 131, 133
Hendrickson, Helena C., 91–92, 95, 109–10
Henry, Dora, 48, 60
Holberton, Frances E. "Betty," 146–47, 150
Hopper, Grace, 26, 27, 42, 155, 216; on Betty Holberton, 146–47; and "bug" legend, 152–53; character of, 62, 113, 130, 212, 215; and COBOL, 147, 150, 210; contributions to computing, 137, 149, 153, 212; at DEC, 213; early years of, 114–15, 156; at Eckert–Mauchly and Sperry, 145, 210, 218; on ENIAC, 141; on feminists, 63, 151–52, 190; on Howard Aiken, 122, 130–31, 147; on John Mauchly, 146; joins the navy, 118; and Man-of-the-Year award, 30, 152; on Mark I, 135; and Mark II and III, 143; and marriage, 117, 219; on Mina Spiegel Rees, 148, 150; Mina Spiegel Rees on, 169, 189, 198; in naval reserve, 143; at NAVDAC, 210; on programming, 129, 133–35; recognition of, 212–13; on self, 135; and teaching, 210; and USS *Hopper*, 113
Hornig, Lilli, 10
Hotelling, Harold, 159
Hourihan, John, 130
Hunter College, 79, 192; and Mina Spiegel Rees, 155–59, 169, 174, 190, 195, 198, 213; WAVES enlisted training at, 15, 200
Hydrographic Office, U.S. Navy, 33, 61; and aerology, 74; and employment of women, 45; Mary Sears at, 57, 65, 205; publications of, 90; reorganization of, 43–44; war work of, 40; Waves at, 20, 45–47, 60

Neyman, Jerzy, 159, 189
Nimitz, Chester W., 29, 66
Northwestern University, 173, 185
Nudo, Rose, 23

Oceanographic Unit (Hydro), 45;
    becomes Oceanographic Division,
    48, 65; and Luzon landings, 56–57;
    Mary Sears heads, 20, 44, 49, 76;
    and Okinawa invasion, 57; reor-
    ganization of, 54; reports produced
    by, 49, 53–59; sources of informa-
    tion for, 50–54, 59–60; women at,
    47–48
oceanography: in Germany, 34, 38–39;
    government funding of, 33–34;
    influence of Vilhelm Bjerknes on,
    33; in Japan, 34; Mary Sears's
    influence on, 65–66, 201–2; and
    meteorology, 41, 55, 57; and sea,
    swell and surf studies, 41, 60; in
    Soviet Union, 201, 205–6; in U.S.,
    31, 204–5; and U.S. Navy, 37, 39,
    203–4; wartime expansion of, 41,
    44, 48–49
Oceanography (Sears), 201
Office of the Coordinator of Research
    and Development, 120, 173, 189,
    193
Office of Emergency Management, 122,
    165
Office of Information Systems Planning,
    210
Office of Naval Intelligence, 53, 60
Office of Naval Research (ONR), 14;
    computing encouraged by, 148;
    Congress creates, 194; Mary Sears
    at, 203–4; Mina Spiegel Rees at,
    119, 178, 187, 192–98, 213; at San
    Francisco, Calif., 204
Office of Naval Weather Service, 207
Office of Research and Inventions, 193
Office of Scientific Research and Devel-
    opment (OSRD), 9, 125, 170, 174,
    193, 196; and AMP, 184; competes
    for scientists, 127; and employment
    of women, 9–10, 189; establish-
    ment of, 123, 165; and Harvard,
    127; mathematicians employed by,
    172, 179; and Moore School of
    Electrical Engineering, 127; and

ONR, 195; and Reserved List of
    Scientific and Technical Research
    Workers, 126, 180; structure of,
    166; success of, 175, 215; war his-
    tory of, 168, 215–16
Office of Strategic Services (OSS), 10,
    53, 187
Oppenheimer, J. Robert, 126
Orville, Howard T., 76, 110; as Aerology
    chief, 74, 89, 92; and employment
    of women, 70, 82; and Florence van
    Straten, 100–102; heads Naval
    Weather Service, 207; on Japanese
    meteorology, 77; and JMC, 76; and
    Mary Sears, 90; on navy aerology,
    94–95; and weather analyses, 90;
    on weather centrals, 86; on weather
    stations, 104

Pan American Airways, 75
Piore, E. R., 195
Potter, Charlotte, 23
Potter, Virginia Scott, 19
Prager, William, 59, 184
Princeton University, 159, 173, 176, 197
Progress in Oceanography, 201

Radcliffe College: and Mary Sears, 30,
    36, 202, 205; Mina Spiegel Rees on,
    156; war programs at, 13–14
Radiation Laboratory (MIT), 163
Radio Corporation of America (RCA),
    151, 172
Radio Research Laboratory (Harvard),
    123, 127
Radiosonde, 85–86, 101–2
Raytheon, 12, 143
RCA. See Radio Corporation of America
Rees, Mina, 10, 26, 103, 215; as AMP
    chief technical aide, 169, 174; and
    AMP tasks, 161, 173–75, 177–80;
    and AMP War History, 216;
    assesses AMP, 187–88; character of,
    157–58, 175–76, 196, 213, 215; at
    Chicago, 157; at City University of
    New York (CUNY), 190, 213; at
    Columbia, 156–57; and computing,
    139, 180, 187, 196–98; early years
    of, 154–55; on Eisenhower, 199;
    and feminism, 188–90; Grace
    Murray Hopper on, 148, 150;

Rees, Mina (continued),
on Grace Murray Hopper, 189,
198; and Hunter College, 79,
155–59, 169, 174, 190, 195, 198,
213; influence on postwar mathematics, 198; and marriage, 158,
198, 219; as mathematician, 176,
191, 213–14; on military uses of
mathematics, 181; on naval
officers, 177; at ONR, 119, 178,
187, 192–98, 218; recognition of,
197–98, 215; on statistical work,
186, 188; on Vannevar Bush, 170;
and Warren Weaver, 169, 174, 180,
190–91; Warren Weaver on, 190, 192
Reichelderfer, Francis W., 73, 76, 82, 110
Remington Rand. See Sperry Corporation
Revelle, Roger, 36, 45; at BuShips, 42,
65; and Harald Sverdrup, 48, 90; at
ONR, 195; and Mary Sears, 43–44,
47, 64; on Mary Sears, 61, 202
Rockefeller Foundation, 32, 154, 170–71
Roebuck, Rosana J., 91–92
Rogers, Edith Nourse, 2
Roosevelt, Franklin D., 11, 49, 72, 87;
and James Forrestal, 194; and
NDRC, 38, 161, 163, 164; and Van-
nevar Bush, 166, 192
Rossby, Carl-Gustav, 73, 76, 78, 82

Salzberg, Bernard, 138
Scene of Change (Weaver), 190
Schildt, Jan, 138
Scott, Elizabeth, 189
Scripps Institution of Oceanography,
32–33, 53; and aerology, 75; Harald
Sverdrup at, 42, 48, 51, 58; and
NDRC, 39; and postwar funding,
203, 219; Roger Revelle heads, 36;
and war work, 42, 44, 55, 59
The Sea Around Us (Carson), 205
Sears, Leila, 14, 31, 34, 37, 62, 64
Sears, Mary, 14, 26, 27, 90, 163, 219; in
American Men of Science, 30;
character of, 30, 37, 54, 61–63, 215;
and Charles Bates, 218–19; and
Columbus O'Donnell Iselin, 34,
201, 205, 206; early years of, 30–31,
68, 156; as editor, 61, 201; on feminists, 63–64, 190; heads Oceano-

graphic Unit, 20, 64–65; and
Henry Bigelow, 31–32; and Howard
Orville, 90; and influence on
oceanography, 65–66, 201–2, 205,
206; and JMC, 53, 58, 75; joins
navy, 41–42, 117; and Luzon land-
ings, 56–57; in naval reserve, 203–4;
on navy career, 30, 60; and Okinawa
invasion, 57; prepares intelligence
reports, 49, 56, 181; recognition of,
29, 61, 65–66, 201–2, 204–5; and
Roger Revelle, 43–33, 64, 195;
USNS Mary Sears, 206; at WHOI,
32, 34–35, 201–2, 218
Seiwell, H. Richard, 41–42, 44, 48, 54
Selective Service, 2, 7, 9, 117, 126, 180
Shuster, George N., 192
Simpson, Joanne Gerould, 81
Smith, Eugene, 123, 148
Smith College, 17, 23, 31, 189. See also
Naval Reserve Midshipmen's
School (WR); Mount Holyoke
College
Sokolnikoff, Ivan S., 174, 176, 184
Soviet Union: and Mary Sears, 201,
205–6; and mathematics, 196; and
weather forecasting, 80, 101, 104–5;
and women in military, 2
Sperry Corporation, 12, 145, 148, 210
Stanford University, 163, 173
Steere, Richard C., 58, 99
Stewart, Grace, 10
Stewart, Irvin, 168–69
Stibitz, George R., 122, 125, 176
Strong, George V., 161
Sverdrup, Harald U., 42, 51, 75, 76, 203;
reports by, 48; and Sverdrup-Munk
technique, 50, 57
Swallow, Mary, 201

Taussky, Olga, 189
Taylor, Hazel Parker, 26–27
Telkes, Maria, 9
Terman, F. E., 163
Thomas, Mary Ellen, 110
Tizard Mission, 160, 164
Turing, Alan M., 125
Turner, Richmond Kelly, 100

Underwater Sound Laboratory (Harvard), 127, 160

ABOUT THE AUTHOR

Kathleen Broome Williams was born in Charlottesville, Virginia, in 1944. When she was four months old, her father, Maj. Roger G. B. Broome, USMCR, died as a result of wounds received during the invasion of Saipan. She grew up in Italy and England, returning to the United States to attend Wellesley College.

Williams holds an M.A. from Columbia University and a Ph.D. in military history from the City University of New York. She is an associate professor at Bronx Community College, CUNY, and is on the history doctoral faculty at the CUNY Graduate School and University Center. Williams is the author of *Secret Weapon: U.S. High-Frequency Direction Finding in the Battle of the Atlantic,* published by the Naval Institute Press, and is currently researching Grace Murray Hopper for the Naval Institute Press's Library of Naval Biography series.

The Naval Institute Press is the book-publishing arm of the U.S. Naval Institute, a private, nonprofit, membership society for sea service professionals and others who share an interest in naval and maritime affairs. Established in 1873 at the U.S. Naval Academy in Annapolis, Maryland, where its offices remain today, the Naval Institute has members worldwide.

Members of the Naval Institute support the education programs of the society and receive the influential monthly magazine *Proceedings* and discounts on fine nautical prints and on ship and aircraft photos. They also have access to the transcripts of the Institute's Oral History Program and get discounted admission to any of the Institute-sponsored seminars offered around the country.

The Naval Institute also publishes *Naval History* magazine. This colorful bimonthly is filled with entertaining and thought-provoking articles, first-person reminiscences, and dramatic art and photography. Members receive a discount on *Naval History* subscriptions.

The Naval Institute's book-publishing program, begun in 1898 with basic guides to naval practices, has broadened its scope to include books of more general interest. Now the Naval Institute Press publishes about one hundred titles each year, ranging from how-to books on boating and navigation to battle histories, biographies, ship and aircraft guides, and novels. Institute members receive significant discounts on the Press's more than eight hundred books in print.

Full-time students are eligible for special half-price membership rates. Life memberships are also available.

For a free catalog describing Naval Institute Press books currently available, and for further information about subscribing to *Naval History* magazine or about joining the U.S. Naval Institute, please write to:

Membership Department
U.S. Naval Institute
291 Wood Road
Annapolis, MD 21402-5034
Telephone: (800) 233-8764
Fax: (410) 269-7940
Web address: www.navalinstitute.org